DATE DUE	
MAR - 9 2005	
OCT 2 0 2006	
NOV 2 0 2006	
GAYLORD	PRINTED IN U.S.A.

ENVY OF THE GODS

ENVY OF THE GODS

Alexander the Great's Ill-Fated Journey across Asia

JOHN PREVAS

Da Capo Press
A Member of the Perseus Books Group

Designed by David C. denBoer
Set in 10/14 point Trump Mediaeval by The Perseus Books Group

Maps by Abdullah Ayazi

Cataloging-in-Publication data for this book
is available from the Library of Congress.

First Da Capo Press edition 2004
ISBN 0–306–81268–1

Published by Da Capo Press
A Member of the Perseus Books Group
http://www.dacapopress.com

Da Capo Press books are available at special discounts for bulk purchases in
the United States by corporations, institutions, and other organizations. For
more information, please contact the Special Markets Department at the
Perseus Books Group, 11 Cambridge Center, Cambridge, MA 02142, or call
(800) 255–1514 or (617) 252–5298, or email special.markets@perseusbooks.com.

1 2 3 4 5 6 7 8 9   08 07 06 05 04

CONTENTS

fere libenter homines id quod volunt credunt

ACKNOWLEDGMENTS

THE STORY OF THE DEMISE OF ALEXANDER THE GREAT IN the East is my third book on the subject of great leaders from the ancient world, and it was perhaps the most difficult to complete in terms of research, writing, and traveling. Whether that is because the subject itself was so overwhelming in terms of all that has been written about this heroic figure, or because travel to the parts of the world that he conquered is so difficult today, or simply because time is taking its toll on my capabilities both physical and intellectual is hard to say. Perhaps all three.

Travel was the most difficult of the three components necessary to produce this book. I traveled to Iran, Afghanistan, Pakistan, Uzbekistan, Kazakhstan, and the border of Tajikistan. They were not easy trips, but in spite of the expense, the risks, the discomforts, and the anxieties they all proved worth the effort. I saw things that gave me the perspective to understand and I hope convey to my readers what Alexander did and why. My trips also gave me a better, more balanced perspective on the conflict between the Muslim world and the West as well as the differences among the Muslims themselves. The Muslim worlds of Iran, Afghanistan, and Pakistan are, I found, very different from the Muslim worlds of Uzbekistan, Tajikistan, and Kazakhstan.

The one country I could not enter was Iraq. I had planned to travel there at the same time I visited Iran to photograph Babylon where Alexander died. By the time I got to Iran the war was raging in Iraq, and even though I was just a few miles away the border was closed.

Nevertheless, there are current pictures of the little that remains of Babylon in the pages of this book. One of my former students, Marine Major Mike Lindemann, took time out from fighting the war to photograph Babylon for me as the forces under his command passed through on their way to Baghdad.

H. E. Hatem Atallah, the ambassador from Tunisia to Washington, was my conduit to the embassies of Afghanistan, Pakistan, and Uzbekistan and the interests section of the Islamic Republic of Iran. As a Muslim and an ambassador, he opened doors for me that otherwise would have remained locked and helped to secure the contacts, visas, and assistance necessary for me to visit those countries. It took two years of persistent efforts to secure the visa to visit Iran so that I could photograph the ruins of Persepolis for this book. Ambassador Atallah is a good friend. He is a Muslim and a diplomat who is working hard in difficult times to bring East and West together based on mutual trust and tolerance. He is a political and religious moderate and a man of exceptional ability. We are fortunate to have him in Washington.

Former Pakistani ambassador and United Nations emissary Jamsheed Marker and his wife Arnaz helped me in many ways as I made my arrangements for travel to Pakistan. They gave me valuable advice on everything from government regulations, local customs, and politics to the proper way to wear my "pajamas"—the ubiquitous Pakistani long shirt and balloon pants worn by men in that country. It was Ambassador Marker who arranged my meeting with Prince Aurangzeb, the Wali of Swat.

The maps for this book were prepared by Abdullah Ayazi, an engineer from Afghanistan now living with his family in Virginia. Abdullah's knowledge of the history and geography of Afghanistan as well as his cartographical skills helped to produce the maps that I hope will assist the reader in following Alexander's and my route across these troubled lands. Abdullah and I worked closely together over the last year, and even though he has embraced his newly adopted country, his heart I believe is still on the plains of Afghanistan.

I owe a debt to Margaret Carrington of Belleair, Florida. Margaret is a teacher who loves words, languages, and grammar. She is well traveled and is an avid reader interested in history and politics. She reflects the type of educated reader I am striving to reach through my books. She took the time to read the early drafts of each of my chapters and make valuable suggestions from the perspective of a general reader. While we often differed over points of grammar and word usage, she never faltered in her task and remained consistent until the manuscript was finished. I tried her patience on more than one occasion. Many of her suggestions and corrections have been incorporated in the pages of this book, and she has my sincerest appreciation for her efforts.

I owe my drivers and guides in Iran, Afghanistan, Pakistan, and Uzbekistan more than just the few dollars I paid them for accompanying me. They all proved to be hardworking men trying to make a living for their families in difficult times and under circumstances that would prove impossible for most Americans. They did not always understand or agree with American foreign policy, but they were not anti-American—quite the contrary. Each one of them contributed to making my trip successful, and they often experienced some tense moments because of my insistence on pushing the limits of patience and prudence in trying to get that one extra shot of a ruin, climb to that one last ledge for a view, or find out the source of the gunfire over the ridge. Each one of them was with me every step of the way.

I have seen the world change in the four short years since I traveled through that area of the world as I wrote my last book. The change has not been for the better. My Greek passport and dark complexion are no longer guarantees of my safety in those areas, as anger over the Palestinian situation is not just directed toward Americans but toward all Westerners. One night in Pakistan, shortly before I was about to cross the border into Afghanistan, I had dinner with the Wali (ruler) of Swat, Prince Miangul Aurangzeb, along with the commanding officer of the Frontier Constabulary. We were in the tribal areas of the Northwest Frontier on the border with Afghanistan. The commander warned me not to cross into Afghanistan. "They will kill you if they come upon you," he warned, referring to the Taliban, al Qaeda, the warlords, the smugglers, and the bandits who roam those mountains. I asked about the value of my Greek passport to ensure my safety. After all, Greece has a long history of supporting the Palestinian cause. "They will kill you as soon as you open your mouth," he replied. "Then they will look at your passport."

The availability of weapons, not weapons of mass destruction but cheap, reliable Kalashnikovs and rocket-propelled grenades mass produced in mom-and-pop backyard arms factories and sold at flea markets, compounded by an inconceivable level of poverty have made safe travel to that area of the world nearly impossible. The cheap accessibility of the Internet, satellite television, and cell phones ensure that these people know exactly how well we live in the West and how badly off they are in the East. Their frustration with their own impoverished, disease-ridden lives and a future without hope for improvement has been focused on the Palestinian plight, and they see Americans and Jews as responsible for all that is wrong and unjust with the world today.

Alexander and I traveled over the same roads, deserts, and mountains although we traveled nearly twenty-four hundred years apart. The topography has hardly changed, but the world I traveled through to research this book is a far more dangerous and much less peaceful place than it was when Alexander and his Macedonians passed through it.

Finally, I continue to be indebted to my wife, Mavis Gibson, for her support, love, and devotion. Though she did not want me to make these trips because of the dangers, she nevertheless supported me in every way she could once I had made up my mind to go. I know she passed many anxious hours waiting for a telephone call or e-mail confirming that I was safe as I traveled from Dubai to Shiraz, then to Peshawar and Islamabad, on to Tashkent, then to Samarkand and Bukhara, on to Al-Maty, back to Islamabad, over the Khyber Pass toward Kabul, back to Dubai, and finally home by way of France. They were long and arduous trips, but I would not trade the experience or the sights I saw for anything.

CHRONOLOGY

356 B.C.   Birth of Alexander in Macedonia (northern Greece)

336 B.C.   Artaxerxes IV, king of Persia, murdered
            Darius III becomes the new king of Persia (Iran)
            Parmenio crosses into Asia Minor (Turkey)
            Assassination of Philip, king of Macedonia
            Accession of Alexander to the throne of his father
            Alexander elected general of the Greeks

334 B.C.   Alexander invades Asia Minor
            Battle at the Granicus River (Turkey)
            Conquest of Asia Minor

333 B.C.   Battle of Issus (southeastern Turkey and Syria)
            Alexander captures the family of King Darius

332 B.C.   Alexander conquers Egypt

331 B.C.   Spartans under King Agis revolt against Antipater
            Spartans are defeated at the battle of Megalopolis
            Battle of Gaugamela (Iraq)
            Alexander occupies Babylon

330 B.C.   Alexander captures Persepolis, capital of the Persian Empire
            Alexander pursues Darius into the eastern deserts of Iran
            Murder of Darius
            Murders of Philotas, Parmenio, and Alexander the
                Lyncestian

329 B.C.   Conquest of Bactria (Afghanistan)
           Revolt and death of Bessus

328 B.C.   Conquest of Sogdiana (Uzbekistan and Tajikistan)
           Revolt and death of Spitamenes
           Murder of Cleitus in Sogdiana
           Pages' conspiracy and death of Callisthenes
           Alexander's marriage to Roxanne

327 B.C.   Alexander invades India, entering the Swat Valley
           (Pakistan)

326 B.C.   Alexander crosses the Indus River (Pakistan)
           Battle at the Hydaspes River (Pakistan) against Porus
           Mutiny at the Beas River (border between Pakistan and
           India)
           Voyage down the Indus River to the Arabian Sea

325 B.C.   Alexander crosses the Gedrosian Desert (southern
           Pakistan)

324 B.C.   Alexander reaches Carmania (southeastern Iran)
           Purges and executions of the satraps at Persepolis
           Alexander reaches Susa, second and third marriages
           Macedonian and Greek troops mutiny at Opis
           Death of Hephaestion

323 B.C.   Alexander returns to Babylon
           Death of Alexander just short of his thirty-third birthday
           Struggle for the succession begins, division of the empire

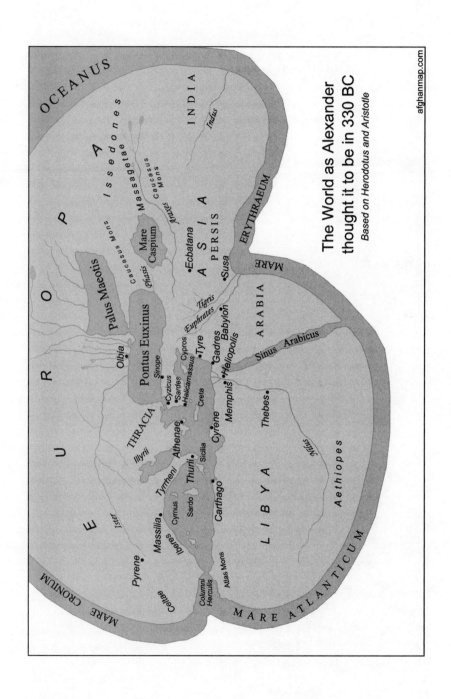

The World as Alexander
thought it to be in 330 BC

Based on Herodotus and Aristotle

afghanmap.com

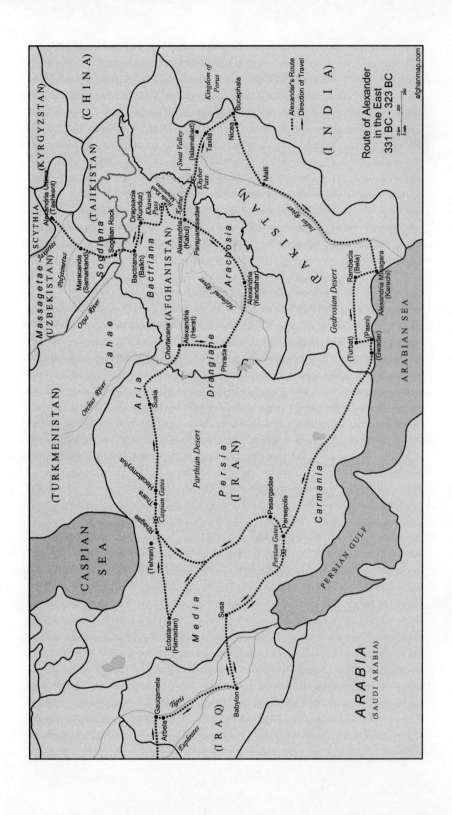

INTRODUCTION

FEW FIGURES THROUGHOUT HISTORY HAVE BEEN MORE written about than Alexander of Macedonia. The image of the conquering young king from Greece who subjugated the vast Persian Empire in the latter half of the fourth century B.C. has evolved over the centuries to symbolize different things to European and Asiatic cultures. The persona and accomplishments of Alexander have reached gigantic proportions and retain to this day a strong appeal. He has become the model and, for many, the ideal of effective leadership. Alexander's methods have inspired generations of kings, emperors, dictators, politicians, generals, and corporate CEOs. He is revered as the master of logistics, a strategic and tactical genius, the consummate multicultural politician, and the ultimate visionary. As seen through occidental eyes, he is the enlightened warrior who brought Greek learning to a barbarian people and the romantic idealist who sought to harmonize the cultures of the East and the West. For Western audiences Alexander is unquestionably a figure of heroic, even superhuman proportions.

Alexander is credited by Western historians with having brought about a significant transformation of the eastern half of the ancient world, both politically and culturally. While the period during which he ruled was short, some thirteen years, the effects of his rule lasted for centuries after his death. Greek language remained the medium of communication in the Eastern part of the world until the advent of Islam and Greek learning set the standards for culture. Some scholars believe that the Hellenistic world established by Alexander

became the medium for the eventual spread of Christianity throughout the Orient. In the romantic sense, Alexander is regarded in the
West as the man who explored and conquered new worlds before he
had reached the age of thirty-three. His short yet glorious career is an
affirmation of the belief that youth, unfettered by the conventional
restraints of its elders and free to pursue its own broader visions,
knows no limits as to what it might accomplish.

When viewed from an Eastern perspective, however, the story of
Alexander the Great takes on a different and much darker shading.
For Persians and Indians, Alexander is not the heroic figure who led
them out of darkness and into the light of Greek learning and culture. From this perspective, the Greeks were the barbarians and the
young Macedonian king takes on a more demonic persona. "Iskander," as Alexander is known today in the East, swept into Asia in
330 B.C. as a Hellenic version of Genghis Khan.

Eastern cultures from Iraq and Iran to Afghanistan and Pakistan
still portray Alexander as the "two-horned" Satan, the "accursed
one" who destroyed some of the most magnificent cities in the Orient
and brought suffering to millions of peaceful and innocent people.
From the Mediterranean shores of western Turkey to the banks of
the Indus River in Pakistan, Alexander and his army slaughtered,
plundered, and enslaved on a scale never before seen in the ancient
world. Eastern scholars condemn the Macedonian king and his
Greeks for having looted and obliterated much of a rich and developed culture they neither understood nor valued.

The bitterness and resentment from the era of Alexander's conquest remain to this day, and overtones of it can be detected in the
current tension between the Judaic-Christian West and the Muslim
East, a tension that threatens the very stability of the modern world.
One cannot help but notice that the source of so much of the hatred
toward the West today and the radical movement to eradicate Western ideals and values comes from those very areas of the world that
were most devastated by Alexander and his Greeks more than twenty-
three hundred years ago: Iraq, Iran, Afghanistan and Pakistan.

When Alexander led the Greeks across the Dardanelles in the
spring of 334 B.C. to invade Persia, he claimed revenge on the empire
that had devastated the Greek homeland in 480. But he also had a

personal agenda, though that agenda did not manifest itself for all the world to see until much later in the Asian campaign.

Alexander came to believe that he was destined to rule over not just Greeks but the entire world—to the ends of the earth. Toward that goal the young Macedonian king plotted, maneuvered, and murdered his way to the pinnacle of power in the ancient world. Alexander was relentless in his pursuit of power both within Greece and throughout Asia. He used whatever means he deemed necessary to accomplish his goal without regard to morality or the cost in terms of human suffering. Through a combination of skill, luck, and circumstances, Alexander rose in a short span of time to become the master of the ancient world, the "lord of Asia." With success his illusions of greatness and eventually divinity became so overwhelming that they supplanted reason and drove his mind to the most destructive recesses of megalomania.

As much as Alexander believed that he was a king and above all other men, he could not come to grips psychologically with the magnitude of his success. Absolute power did not bring the young Macedonian happiness and fulfillment. While his position brought him wealth beyond imagination along with the adornments of power, it also brought him misery, anguish, and an early death. There is no better example in history than Alexander of Lord Acton's famous warning that "power corrupts and absolute power corrupts absolutely."

Alexander was a young man who could not make the best use of his material success. For all his gifts and genius, Alexander had a fatal flaw that made happiness and true success unobtainable for him. Without self-control, no amount of success can bring a man happiness, and this self-control is what Alexander lacked. Power for him became an aphrodisiac that he could not use wisely and prudently. Alexander's was a complex personality with its own particular combinations of strengths and weaknesses. In spite of his ability to command others, he seemed incapable of achieving that measure of self-control necessary in order to bring about his own personal happiness. Alexander, "protector of men" as his name means in Greek, was a powerful leader continually torn between the emotional nature he had inherited from his mother and the practical yet focused and sanguinary nature he had inherited from his father. This complex interplay of personality traits often manifested itself in all aspects of his life, from his military actions to his political and personal decisions. For all his heroic qualities and accomplishments, in the end, for whatever reason, Alexander could never maintain that proper balance of self-control and emotional maturity that in any age and under any set of historical circumstances are the sine qua non of holding power while maintaining a sense of proportion.

The book begins with Alexander's capture of Persepolis in the winter of 330 B.C. and ends seven years later with his death at Babylon in 323 B.C. The heart of the story is contained between those two events and represents the tragedy of Alexander's demise. In the ancient capital of the Persian kings, among the splendor and luxury of the empire's finest city, Alexander first came to grips with the enormity of what he had done and the extent of the wealth that had fallen into his hands.

By the time he reached Persepolis, Alexander had fulfilled his promises to the Greeks. He had conquered most of Asia Minor for them, and by burning the imperial palace and driving the last Persian king into the deserts of Iran, he had extracted the promised vengeance. Now Alexander was master of Persia, and he possessed the resources to establish Greece as the largest and most powerful force in the ancient world.

The conquest of Persia would have satisfied the most ambitious of men. But Alexander was a man who could not rest, and he was no longer concerned with Greece. He had within him an all-consuming desire, a pathological compulsion, to keep pushing the limits of what could be done—what the ancient Greeks called "pothos" and the Romans "ingens cupido." Even after he had conquered all of Persia, he was driven to explore further and bring within his dominion the farthest recesses of the ancient world. He had to travel farther east to distant and mysterious lands where legend said that only gods and mythical heroes had dared to venture. Alexander was compelled to move into unexplored territory and search for himself the limits of the earth. He had to see the great "Ocean," which he had been told lay beyond India at the end of the earth.

Alexander left Persepolis in the spring of 330 B.C. and pursued the defeated Darius into the deserts and wastelands of eastern Iran. After finally catching the dying Persian king, Alexander moved farther east as he pursued the last of the satraps (governors) who had served the Persian monarch and were the final source of resistance to his new regime. In the course of this pursuit, Alexander made his way through what is now modern-day Afghanistan and into the high snow-covered passes of the Hindu Kush Mountains. He moved his army as far north as modern-day Uzbekistan and Tajikistan, founding cities colonized with unwilling soldiers and the enslaved local populations.

Eventually Alexander and his army made their way into the kingdoms of India and to the shores of the Indus River. It was in India that Alexander's men revolted and refused to move forward any farther. They were tired and worn out. They had endured months of incessant monsoon rains, disease, hunger, and fighting. They no longer shared Alexander's vision or believed in his invulnerability. They would not follow him any farther east to find the Ocean he believed marked the boundaries of the earth. The Greeks and Macedonians threatened mutiny if he did not lead them home.

For the first time as king, Alexander was forced to submit to a will greater than his own. Reluctantly, he complied with the demands of the army and agreed to turn back. He led the army south as they followed the Indus River to the Indian Ocean and the site of the modern-day city of Karachi. From there Alexander turned west and led his army through the scorching and arid Gedrosian Desert, one of the most desolate and inhospitable places on the face of the earth. It was in this desert that he suffered the greatest defeat of his career, not at the hands of a rival king but by nature and his own hubris.

The casualties in Gedrosia were the worst that Alexander and his army had ever experienced in their years of campaigning. The losses stemmed mostly from Alexander's vindictive nature and poor judgment. He had been bent on punishing the army, which had thwarted his will, and at the same time he wanted to cross the desert and duplicate a feat that only a legendary hero had dared to undertake before him. The few who survived the long march through Gedrosia with Alexander returned to Persepolis, where they had begun their odyssey seven years before, with little faith in the god-king they once regarded as infallible.

When Alexander left Persepolis and moved deeper into the Orient, his persona and power grew beyond anything ever seen in the ancient world. He defeated kingdom after kingdom as he accumulated even more wealth and amassed greater power. The result of his success was his own undoing. He came to believe that he was following in the footsteps of the gods as he pushed himself and his men farther east. The deeper he moved into the Orient, the more reason was replaced by fantasy. His mind became filled with romantic notions of the legendary accomplishments of heroes and gods such as Heracles and Dionysus, and he came to believe that only among the gods could he find his rightful place.

Alexander became estranged from the values of his allies, the mainland Greeks—values such as democracy and the right of every Greek to be heard. Alexander's was an autocratic regime, and his personality would not tolerate dissent from any source. Alexander's Persian retinue and some of the more obsequious and opportunistic Greeks and Macedonians around him played into his image of himself. They equated his victories in Persia and India with the greatest accomplishments of legendary heroes. They attributed to him god-like qualities and pointed out that he had long surpassed the accomplishments of his mortal father, Philip. Finally, following in the footsteps of the gods no longer sufficed, and Alexander came to believe that he was himself a god. Persian manners and mores played perfectly to his perception of his divinity as he slid deeper and deeper into the world of illusion.

The more Alexander came to regard himself as divine, the more he endured in terms of physical pain and deprivation. Along the march he suffered as much pain as he inflicted. In every battle and skirmish, he placed himself in harm's way and took every opportunity to lead his men into the worst of the combat even when there was no need for him to do so. By the time Alexander and his army had crossed the Gedrosian Desert, he had driven himself and his men to the limits of physical endurance and sanity.

In retrospect, Alexander should have followed the sage advice given him by his most senior commander, a man whom Alexander had murdered. Shortly after the victory at Issus, Darius offered to relinquish all of Asia Minor. This was an opportunity for Alexander to colonize Persia for the Greeks and Macedonians and to build perhaps the greatest empire the ancient world had ever seen. Parmenio, Alexander's most senior general, advised him to accept the Persian king's offer and content himself with what he had accomplished.

Instead, Alexander's ego prevailed over the interests of his people and he rejected the offer, preferring instead to accept the risks in pushing the army all the way to the mythical limits of the earth. In the end, when he finally returned to Babylon, all he had done was to squander his resources and wear out his soldiers and himself conquering vast areas of wasteland that no man could or ever would want to hold. When the end came for Alexander at Babylon, he was a man worn out before his time. He died in June 323 B.C. a month short of his thirty-third birthday. On the day that Alexander died, his soldiers mourned the passing of their leader, but at the same time the army and the ancient world collectively breathed a sigh of relief to be rid of him.

In the final analysis, Alexander was no better or worse than any man who attains power equal to his passion, no matter in what age or era, ancient or modern. Central to this story of his demise is the biblical injunction that historically has warned men against striving to gain the world lest they lose their souls in a sorry bargain. It is an axiom that men at the highest reaches of power have continued to ignore from one age to the next as history repeats itself in a tragic, seemingly endless, and needless spiral of human suffering. As the story of Alexander shows, power in any age never comes without cost. In the end it consumes those who pursue it and corrupts beyond redemption those who attain it. All the while, it causes horrendous amounts of suffering to incalculable numbers of innocent people.

CHAPTER I

THROUGH THE GATE
OF ALL NATIONS

PERSEPOLIS WAS A RELATIVELY YOUNG CITY AND AT THE pinnacle of its beauty when its garrison surrendered to the Macedonian conqueror in January of 330 B.C. The city had been built as the new capital of the Persian Empire by the two kings most reviled by the Greeks: Darius I and his son, Xerxes. The original name of the city as found in very early fragments of manuscripts was Parsa. The name most familiar to modern readers, Persepolis, was probably a merging of the Greek word for Persians with the word for city. Construction of the city had been started around 518 B.C. by Darius,[1] the third Persian king since the founding of the empire in 553 B.C. The city was completed in 464 B.C. just before or shortly after the death of his son and successor Xerxes I.[2] These two kings were the father and son whose armies had invaded Greece in the fifth century, and Xerxes had even succeeded in reaching and burning Athens. For the Greeks, especially those who were with Alexander when the city surrendered on that January day twenty-three hundred years ago, these two men were the most hated of all the Persian kings, hated more so than Darius III, the current king they were pursuing.

The city was isolated in the remote southwestern part of Iran at the foot of the Zagros Mountains. Because of this location, it was removed from the mainstream of the commercial and governmental activity of the empire, which was carried out in the larger cities farther north—Susa, Ecbatana, and Babylon. Because of its isolation, Persepolis evolved into a sacred place for the subjects of the Persian Empire, similar in many respects to what Mecca and Jerusalem have become today for Muslims and Jews.[3] The city became the symbolic residence for generations of Achaemenid kings and, for most of them, their final resting place. When the kings of Persia died, traditional practice was to expose their bodies on a high rocky ledge where they were picked clean by vultures. Then the remains were covered in wax and placed in rock tombs carved into the sides of the surrounding cliffs. Two of those tombs are located just behind the palaces at Persepolis, while several others are found in the cliffs of Naqsh-e-Rostam and Naqsh-e-Rajab a few kilometers from the city.

Persepolis was also important because it was the location for the most important annual event in the empire, a celebration of the New Year that was held each spring at the vernal equinox. The equinox was the traditional time of the year when thousands of ambassadors, envoys, and visitors from the subject nations of the Persian Empire converged on the city bearing vast amounts of tribute for the king. As a result, the city prospered and became the repository for the accumulated wealth of generations of Persian kings. The tradition of celebrating the New Year during the spring equinox is still maintained throughout Iran today.

The garrison at Persepolis surrendered the city to Alexander without resistance—and could not have done otherwise given its location. Persepolis lies nestled at the foot of low rocky hills overlooking the large and fertile Marvdasht plains of Iran. When Darius planned the city, the Persian Empire was at the height of its power; that any foreign enemy could penetrate far enough into its interior to threaten the capital was inconceivable to him and his successors. The site was chosen more for its natural beauty than from considerations of defense. The walls that surrounded the terrace were far from impregnable, and any invading army could easily have occupied the heights above the city. Persepolis could never have resisted a siege by Alexander and his army for any length of time.

Within the center of Persepolis, the early kings had commissioned the building of a massive foundation nearly half of a kilometer square. This foundation was constructed of a filling of sand contained by thick blocks of stone and towered nearly twenty meters above the level of the streets below. A terrace of carefully interlaced bricks had been laid on the top of this foundation, protected by high

walls and a series of square watchtowers. Twin ceremonial staircases
led up and along the northwestern face of the foundation to the terrace. Each of these monumental stairways faced the other at the base.
As they rose along the foundation, they moved away from each other
until they reached a height of some nine meters, where they turned
and rose the remaining distance to converge at the entrance to the
terrace. Even today these staircases are an impressive reminder of
the elegance and architectural sophistication of that ancient city.

The city and its inhabitants were calm that day as they awaited
with apprehension their fate under the new conqueror. When Alexander entered Persepolis, he was awed by what he found there, just
as visitors continue to be even today. The young king mounted one
of the two symmetrical staircases leading up to the terrace, and he
could not have failed to note that the stairs had been designed so that
each tread was very wide with a shallow rise. Every fourth, fifth, and
sometimes sixth step had been skillfully carved out of a single boul-
der, each placed perfectly into position. For many years the accepted
thinking among scholars was that the staircases at Persepolis had
been constructed in this manner so that horses and other large animals could be easily led up and onto the terrace for ceremonies and
sacrifices.[4] The most recent thinking, however, is that the shallow
rise of the steps was designed more out of considerations of protocol.
The shallow design of the staircases allowed groups of nobles, government officials, and envoys from the subject nations, dressed in
their finest attire for their audience with the king, to ascend to the
terrace with a minimum of effort and thus maintain the dignified
bearing befitting a royal ceremony. A similar consideration in the
design and construction is evident in all of the staircases on the terrace at Persepolis, especially those leading to the palaces and audience
halls. This accommodation allowed the king to ascend and descend
from the various buildings on the terrace while retaining the ethe-
real airs that were important to his image as a divinity.

When the young Macedonian conqueror reached the terrace, he
passed through an entry portal, fourteen meters high, known as the
Gate of All Nations. On either side of this massive entryway two
ominous and massive stone bulls, each seven meters high, stood
guard.[5] The portal is sometimes referred to as the Gate of Xerxes

because of the great carved letters inscribed over the entryway. Over the portal is written successively in three languages (Elamite, archaic Persian, and Babylonian) "I am Xerxes the great, king of kings, king of this great earth far and wide."

Through the Gate of All Nations Alexander passed into a hedonistic world of self-indulgence and fantasy that would come to stress the weaker aspects of his character. The young king from rustic Macedonia must have been taken by the scale and splendor of everything he saw. Buildings of monumental proportions and elegance abounded on this vast terrace. Persepolis was the ceremonial center of the Persian Empire, and the terrace was a symbolic representation of the power of the Achaemenid kings. It was a structure that had been designed and built to impress, and impress it does even today in its ruined state. Alexander had seen Babylon, but Persepolis was unique and he would not see anything to rival it until he entered the kingdoms of India.

To the right of the great gate leading onto the terrace was an ornate open-air audience hall known as the apadana. This was the largest and most impressive of all the buildings at Persepolis, and the idea for this great hall had been copied by Darius I from the palace of Nebuchadnezzar at Babylon.[6] In the apadana, generations of Persian kings had received representatives from the subject nations of the empire, often with several thousand people in attendance. The apadana consisted of a central hall, square in shape, covered by an elaborate roof supported by thirty-six columns that rose to a height of nearly sixty feet above the floor. At the top of each column was a capital upon which perched an ominous-looking double-headed gargoyle that leered down on the ceremonies below as it shouldered the burden of the massive cedar roof beams above. Attached to the apadana on the north, east, and west faces are smaller terraces with staircases. On the southern wing are indications of the remains of a number of rooms, probably built to house the servants and guards who attended the king during the audiences. The interior as well as exterior surfaces of the sun-dried brick walls were decorated with elaborate color-glazed tiles.

As Alexander climbed the north staircase to the apadana, he must have lingered for a moment or two to examine the elaborate details in the architecture of the walls. Today the walls of the main staircases on the northern and eastern facades contain the remains of elaborate bas-reliefs that depict Iranian nobles, soldiers from the king's royal bodyguard, and gift-bearing ambassadors from the subject nations of the empire. The eastern bas-reliefs are better preserved than those on the northern facade, which have been badly weathered over the centuries. To a length of nearly one hundred meters along the north and east faces of the apadana, these detailed bas-reliefs reflect the remnants of ancient Persian art at its best. There are two smaller and less elaborate staircases located at the far corners of the apadana terrace.

Adjacent to the apadana on the southeast corner is a small structure known as the council hall. It was here that the Achaemenid kings consulted with their military commanders, ministers, and other high government officials on a more intimate basis. A double stairway decorated with bas-reliefs depicting Persian and Medean nobles connects the eastern entry to this council chamber with the apadana. Scholars have speculated that this hall could have played an important role for the Persians in the determination of their celestial order, and perhaps it served as the basis for fixing their calendar. It is interesting to note that this council hall is the only structure in Persepolis where the capitals of the pillars supporting the roof were cast in the form of human heads on animal bodies.

Just a few yards east of the apadana are the remains of the hall of a hundred columns. It is the second largest building in the Persepolis complex and has a central audience hall larger than the one in the apadana. The roof of this hall was supported by one hundred tricolor wooden columns set on massive stone bases and placed in rows of ten. The columns rose to a height of fourteen meters. Twelve wide and elaborate stone doorways led into the hall from each side. On the walls of the eastern and western entryways are the remains of intricate carvings that depict the Persian kings contending against the worst demons hell could conjure from its depths. Figures of animals and demons such as these played a large part in the decorative motif of the art at Persepolis and lead to tantalizing speculations about the psychology of the Persians. The hall of a hundred columns must have functioned as another audience hall for the king but the redundancy of these two halls has never been satisfactorily explained by scholars.

At the height of the Achaemenids' rule, those who entered these audience halls were required to prostrate themselves in adoration, for by Persian custom the king was regarded as a divinity. This act of prostrating oneself before the king was called "proskynesis" by the Greeks. It was considered a particularly debasing practice characteristic of Orientals. In addition to proskynesis, during the royal audience those in attendance were required to be keep their hands hidden in their sleeves. While the exact reason for this practice is uncertain, it was perhaps used as a safeguard against the risk of assassination.[7] After the audience, when the king had retired, his subjects were allowed to come forward. They were permitted to marvel at the ornate throne, though it was an offense punishable by death for anyone but the king to sit on it.[8]

To the south and west of the throne hall was the area of the terrace where the residences of the Achaemenid kings had been built. In this quarter Alexander discovered the palace of Xerxes I, the most elaborate of all on the terrace. The palace quickly captured the attention of the young conqueror. It had been constructed on the highest point and consisted of a central hall with thirty-six columns, a pillared terrace on the north face, and a number of rooms in the east and west wings. A veranda on the south side led discreetly down two small stairways to the harem.

A second smaller palace is located just next to the main one. This smaller palace is also believed to have been commissioned by Xerxes and contains carved bas-reliefs on the stairways and door frames that depict the king fighting lions and demons. These images appealed to Alexander's sense of fantasy and played into his preoccupation with legends of heroic deeds. Other more mundane reliefs on the walls of this palace showed the activities of daily life in the royal household, such as servants carrying food for the king's table and attendants shielding the king from the sun with umbrellas while he sat on the throne.

Alexander moved through one of the main doorways and strolled into a nearly deserted courtyard of the palace. The afternoon sun, warm even in January in the southernmost area of Iran, caused him to remove his helmet and undo his breastplate. Standing bareheaded, he gazed down with wonder and then admiration at the face of a stone statue that had been toppled onto the courtyard floor[9] and now lay broken on its back. Persians had pulled the statue over earlier that day hoping no doubt to curry favor with their new master. Some of them cowered in the shadows and doorways of the adjacent buildings as they waited to gauge the new king's reaction to what they had done. Only if he reacted favorably would they dare to approach him to pay homage and ask for his favor.

For the moment, though, Alexander was alone with his thoughts in the courtyard as he contemplated the fallen and broken statue of a once great king. It had been a skillfully sculpted piece, done perhaps by a Greek artisan nearly a century and a half before. The statue mirrored not only the features of the man who had commissioned it, but by its size and majesty it proclaimed to all who entered the palace that here was the king who had held sway over the greatest empire in the ancient world.

This was Xerxes, the king who had brought the proud Hellenes to their knees in 480 B.C. This was Xerxes, the king who had bridged the Hellespont and led an army to invade Greece. This was Xerxes, the king who had slaughtered the Spartan defenders at Thermopylae and then marched triumphantly into Athens, that most beautiful of Greek cities, and burned her sacred temples. This was the king who had committed sacrilege when he ordered his soldiers to sack the Greek temples and carry off their treasures to adorn the Persian palaces. It was the hatred of the memory of this man, now dead for more than a hundred years, and of his father before him, that had helped Philip of Macedonia and then Alexander to unite the otherwise factious and independent Greeks. Alexander exploited and manipulated this hatred for the Persian to keep his Macedonian and Greek soldiers motivated as he led them over the Hellespont to Asia Minor and then Egypt, and then across the deserts of Syria and Iraq. Finally, after nearly seven thousand kilometers and four years of fighting, they had reached Persepolis and the completion of their crusade of vengeance.

Now the image of that once mighty Persian king lay broken, like his empire, at the feet of a Macedonian conquer. Xerxes and his empire were no longer great, and history had once more shifted and readjusted the fortunes of men and nations. Now it was the twenty-five-year-old Alexander of Macedonia who was "king of this great earth far and wide." Under Alexander's command, the Greeks and Macedonians had defeated the Persian armies sent against them in three decisive battles—Granicus, Issus, and Gaugamela. Three times the last of the Persian kings, Darius III, had sued for peace and offered generous concessions. Each time Alexander's most senior military advisor had urged the young conqueror to reach an accommodation with the Persian king, and each time Alexander had refused and pressed forward deeper and deeper into Persia.

Now the last and weakest of the Persian kings was on the run. Darius III had deserted Persepolis and taken refuge in the northern mountains of Iran at Ecbatana. His mother, two daughters, and young son had fallen into the hands of Alexander following the battle of Issus nearly three years earlier. His wife, also captured at Issus, had died less than a year earlier just before the battle at Gaugamela. Some ancient sources have speculated that she died giving birth to Alexander's child. Other sources refute the notion and maintain that Alexander's "nature" would not allow him to "rape captive women."[10]

As Alexander stood on the terrace of the palace of Xerxes that afternoon, he looked out over Persepolis and the wide lush valley beyond. This would be his greatest moment, and there would never be another like it in his short lifetime. He had defied convention and the odds, and now he stood in the palace of Xerxes as conqueror and master of Persia. Alexander pondered the broken statue at his feet and the memory of the man it represented. As a few of his closest companions and senior officers came into the courtyard and surrounded him, he addressed that broken slab of marble as if he were speaking directly to the Persian king himself. Alexander asked rhetorically whether he should suppress his hatred for the memory of this enemy king and recognize that he had accomplished many great things, not the least impressive of which was the completion of this magnificent city. Should the Macedonian conqueror pay this long-dead Persian king the respect due him as the builder and ruler of a once great empire? Should he order the statue repaired and set upright once more to commemorate the memory of Xerxes?

Alexander's companions urged him to leave it overturned and

broken, a fitting symbol that the "hegemon"[11] of the Greeks had punished the Persian Xerxes. So Alexander left the statue where it lay and moved on to survey less symbolic but infinitely more lucrative areas on the great terrace. Alexander of Macedonia would do more to this city in the coming days and weeks than just leave a broken statue lying on its back in the courtyard of an empty palace.

The repository for the royal treasury was located adjacent to the palaces on the southeast quadrant of the terrace. Alexander was anxious to take control of its contents, for he had captured what at the time was probably the richest city in the ancient world. While revenge against Persia had motivated the Greeks and Macedonians into coming so far, money was the principal reason Alexander had come to Persepolis. So anxious had Alexander been to secure the treasury that he had broken off his pursuit of Darius at Susa a month or so earlier and allowed the king to escape. Alexander had fought his way south through hostile mountain tribes and a murderous ambush to reach Persepolis and capture the treasury. He anticipated that the wealth of the Persian kings, most of it stored at Persepolis, would make him financially independent of the mainland Greek city-states. This financial independence would allow Alexander to pursue his own agenda in the East, an agenda that was evolving and would become very different from that of the Greeks and Macedonians he had led over the past four years.

At the entrance to the treasury building Alexander was greeted by Tiridates, the Persian noble who had served Darius III as the guardian of the royal wealth. Now Tiridates was equally as eager to serve the new Macedonian conqueror. A few days earlier, in the mountains some sixty kilometers from the city, the loyal Persian satrap Ariobarzanes with a contingent of infantry and cavalry[12] had attempted to defend Persepolis by holding Alexander's army in a narrow defile called the Persian Gates. That battle, where a small force held a much larger invading army at bay in a narrow space, was an uncanny replay of the famous battle of Thermopylae in 480 B.C., except this time the sides were reversed. Alexander and his army, searching for the shortest route to Persepolis, had been drawn into a mountain defile and then trapped by Ariobarzanes and his forces like animals caught in a hunter's pit. A century and a half earlier on the Greek mainland, a massive Persian army under Xerxes had been blocked in a similar manner in the narrow plain of Thermopylae by a small force of Spartans.

From the heights above, the Persians rolled huge boulders down on the Greeks and Macedonians. Many of the boulders were so large that they crushed entire groups of men trapped below. It had been a well-planned and executed ambush by an experienced Persian commander, and Alexander had walked right into it. It was his worst defeat of the entire campaign, and his casualties were high. Alexander was infuriated not so much by his hatred of the Persians who held his forces pinned down in the defile, but by his own stupidity in having being drawn into the trap in the first place. The Greeks and Macedonians were forced to slowly retreat, sustaining additional losses from the Persian arrows raining down incessantly upon them. When the soldiers who survived the carnage finally returned, exhausted, to the safety of their camp, Alexander was ashamed to face them. Not only had he failed them as their commander by leading them into a trap, but he had left their dead behind. Among the Greeks and Macedonians, nothing was more disgraceful than to retreat from the field of battle leaving fallen comrades behind, and no duty was more sacred than the recovery and proper burial of those who had fallen in combat.[13]

While Ariobarzanes was fighting to keep the Greeks and Macedonians from taking the city, Tiridates, through a secret messenger, had been negotiating with Alexander to surrender it. The imperial treasurer knew that resistance was futile, and he took the more practical route of offering to cooperate in return for his life and a possible future. He secured the treasury for Alexander but warned that any further delay could result in it being plundered by the people of the city and elements of the garrison.[14] The bottleneck at the Persian Gates was finally broken when a man who knew the area showed Alexander a path by which a contingent of his best soldiers were able to climb up through the surrounding mountains and come down from above and behind the Persian defenders. Here was another similarity to the sequence of events that had transpired at Thermopylae.

When Alexander's forces descended on the Persian position, Ariobarzanes and his soldiers were caught by surprise and the tables were turned. Attacked from above, the Persians could no longer hold the pass. Alexander's main force was able to breach the defile, and the satrap fled to what he expected would be the safety of Persepolis. When Ariobarzanes and the remnants of his forces reached the gates of the city, they found them closed. Tiridates, standing on the battlements of Persepolis, turned a deaf ear to their pleas and left the valiant commander and his men outside the walls to be killed by the pursuing Macedonians.[15]

For betraying the city and the prospect of future services, the royal treasurer anticipated that he, like the Persian quislings Mazaeus of Babylon and Abuletes of Susa, would be retained in a prestigious and lucrative position to advise and assist the Macedonian king.[16] At Susa, Alexander had taken possession of one of the larger treasure depots of the Persian kings with the full cooperation of the satrap. While Alexander had allowed Abuletes to remain as satrap as a reward for his role in surrendering the city, he nevertheless took the satrap's son as hostage and then placed two Macedonians as commanders of the city garrison. While Alexander would readily reward Persians for their cooperation, there was no indication as yet that he trusted them. All that, however, would change in the coming months and years as Alexander would move away from his Macedonians and Greeks and closer to the Persians.

Tiridates led Alexander into a large building behind the palace of Xerxes that served as both an armory for the royal bodyguard and a repository for the king's wealth. Diffused light filtered through a series of openings in the roof above and washed gently over the tons of gold and silver bullion that had been neatly and methodically stored there. Within the treasury building were 120,000 talents[17] of bullion, the largest single concentration of wealth to be found anywhere in the ancient world.

Darius I had imposed a tribute of precious metals in addition to a tribute of goods on his satraps and on the subject nations of the empire. Instead of converting that tribute into coins that could then have been put into circulation, Darius and his successors had it melted and then formed into ingots of gold and silver. The bars were stored in the palace treasury, and when the kings of Persia needed to finance particular projects, wars, or adventures, the precious metals were cast into coins. It was Darius who had introduced the coining of money into the empire; hence, the Persian coin became known as the Daric. Until that time, the empire had been administered largely on the basis of barter.

Successive generations of Persian kings had dipped into the treasury and spent vast sums on themselves. Over the years, they had spent great amounts on administering and expanding the empire and had dispensed large sums in fighting, hiring, and bribing the Greeks. Yet no matter how much money the kings spent, every year at the New Year ceremony more came in to replenish and add to the royal coffers. In the treasury building at Persepolis, Alexander was shown the full measure of how wealthy the Achaemenid kings of Persia had been and how wealthy he had now become.

Alexander found so much bullion in the royal treasury that day that he became, without question, the richest man in the ancient world.[18] Combined with the treasure he had taken from the Persians over the past two years, first from the royal treasury at Damascus then later from Babylon and Susa, the wealth that Alexander controlled is said by the manuscripts to have been beyond belief.[19] And it was all his. Now Alexander had all the money he needed to complete his war against Darius and to finance his future plans without depending on his Greek allies or anybody else. Alexander was his own man. Twenty thousand mules and between three to five thousand camels were brought from Susa and Babylon in order to transport Alexander's treasure to a central repository, which was first planned for Susa but later became Ecbatana.[20]

In the short space of a few months, Alexander had amassed what was probably the greatest hoard ever taken by a conqueror. The total from the imperial treasuries at Damascus, Susa, and Persepolis came to between 180,000 and 200,000 talents of gold and silver bullion as well as a considerable amount in coins.[21] Added to this already enormous treasure were an additional 6,000 talents taken at the surrender of Pasagardae.

Pasagardae, the former capital of the Persian Empire under its founder and first king, Cyrus the Great,[22] was a much smaller city than Persepolis and was located in a more isolated but equally beautiful valley some eighty-five kilometers northeast of Persepolis. The city had been maintained over the years only because of its historical associations with Cyrus and was used as the ceremonial site for the coronation of the Persian kings. The satrap of Pasagardae had quickly surrendered the city to Alexander after the fall of Persepolis in the hope of avoiding a massacre of his people. When Alexander arrived at Pasagardae, he visited the tomb of Cyrus where he was moved by the simplicity and modesty of this great king's final resting place.

Alexander was favorably inclined toward the memory of Cyrus the Great, even if he was the founder of the Persian Empire. As a boy Alexander had probably read and been influenced by the writings of the Athenian philosopher and general Xenophon.[23] Xenophon had been one of the leaders of a Greek mercenary expedition in Persia the century before and had written extensively about his experiences. Xenophon had admired Cyrus and believed that an absolute ruler, an enlightened monarch such as this first of the Persian kings, was the best form of government for Greeks as well as barbarians. This was an idea that appealed to Alexander and one he was increasingly prone to try to put into practice as his power increased. But it was also an idea that ran counter to Greek ideals of democracy and would bring the young conqueror into conflict not only with the Greeks but with his own Macedonians as well.

So moved was Alexander by this great ruler's tomb that he provided money for its restoration and assigned one of his own officers, a Macedonian, to protect this final resting place of Cyrus the Great. A few ruins from Pasagardae still remain today. Although the natural beauty of the site is exceptional and tranquil, the ruins are not nearly as impressive as Persepolis. What remains of Pasagardae are the foundations of a few buildings and the tomb of Cyrus in a little valley where gentle whirlwinds and miniature cyclones sweep through with an amazing regularity. It is almost as if the spirit of the Achaemenid king is contained in these whirlwinds as they blow from one end to the other in this picturesque valley, hidden off the beaten track and just a few kilometers from the modern highway that leads to Isfahan.

With the wealth Alexander took from Persepolis, his financial supremacy in the ancient world was assured. His situation had improved dramatically since he had first landed on the shores of Asia

Minor near the ruins of Troy in the spring of 334 B.C. He had leaped
onto shore from his ship and claimed all of Asia as "spear-won territory." This was a tall claim for a young man with only his self-
confidence, a small army made up of restless allies, a month's
provisions, and seventy talents to sustain him. Alexander had been
perilously close to bankruptcy at this point in the expedition, and
it was questionable if he would have been able to pay his men. To
finance the expedition he was dependent on help from the Greek
mainland and whatever income his soldiers could generate by looting as they moved east. The entire story of Alexander the Great could
easily have ended on the shores of Asia Minor as the tale of Alexander the Little, an insignificant little tyrant whose career warranted
little more than inclusion into one of history's footnotes. In addition
to his financial problems, the young Macedonian king took unnec-
essary risks in those early months of the campaign. He had been so
anxious to secure his first victory that he came close to being killed
in his first battle against the Persians at the Granicus River. Alexander was saved by a friend he would later murder. In addition to the
enemies in front of him, Alexander was facing rebellions against
his authority in southern Greece. He had discontented and restless
allies among the Greeks, which combined with his financial problems threatened to end not only his campaign against Persia but also
his life.[24]

After a rocky start, however, fortune smiled on Alexander, and
over the next four years he did well. As a result he was able to send
money to Antipater, his regent in Macedonia, to quell the rebellions
against his authority that were developing on mainland Greece.
When Alexander took Persepolis, he freed himself from any further
financial dependence on the Greek city-states. With the wealth he
took from the Persians, he could afford to raise his own armies and
pursue his own agenda independently of the Greeks. Alexander was
pleased with the extent of the treasure he found at Persepolis, and
Tiridates was in turn rewarded for his cooperation. The Persian treasurer was left temporarily in charge of the vast wealth at Persepolis,
but, as at Susa, with Macedonians to guard it.[25]

In spite of the wealth he found at Persepolis, Alexander would not
be merciful toward the city. He had a final obligation to fulfill to his

Greek allies, one that demanded satisfaction through Persian suffering. According to at least one of the ancient sources, Alexander held a "bitter enmity" toward the people of Persepolis and intended to destroy them and their city completely.[26] Given that the people of Persepolis had surrendered to him without a fight and cooperated with him in every way, and in light of examples from Alexander's past that often included the generous and humane treatment of cities that surrendered without resistance, this hatred makes little sense. While it is true that Ariobarzanes and his forces had inflicted severe casualties on the Greeks and Macedonians at the Persian Gates, there can be little doubt that once Alexander entered the city the inhabitants blamed the resistance entirely on the dead satrap and extolled the cooperation of Tiridates. Alexander's hatred must have either been contrived for political reasons or derived from a covert source of anger and frustration deep within him.

The political reasons for Alexander's hatred of Persepolis are obvious and understandable in the context of the war he was waging against Persia. Shortly after the assassination of his father Philip in 336 B.C., Alexander had been appointed strategos, supreme commander of the Greek forces, by the League of Corinth. This was not a permanent appointment but only for the duration of the war against Persia. The surrender of Persepolis signaled the official end of the war even though Darius III had not been captured. In that context, Alexander prepared to discharge the last of his obligations as strategos to both his army and the mainland Greeks. Revenge against Persia had been the theme for this war and the reason the Greeks united to fight it. The taking of Persepolis was uneventful, and it is impossible to imagine the warlike Greeks and Macedonians accepting a peaceful and uneventful surrender of the city that symbolized all they hated about Persia. There had to be a psychological closing to this chapter in their history, and it had to be violent and filled with retribution.

On a personal level, Alexander probably held no more animosity toward these unfortunate people then he did toward any enemy he faced. But he had motivated and led the Greeks by the use of a common and focused hatred of the Persians. Now circumstances compelled him to the logical culmination of that hatred—the destruction of their capital. There were additional pressures on Alexander from his army to fulfill the customary expectation that as conquerors they would kill the men of the city and enslave the women. The luxury of Persepolis, the opulence of a city that exceeded all others, inflamed the desires of his soldiers to enrich themselves.

Alexander was compelled by his role to fulfill the expectations of the Greeks on the mainland and the demands of his army. The sacking of Persepolis would be a sign to the entire ancient world that the war of revenge was over and that it had been decisively won by Alexander and the Greeks. The city had to be looted and its people massacred. It was the only acceptable conclusion to the war. Alexander had taken what he needed—the treasury. Now the Greeks and Macedonians eagerly awaited their turn at the spoils. All they needed was word from their commander so that they might unleash their fury on the helpless people of the city.

While Alexander secured the treasury at Persepolis, his soldiers, camped outside the city walls, were becoming increasingly impatient. They were anxious to exact vengeance on the Persians for the transgressions of their ancestors against the Greek homeland. At the same time, they relished the opportunity to slaughter, rape, and pillage a defenseless and prosperous population. Sacking had been the pattern when the Greeks and Macedonians took the cities of Tyre and Gaza on the southeastern Mediterranean coast two years earlier. At Gaza, Alexander had set the example when he tied the city's satrap and defender, Batis, behind his chariot and proceeded to drag him around the city walls. This was done in emulation of the Greek hero, Achilles, who nine hundred years before had dragged the lifeless body of the fallen Trojan prince, Hector, around the walls of Troy in a similar manner. What occurred at Gaza had been a sadistic and barbaric episode, yet it was an incident that was consistent with Alexander's romantic notions and neurotic misconceptions of himself as a Homeric hero like Achilles.

Since that incident, Alexander had tried to temper this image of himself and his men as barbaric invaders. He had restrained himself and his soldiers as they moved farther east, possibly because he was seeking to court the Persian nobility into accepting and legitimizing his rule as the divine heir to the Achaemenid throne. When the cities of Babylon and Susa surrendered, Alexander held his army in check.

He treated these two cities with remarkable generosity and showed great leniency to their people. In return, the inhabitants responded graciously, obsequiously, and appreciatively, especially the residents of Babylon, that "mother of all whores."[27] This was a city that had a reputation throughout the ancient world for entertaining visitors in its own unique style.[28] Babylon, much more than Susa, was a wide-open city. One reason it received such lenient treatment at the hands of Alexander was no doubt because its residents flattered the ego of the Macedonian conqueror and catered salaciously to the needs of his soldiers. Yet Alexander, for all his restraint, had not at Babylon and Susa been recognized as the legitimate heir to the throne of Darius by the Persian nobility, and this was what he had begun to crave.

Persepolis was the symbolic capital of the empire, and no doubt Alexander anticipated that the Persians would proclaim him as their new king when he occupied it. But his recognition, with all the implications of divinity that he craved, did not materialize. Political reasons alone do not suffice to completely explain why Alexander allowed the looting of this magnificent city and the massacre of its defenseless population. For a complete explanation, one is forced to look deeper into the psyche of the man who led the Greeks and Macedonians. By the time Alexander had reached Persepolis, there were indications that he wanted more from this war than to be recognized as a conqueror. Alexander had begun to formulate aspirations of attaining if not the status of a god among men at least the status of hero. A hero to the Greeks was a man who through his exceptional deeds on earth was in his lifetime or upon his death allowed to join the company of the gods. Heracles was the classic Greek example. The idea of joining the gods in his lifetime played directly into Alexander's heroic and divine notions of himself as the second Achilles and the new Heracles for his age.

The Orient, with its slavish adulation of its kings, its sensuality, luxury, and decadence, was beginning to affect the young Macedonian. The more he conquered, the more the Orient played into his fantasies and flamed his desires. He had been recognized in Egypt as a pharaoh, and with this recognition had come at least the implications of a quasi-divine status. While in Egypt Alexander had made a pilgrimage out into the desert to the oasis sanctuary of the god Ammon. This sanctuary was a respected and established oracle. It was familiar to the Greeks, who regarded the Egyptian god Ammon as a local manifestation of Zeus. Alexander believed that his ancestor Heracles had consulted this oracle, and so he turned to Ammon for advice.

In the desert the high priests of Ammon told Alexander what he longed to hear. They addressed him as the son of Zeus-Ammon, and for Alexander the oracle had acknowledged his divine lineage and enhanced his "Greek character" among his soldiers.[29] Alexander's mother, Olympias, played further into the fantasy when she wrote her son that she had been impregnated by the king of the gods prior to her wedding night.[30] From then on Alexander referred to Philip as his putative father, and up until his death all his words and actions reflected his belief that Zeus—king of the gods, ruler of Olympus— was his true father.[31]

The farther Alexander moved into the Persian Empire, the deeper he was drawn into a world of oriental influences and the more those influences would play into his evolving perception of himself as divine. This was something that did not play well with either the Greeks or the Macedonians in his army. It would only take time and the right set of circumstances for his aspirations to burst forth with all the passion of which he was capable and bring him into conflict with the more conservative elements in his command structure. For the Greeks, no man was divine and any man who thought himself so was a threat to their much-cherished notions of freedom.

By the time Alexander reached Persepolis, he might have been questioning any ideas of his conciliation with the Persian nobility. It was doubtful that he would be recognized as the divine successor to the throne of Darius by the Persian aristocracy. There were many among the Persian nobles who had served Darius and were now all too ready to cooperate with Alexander. However, few among them would accept Alexander as a god-king to be worshiped in the same manner as the Achaemenids had been. For the high priests of Persia as well as the Iranian aristocracy, Alexander and his Macedonians were little more than "godless, violent, foreign usurpers."[32]

For what the Persians would not give, Alexander would now punish the people of Persepolis by murder, rape, and pillage. Persepolis would serve as an example of the consequences of incurring the Macedonian king's displeasure and perhaps stimulate the subject nations of the Persian Empire to pay him homage in the spring during the annual New Year celebration. This may help in understanding why Alexander allowed his soldiers to sack Persepolis even though Tiridates had surrendered the city without resistance. If Alexander could not obtain the Persian crown by the approbation he craved, then he would take it by force. He would show himself to be a demon from hell worse than anything the Persians had ever seen depicted on the walls of their palaces.

Alexander prepared the army for the sacking of the city. He assembled his officers and began by telling them that no city was more hateful to the Greeks than Persepolis.[33] Then he told his soldiers how from this very city, which they now held, the orders had been given— first by Darius and then by his son Xerxes—for the Persian armies to invade Greece. Persian kings, he railed, had made godless war upon Europe. Now the time had come for the Persians to pay as the Greeks fulfilled their sacred oaths of vengeance to their forefathers.

It was nearly all propaganda, and like most propaganda ancient or modern very little of it was true. Before Alexander took the city, few if any Greeks on the mainland had heard of Persepolis because it was so remote and isolated.[34] The cities the Greeks associated with Persia were Babylon and Susa, the commercial and administrative centers of the empire and along with Ecbatana the three principal residences of the Achaemenid monarchs. Susa was the winter palace of the Persian kings and was the place most associated with the invasions of Greece. In addition, it had been at Susa, only fifty-seven years before (387 B.C.), that Artaxerxes II[35] had acted as a power broker among the Greeks. The Persian king had dictated a harsh peace to the humbled ambassadors that ended the fighting between the city-states of mainland Greece.

When Alexander entered Susa he found many of the treasures and works of art that the army of Xerxes had looted from Athens in 480 B.C. Yet in spite of all these reasons to extract revenge, Susa was left untouched. It was Persepolis that bore the full wrath of Alexander's anger, which is difficult to understand considering the minor role the city played in affecting the affairs of the Greeks.[36] Persepolis suffered because it was a symbol, not for anything its people had done.

Then to further incite his army for what they were about to do, Alexander reminded them of the most recent example they had seen of how cruel the Persians could be. Alexander and his army had encountered a large group of old men on the road to Persepolis. They were Greeks who had recently been freed from years of Persian captivity. Some had been captured soldiers or mercenaries in earlier wars, while others had been carried off as slaves by the Persians in Asia Minor. These Greeks had lived around Persepolis as slaves, many of them for decades, and only recently had they been freed by their masters in a vain attempt to curry favor with Alexander. All of these Greeks had been crippled or maimed in some horrible way. Some had a foot amputated, others a hand or ear or nose. Their flesh had been branded in barbarian letters to mark them for life as slaves.[37] Alexander had wept openly when he saw their condition. He offered them money and provisions to return to Greece but most refused, considering themselves too grotesque to be able to return to their native land. That, for Alexander's soldiers, was justification enough for what they were about to do.

On the night Persepolis was looted greed and cruelty accompanied the Greeks. The looting of the city began shortly after dusk, although at least one ancient source contends that the Greeks began the looting immediately upon their entry into the city on the first day.[38] While the soldiers broke into the homes of the common people, Alexander and his senior officers looted the palaces on the terrace. The treasury was off-limits to everyone, as this was the exclusive property of Alexander. Because Persepolis housed the wealth of Persia, accumulated over the last two centuries, and because it had become the ceremonial center of the empire, the inhabitants of the city had prospered. Not only gold and silver in great quantities were stored in the treasury, but vast quantities of expensive clothing, the finest cloth, intricate furniture, and valuable household items adorned the homes of not only the nobles but many of the merchants. Even the homes of the common tradesmen in Persepolis contained furniture and clothing.

The rampage began with the slaughter of the Persian men and boys—not just those who resisted but all of them. Then the Greeks and Macedonians turned their attention to the unfortunate women and girls. Often the soldiers dragged them away from their homes more because of the value and beauty of the clothing and jewels that they wore than for their use in gratifying lust. The women and girls were stripped and then devoured by a mob of what had once been disciplined soldiers. Garments and jewels were ripped from the bodies of the living as well as the dead.

The orgy of looting, murder, rape, and mayhem continued all through that night. Ordinary people as well as the wealthy were indiscriminately cut down by the Greeks and Macedonians. Many of the unfortunate, resigning themselves to their impending deaths, chose to take their own lives rather than wait to be butchered. Entire families, dressed in their best clothing and clinging to each other for emotional strength, hurled themselves from the roofs of their barricaded homes as the Greeks and Macedonians beat down their doors. Some families set fire to the interiors of their homes and chose to perish in flames fueled by the luxury that had once surrounded and comforted them in better times. That night in Persepolis, human life became the least valuable commodity as the Greeks and Macedonians rampaged through the city.

Alexander and his officers entered the palace of Darius III. It was modest compared to the other palaces that surrounded it and had been recently completed in the only space remaining on the terrace, a corner section bounded on the north by the palace of Darius I and on the east by the palace of Xerxes. The palace was similar to that of Xerxes yet on a much smaller and more modest scale. There was no great double stairway to the north—just a relatively simple entrance. They proceeded to empty the king's cushion, a large chamber with five thousand talents of gold at the head of the royal bed. Then they looted the king's footstool, a smaller chamber with three thousand talents at the foot of the bed. Alexander had his men dismantle and carry away the golden vine, an elaborately crafted rope of braided gold that was embedded with jewels and entwined throughout the posters and rafters of the royal bed.[39]

As the night wore on, the looting reached such a level of insanity that Greeks and Macedonians began to kill each other in a mindless frenzy of greed and lust. Priceless works of art were destroyed, and the looters became so crazed that they even carried off the worthless limbs of broken statues. At last Alexander was forced to order a stop to the slaughter and the looting. Calm began once more to prevail among the army units. The remaining Persian women and girls were spared so that they could be used as slaves and harlots for the troops in the coming months.

Persepolis, which had once been the richest and one of the most beautiful cities in the ancient world, now "exceeded all others in misery."[40] Why the city and its people were handed over to the soldiers in such a violent way is something contemporary scholars, especially those who admire Alexander as a heroic figure, have expressed difficulty in understanding and accepting.[41] There was no need to do it. If anything, Alexander should have treated this city with respect if he had any hope of inheriting the Achaemenid crown by legitimate means.[42]

Persepolis had surrendered without resistance, and the Greeks had found plenty of gold and silver to make them wealthy. Even allowing for the looting of the private homes, there seems to have been no reason for the killing of the men and boys or for the rape, murder, and enslavement of the women and girls. All this horror Alexander justified because of the mutilated Greek captives he encountered outside the city the day before and because of the vengeance the Greeks needed to extract for the Persian wrongs against their country a century and a half earlier. It did not matter that generations of Greeks had been in Persian service over that same period of time or that substantial numbers of Greeks were still in Persian service. In fact, over the last several years, Alexander faced more Greeks on the battlefields fighting as mercenaries with Darius than he had in his own army.

For decades Greek politicians on the mainland had willingly accepted money in return for allowing Persian kings to influence the affairs of their city-states. Even as Alexander prepared to face Darius on the field of battle at Issus, his allies—the Athenians and the

Thebans along with the Spartans—had sent ambassadors behind his back to negotiate with the Persian king.[43] Had the city of Persepolis resisted Alexander to its last defender it could not have been treated worse than it was after it surrendered peacefully. When it was over, Alexander boasted in letters he sent home how he had ordered the Persian captives to be massacred.[44] As the looters hauled their goods and dragged their new slaves back to their camp, they passed with hardly a glance beneath the once proud words of Darius I chiseled upon a wall overhead: "This is the land of Persia, which Ahuramazda [Persian god] granted me, it is fair, rich in men and horses, and trembles before no enemy." Those days were over. The glory and might of Persia were finished, and all the empire would tremble before Alexander and his army by the time he was finished.

When the looting and killing finally ended, an eerie calm settled over the city. The soldiers, exhausted from murdering defenseless men and boys, raping their women, and looting their homes, took the time to rest and take stock of all they had amassed. Alexander chose Persepolis to end his holy crusade against the Persians and fulfill his final obligation to the Greeks who had appointed him strategos. With the looting of the city, he owed nothing further to his army or the Greeks on the mainland. Alexander had avenged Greece and at the same time made most of those who had accompanied him wealthy men relative to the poverty of their countrymen on the Greek mainland. Joining Alexander on his expedition had proven to be a profitable venture for most of them. Casualties, relatively speaking, had been light. Massacring the defenseless was easy. Their thoughts turned now to going home.

No matter what his men thought or might have hoped for, Alexander had no intention of returning to Greece, at least not in the foreseeable future. He moved his quarters into one of the palaces on the terrace and spent the next few months in and around Persepolis ostensibly for the purpose of resting his army through the winter months. When Alexander sat on the empty throne of Darius for the first time, an old Greek, a family friend who had accompanied the army, wept openly at the sight. When asked why on such a joyous occasion the old man was given to tears, he replied that it saddened him to think that the Greeks who had died fighting the Persians over the last two centuries had been denied the chance to witness this historic moment. Now a king of the Greeks sat upon the Persian throne.[45] This was not, however, the first time Alexander had sat upon a Persian throne. Months earlier, when he captured Susa, he had tried out the king's throne, but because Alexander was a man of short stature and the Persian king had been so tall his feet had been unable to touch the floor. The embarrassing scene was quickly remedied when one of Alexander's officers brought a low table to place under his feet.[46]

As the weeks passed at Persepolis, Alexander believed that his officers were becoming increasingly more used to the luxury of their surroundings and to their newfound wealth. Most had amassed fortunes due largely to Alexander's generosity, but now the king found that they were becoming lazy and extravagant. The wealthier Alexander had become, the more generous he was with his friends and officers as well as his family back in Macedonia. To his mother, Olympias, he sent vast quantities of treasure, and she in return wrote him back warning him to be less generous with his officers and friends. Excessive generosity, she warned, diminished his stature as a king and could breed a dangerous excess of familiarity, even contempt, among his officers that could become troublesome for him later on.

During the next four months at Persepolis, Alexander kept himself busy, at first hunting and then in carrying out a number of minor military operations against the mountain tribes in the area. Alexander craved action and could not remain idle for long. With a picked force of infantry and more than a thousand horsemen, he set out into the interior of Persia. He pushed ever deeper into the surrounding countryside and mountains, intent on subduing the tribes who were living there. This happened, according to the ancient sources, at the setting of the Pleiades,[47] probably in March or April of 330 B.C. when there was still a considerable amount of snow in the mountains.

Due to the time of year, the conditions, especially in the mountains, were difficult. Nevertheless, Alexander pushed his men on through the snow and cold, usually by setting an example for them when it came to stamina. The people he was pursuing were a rustic, simple country folk who paid their tribute to the Persian king and in return were used to being left alone. Alexander attacked them at a time when they least expected him to invade and were ill prepared to defend themselves. They quickly came to terms with their new master, and in the end whether they paid a Macedonian or Persian king made little difference in their difficult and isolated lives. In return, Alexander promised them fair and humane treatment and, after extracting his tribute, returned to Persepolis.

After Alexander subdued the mountain tribes he reduced many of the villages at the lower elevations around Persepolis to ruins. All the tribes eventually fell to him, and within a month he returned to distribute what he had taken among his friends. There were banquets in his honor, games, and the usual sacrifices to the gods to commemorate the success of the campaign. Many of Alexander's friends and officers did not join him in his military forays into the countryside and instead preferred to enjoy their idleness at Persepolis. Many had become lazy and openly critical of Alexander's attempts to keep them active through military expeditions. According to the ancient sources, Alexander tolerated this criticism at first and would even joke that it was the lot of a king to be generous and confer favors on others only to be criticized in return.[48] At this point in his career, Alexander apparently still retained a remarkably mild and conciliatory disposition toward his officers and friends, even those who criticized him or disagreed with him. All this would change drastically in the coming months as he moved the army farther east and began to put into place his own agenda.

While Alexander had been campaigning in the mountains, a steady stream of opportunists seeking to benefit from the success of the young king had filed into Persepolis. They had come all through that winter and well into the spring from the Greek mainland, a collection of the types who are eager to profit from the misfortunes of others. Among those who came to Persepolis that spring was an Athenian courtesan, Thais, a young woman who would bring as much misery and destruction to the city as Alexander did.

While the looting of Persepolis and the violence against its defenseless population of noncombatants were reprehensible by any standards in any age, what Alexander did a few months later as he prepared to leave the city has raised more argument, debate, speculation, and apology among generations of scholars than probably any other incident in his entire career. As if the city and its people had not suffered enough from the barbarities of the looting, the violence, and the occupation, in May of that same year, Alexander ordered the magnificent palaces and audience halls on the terrace burned shortly before he left to take up the pursuit of Darius.

The circumstances that immediately precipitated the burning of Persepolis are not entirely clear. That Alexander ordered and with his own hands set the fires seems to most scholars a virtual certainty. The precise reason behind the burning of the city and the circumstances leading up to it have given rise to considerable speculation, ranging from the burning as a matter of calculated policy to an act of vandalism. Whether it was a matter of policy, a premeditated or calculated act, or something done impulsively out of anger is a question that scholars over the centuries have been unable to answer with certainty. The incident is noteworthy because it constitutes an important aspect in the never-ending speculation, disagreement, and debate about Alexander's character.

There have been three main lines of argument advanced over the centuries as to why Alexander burned the palaces on the terrace at Persepolis. The first argument looks to a covert, pseudopsychological motive and maintains that Alexander burned Persepolis out of anger over not being recognized as the divine successor to Darius. The second argument maintains that Persepolis was burned as the logical and dramatic conclusion to the war of vengeance that Alexander had led. It was intended as confirmation to the Greek city-states that the objectives of the war had been fulfilled. The third and most intriguing argument is that the burning of the palaces on the terrace was nothing more than an impulsive act committed by Alexander during a drunken orgy and later regretted when he was sober. All three theories have their advocates and critics within the realms of Alexander scholarship, and the debates among them have raged from ancient times to this day without being settled.

The question has often been posed as to why Alexander did not burn the city during the initial rampage that winter. The answer seems evident enough. He spared the city because he thought he would need the palaces and audience halls intact for the spring cele-bration of the Persian New Year. Alexander anticipated that in April, as was their annual custom, ambassadors and envoys from the sub-ject nations of the empire would be arriving in Persepolis, this time to honor him as their new king. Alexander needed the audience halls and palaces to receive them, not only in a style befitting his evolv-ing perceptions of himself as the new ruler of Persia, but in a manner that would reassure the envoys that the monarchy and its institu-tions would continue in the manner they knew.

Recognition and tribute from the ambassadors of the empire were important to Alexander. The effect produced by the arrival of these emissaries at Persepolis to pay him homage would be invaluable, both for the psychological gratification that it would afford his ego and for what it would do to legitimize his position as the new king of the empire. The news that Alexander had been recognized as the heir to the Achaemenid dynasty at Persepolis during the New Year celebration, perhaps with the mother and children of Darius in attendance, would spread throughout the empire to reach even the unconquered portions in Central Asia and India. There, in the far-thest reaches of the empire, Alexander anticipated that the news would lessen any further resistance to his rule and spare him a long and arduous campaign. With recognition as the new king, Alexander would become elevated, in Persian eyes if not in Greek and Mace-donian, to the status of a divinity. And this is what he was beginning to crave the most, far more than wealth.

Much as Alexander might want to be recognized as the king, he had failed to impress the Persian aristocracy that he could take the place of Darius as their god-king. That spring no tribute-bearing ambassadors from anywhere in the empire came to Persepolis. Per-haps no one came because Darius was still alive and active in the northern part of Iran. Alexander's anticipation of their arrival became disappointment that in turn gave way to anger. The anger, fueled by alcohol, resulted in the burning of the palaces.

Certainly burning the palaces ended any possibility Alexander might have had of legitimizing himself as an Achaemenid heir by peaceful means. Just how realistic was it for him to think that after

looting the city in January, massacring most of the people, and en-
slaving the survivors, the rest of the empire would be inclined to proclaim him its god-king during the Persian New Year? Would fear of
Alexander motivate people to such a degree in the farthest reaches
of the empire not to resist him, or would it just confirm their resolve?

When it became painfully obvious that no one was coming that
spring of 330 B.C., Alexander prepared to leave Persepolis and take up
the pursuit of Darius. Darius had to be captured, and if he could not
be forced to abdicate to Alexander then the remaining areas of the
empire would have to be conquered and their people forced into submission. The palaces of Persepolis were burned as well because they
symbolized nearly two centuries of Achaemenid rule. As Alexander
prepared to move north, he took the necessary steps to ensure that
the city would not become a symbol of resistance in the empire, on
either religious or political grounds.

The second argument advanced for the burning of the palaces is
that they were burned as a matter of policy, a premeditated act with
a very rational or at least understandably political motive behind it.
The burning of the palaces was carried out as a policy of calculated
retaliation for the Persian burning of Athens and the looting of the
Greek temples by Xerxes more than a century before. The burning
of the city was the logical conclusion to the end of the war of
vengeance. It was a symbolic act by which Alexander conveyed to
the ancient world and especially to the Greeks on the mainland the
message that the campaign of vengeance had been fulfilled. From this
perspective the burning was not a demonstration to impress the Persians throughout the empire—they were painfully aware of what
Alexander was capable of inflicting. Rather, it was a message to the
mainland Greeks and to the Macedonians back home that the war of
vengeance was over. It was also a warning to the Greek city-states
and to the Greek cities along the coast of Asia Minor that they had
best remain loyal to Alexander while he was in Asia. The Spartans
on mainland Greece had recently rebelled against his authority, and
the burning of Persepolis might have served as a timely reminder to
the other city-states of what he could do to those who rebelled.

Scholars who have accepted the idea that the burning of the city
was a matter of policy point to indications that the palaces had been

picked clean before the fire, something made "perfectly clear from the excavations of the treasury."[49] The treasury may well have been cleared of bullion before the fire, but that does not prove that the burning was planned in advance. Alexander had early on decided to move the bullion to a central repository, which was later established at Ecbatana, and requisitioned the means necessary to do it.[50] The gold and silver must have been removed from the treasury and placed in a single easily guarded assembly point for packing and shipment well in advance of the burning.

It seems likely that the reason Alexander waited to burn the city was that he needed it. With its magnificent audience halls and palaces intact he could receive the tribute-bearing guests if they came in the spring. If the burning of the city was "a matter of policy," then as one ancient source commented it "was bad policy."[51] Scholars through the ages have agreed with that assessment and faulted Alexander for having made a serious miscalculation, though they differ among themselves as to his motives.

There are references in the sources that Alexander regretted the burning afterward and that the act only further widened the rift that was developing between him and his most senior commanders. Parmenio was Alexander's principal advisor and the most senior military member of his staff. He recommended against burning the palaces and maintained that it would be foolish for Alexander to destroy what had essentially become his own property by conquest. Parmenio warned that such an act could alienate the subjects of the empire by making Alexander seem like a conqueror rather than a king who was there to rule Asia. Yet according to some sources, Alexander rejected his advice.[52]

Alexander replied to Parmenio that he was burning the city in revenge for the Persian invasion of Greece and the burning and looting of the temples in Athens. The burning of Persepolis was the culmination of the Greeks' revenge. The burning would be a dramatic confirmation that the Greeks had triumphed and extracted vengeance against Darius and Xerxes for the Persian acts of sacrilege against the Greek temples. The news would reach Greece that Alexander had defeated the Persian Empire. This news would strengthen the hand of Antipater, Alexander's regent in Greece, and encourage the city-states to remain loyal to the alliance.

Parmenio argued back that to burn Persepolis would alienate the Persians, who would regard the Macedonians as no more than conquerors and ravagers. The Persians would see the burning as mere destruction. Parmenio was nearing seventy, and he was several generations removed from Alexander and his closest friends who were in their twenties. A serious generational gap was developing between Alexander and the older Greeks and Macedonians on his staff, men in their fifties, sixties, and, like Parmenio, early seventies.

Parmenio was a respected figure among Greeks and Macedonians. He had been the principal advisor to Alexander's father Philip and the general who led the Greek expedition to Asia Minor in the spring of 336 B.C., the precursor to Alexander's invasion. It was Parmenio in concert with Antipater who had helped Alexander stabilize his regime in the early days and weeks following Philip's assassination. But now because of his age Parmenio was falling out of favor with Alexander. He was viewed as old and resistant to the tides of change that were sweeping into the ancient world under Alexander. The more Alexander succeeded in the East, the more critical and openly hostile he became toward Parmenio and his senior staff.

When Philip was assassinated in 336 B.C., Parmenio and Antipater were the two most powerful figures in the old regime. They supported Alexander in the first few crucial days after the murder of Philip and thus enabled the young prince to stabilize himself upon his father's throne. When Alexander left for Asia Minor, Antipater had remained behind to govern Macedonia as regent and to keep the Greeks in line. Parmenio accompanied Alexander to Asia Minor as his chief of staff, and Alexander had been dependent on both men in the beginning of his reign for guidance on military as well as political affairs.

The three sons of Parmenio all held senior positions in the command structure of Alexander's army, and the old man was himself Alexander's second in command when they had crossed into Asia. In the major battles it was always Parmenio who commanded the solid left wing while Alexander executed the flanking movements on the right. It had been a winning combination that allowed Alexander to triumph in each of the three major battles against numerically superior Persian armies. Parmenio was always there, holding firm on what became the main line, solid and dependable, while Alexander was free to improvise with his cavalry on the flank and turn the tide of battle.

The last of the theories, however, is the one that generates the most controversy and raises the greatest level of interest among readers. According to this theory the burning of the city was an accident. It happened as a result of a drunken orgy and was carried out by an impulsive young man urged on by an Athenian whore. For many scholars, this is nothing more than fiction. Scholars skeptical of the story of the Athenian courtesan, Thais, tend to believe the fire was a deliberate act of policy on the part of Alexander, opposed by Parmenio.

These scholars point to an account of the episode written some years afterward by Ptolemy, one of Alexander's generals and close boyhood friends. Ptolemy was one of the successors of Alexander and later became pharaoh of Egypt. He wrote his account shortly after Alexander's death, and it has come through to modern times contained in the works of a series of historians. In his account Ptolemy explained the burning of the palaces as the outcome of a disagreement over policy between Alexander and Parmenio. The problem with Ptolemy's account is that Thais was also his mistress, and over the years she bore him a number of children. Thus, some scholars are justifiably skeptical of his objectivity when it came to her role in the burning of Persepolis. They have concluded that he may have tried to protect her by omitting her role in the unpleasant affair.[53]

In searching for the reasons Persepolis was burned, it is important to recognize that by this time in his life Alexander had begun to drink, perhaps more heavily than had been his nature.[54] The months of leisure in Persepolis and the luxurious living had affected him as well as those around him. He began to change, with the most notable feature being a loss of temperance. Where once he drank only a small amount of wine mixed with water, he now developed a strong taste for unmixed wine. He began to participate in prolonged drinking bouts. His character became "sullied by an excessive love of wine."[55]

One of the most respected of the ancient sources tells us that Alexander did not show good sense when he burned the city, and that he punished the people of Persepolis for what their ancestors had done long before.[56] But this would not be the last time Alexander would show such brutality toward a people for the alleged transgressions of their ancestors. It would happen again.

The corruption of Alexander's character probably began after his defeat of Darius at the battle of Gaugamela. Following the battle, Alexander and his army entered Babylon where they stayed too long—thirty-four days to be exact. Furthermore, it has been written that no other city in Asia did more to undermine the discipline of the Greek and Macedonian soldiers than Babylon.[57] Amid a luxury and splendor such as Alexander had never seen before, he started taking part in frequent banquets with his closest companions that began early and lasted until late.[58] The last of the great battles in this war was over, and they celebrated what they thought was the end of the heavy fighting. They thought the road ahead would be easy for the victorious Macedonian king and that the worst was behind them. The entire Persian world was at their disposal. Alexander moved on from the debauchery of Babylon to the luxury of the king's palaces at Susa and Persepolis. He entered a world where every conceivable pleasure that the sensual oriental mind had ever conceived was his upon command. But as the historian Herodotus commented, when it came to sex it was the Greeks who taught the Persians the salaciousness of "unnatural lust."[59]

Although Alexander had conquered much of the Persian Empire, he was still a young man discovering the extent of his appetites. His youth in rustic Macedonia had been characterized by a life of self-restraint where the pleasures of the body had little hold on him. At that stage in his life, he had enjoyed banquets and the symposia that followed, more for the conversation than for the wine.[60] He was, in this respect, the complete opposite of his father Philip, who had been a heavy drinker and a prolific womanizer. Some of the sources mention that in the beginning Alexander had been a young man of great mental endowments and exceptional abilities. Many of the ancient writers saw in the young pupil of Aristotle a man who exceeded all others in his ability. They found him to be quick and efficient in carrying out his plans, honest in keeping his word to those who submitted to his will, and merciful in his treatment of prisoners. In the early years they found Alexander to have been temperate in all the lawful and usual pleasures.

As the campaign in Asia progressed and the years passed, Alexander became a heavy drinker of wine. It was the "heat of his body" coupled with the hot dry climate of Mesopotamia, one ancient source wrote, that made him drink so much. When it came to women we learn that Alexander was naive. He had never known a woman until he took Barsine, a much older Persian woman, as his mistress following the battle of Issus.[61] That too would change after Babylon as he began to know the pleasures of the king's harem.

The night the fires were set at Persepolis, Alexander had been drinking with his friends. They had invited a number of women, Greek and no doubt Persian, to share the wine and add to the pleasures of the evening. As one source commented, "it would not be a crime to violate" these women. They were women "accustomed to living with armed men and with more license than was fitting a decent woman."[62]

As the drinking continued and most of the company became thoroughly inebriated, Thais asked permission to give a speech. Alexander consented and she rose to give her speech, which one source wrote was "befitting the character of her native country" but "too lofty for one of her kind."[63] She recounted to the assembly all the hardships she had endured the last few months while traveling through Asia. But it had all been worth it now that she was with her fellow Greeks, heroes all of them, and reveling luxuriously in the splendid palaces of the conquered Persians. It would be even a greater pleasure for her to see the Greeks burn the house of Xerxes, the king who had set fire to Athens and defiled their temples. She herself would be pleased to set the first fire, if the young king would permit. Thus, a tradition might be born and spread throughout the ancient world that the women of Alexander inflicted more punishment upon the Persians on behalf of Greece than did the men in his army.

Her words were heard by men who were young, intoxicated, and easily inflamed. They were so thoroughly inebriated by the time she gave her speech that "madness had taken possession of their minds."[64]

They turned to Alexander and shouted out their approval. They cheered Thais and urged the young king to allow her to set the first of the many fires that would engulf the palaces that night. Alexander, himself intoxicated, yielded to the passion and excitement of the moment. Reclining on his drinking couch, he had become "more greedy for wine than able to carry it"[65] and ordered the company to form a victory procession in honor of Dionysus.

The dangerous combination of youth, ego, and too much wine all skillfully and cunningly manipulated by the Greek woman proved fatal for Persepolis that night. The company, followed by the accompaniment of musicians, formed a procession in honor of Dionysus and set out to burn the palace. The Athenian whore and the drunken Macedonian king, torches in hand, led the way.

Alexander was the first to throw a torch into the palace of Xerxes, followed by Thais. Then his companions and their harlots took their turns. The palace ceiling contained large amounts of cedar, and heavy cloth tapestries hung from the walls. All of these caught fire quickly. From that point on the flames spread rapidly. The soldiers encamped just outside the city walls saw the fire and, thinking it accidental, rushed in to aid in putting it out. When they came up on the terrace and saw it was Alexander setting the fires, their alarm turned to joy. They took up torches and joined in because they saw the burning of the palaces as an indication that their king was preparing to take them home.[66] Torches by the thousands were lit, and that night the Greeks burned the terrace at Persepolis, one of the most magnificent structures in the ancient world.

The spirits of the soldiers soared when word spread throughout the camp of what was taking place on the terrace. They looked up at what had just a few minutes earlier been the dark Persian sky above Persepolis; now it seemed ablaze from the reflection of the fires raging below. The Greeks were rejoicing, thinking their strategos had signified an end to the long campaign. Perhaps their actions indicate that there was considerable pressure on Alexander to stop the war and leave for home. The fire encouraged many of the older Macedonians in the army, men such as Parmenio, to come forward and press Alexander for an end to the war. But, this was the last thing Alexander contemplated.

One plausible explanation is that the decision to burn the city had been made in advance and the actual setting of the fire was then later stimulated by the lethal combination of Bacchus and Thais. There is every possibility that Alexander was planning to burn the city all along and, on the night in question, given the quantities of wine consumed and the mood, did it spontaneously in the course of the revelry.

All the sources agree that Alexander realized his error and regretted having burned the palaces. The question is when. It is on this point that they disagree. There are those among the ancient historians who write that Alexander realized his error immediately after the fires had been set and ordered them extinguished.[67] But it was too late—by that time the fires were out of control. Some say Alexander regretted what he had done only after he had recovered from his drunkenness the next day.[68] Others wrote that he regretted the act years later when he returned to Persepolis from India.[69] Even contemporary Alexander scholars differ as to exactly when he regretted his actions. After it was over, Alexander declared that he wished he had spared the city, for it would have been a more effective punishment to have forced the Persians to worship him in the palace of Xerxes rather than to have burned it.

After Persepolis, Alexander seemed to have much less need of Parmenio. In the coming months the aging general and his sons would fall victim to the purges that were about to begin and that would frequently characterize the final years of Alexander's reign. Alexander was now wealthy, his obligation as hegemon to the Greeks had been fulfilled, and he was preparing his own agenda. This was an agenda in which Parmenio and his sons, as well as many of the senior Greek and Macedonian commanders, would play no part.

Alexander was young, only twenty-five, when he captured Persepolis. Impulsiveness and outbursts of temper were already developing trademarks of his often troubled character, but those characteristics had not as yet consumed his personality to the destructive degree they would in the coming years. There is little doubt that Alexander acted impulsively when he burned Persepolis. He probably instituted the burning with his own hand, because it is an action consistent with so many other spontaneous and impulsive aspects of his character and events in his career. The pattern of destructive and violent behavior followed by a period of immediate and intense, even hysterical, remorse is one that was repeated often in his short life. Just as at Thebes, Tyre, and Gaza—cities where the will of Alexander had been thwarted by the resistance of their defenders—when he vented his displeasure, it was something that clouded his judgment and produced the most outwardly violent reactions. The destruction of Persepolis followed the pattern and showed what was yet to come.

Not as civilized as they thought or portrayed themselves, the Greeks and Macedonians proved at Persepolis that they were a race capable of the most barbaric savagery. They could inflict on others suffering as cruel as could be found anywhere in the uncivilized world. The Greeks with Alexander were men so limited that they could not see beyond their own avarice and anger in order to spare a magnificent city and the people who had surrendered to them without resistance. That night the Greeks and Macedonians only wanted to destroy, and they easily found the rationale to justify their actions. They inflicted a mindless revenge on Persepolis for Persian offenses against their country, offenses that had been carried out more than a hundred years before most of them had been born. What the Persians had done to them they had done to others time and time again, even to their own people. The burning of Persepolis shows just how thin was the veneer of the Hellenic civilization that many of Alexander's biographers over the centuries would have us believe he was carrying to the East.

This was the end of the capital of the Persians, the birthplace of a line of noble kings, the nemesis of the Greeks, and once the envy of every city in the ancient world. With the burning of Persepolis, the last of the great Mesopotamian empires came to an end. There would never be an empire like it in size and longevity until the advent of Rome, nearly three hundred years later. There are conflicting views, however, on how the burning of the city affected its continued existence as the capital of the area of southwestern Iran that became known as Persis. Peucestas, an officer and successor of Alexander, is said to have established his court there in the period after Alexander's death.[70] There are scholars who maintain, conversely, that after the fire the city was never again occupied, given modern archeological evidence indicating that the palaces and audience halls were never rebuilt.[71]

Alexander left one of his officers, Nicarchides, with three thousand Macedonian soldiers to hold the citadel of an empty, plundered, and burned-out city. Tiridates, the Persian who had surrendered the city to Alexander in the months before, was given his reward. He was left in the same rank as he had enjoyed under Darius and remained a royal treasurer but with no treasury to guard. Alexander now turned north and set out after Darius.

CHAPTER 2

BEYOND THE CASPIAN GATES

WHILE ALEXANDER HAD PASSED A TEMPERATE WINTER IN the southern reaches of Iran, reposing in the luxury of his newfound wealth at Persepolis and waiting for the spring, several hundred miles away to the north, Darius III, the last of the Achaemenid kings, spent a cold and depressing winter sequestered in what in more tranquil times had been his summer palace at Ecbatana.[1] There he was surrounded by the remnants of what had once been the largest and, on the surface at least, the most formidable army in the ancient world. What was left of that army was now led by commanders from the far eastern provinces of the empire and still remained a threat to Alexander. However, the men who led that army had come to question not only the competence of Darius as a military leader but his continued value as a king.

It was a dismal time for this last and perhaps most tragic of the Persian kings. A mood of apprehension had set in, and it affected not only the king but also all those around him. Darius had lost those who had meant the most to him—his family. His wife, the beautiful and regal Stateira, had died in the camp of Alexander a few months earlier. His mother, two daughters, and young son were captives. As the months of that winter passed, Darius pined for them and sank deeper into despondency. His only comfort at court was a loyal and longtime friend, the elderly satrap Artabazus.

Artabazus was related to the king by marriage and, more than any of the others around Darius, he shared the king's grief the most. His own daughter Barsine had been captured at Issus along with the

family of Darius. She had become the mistress of Alexander and carried his child. Artabazus knew Alexander and the Macedonians better than any of the king's other advisors. He had been welcomed at
the court of Alexander's father Philip some years before after he was
exiled from the Persian court by the prior king.[2] Living in Macedonia
for several years, Artabazus had come to know Alexander and had
been impressed by the young boy's maturity and interest in learning
about the Persians and their customs. Thus it became Artabazus more
than any of the others who advised Darius on how to deal with Alexander, and there can be little doubt that the old satrap was probably
the architect of the failed Persian peace initiatives.

Darius was an unusually tall and handsome man in his early
fifties. From the vantage point of appearance, he was the ideal king.
With his regal bearing and often-somber countenance, he inspired in
his subjects the belief that he was truly a god-king. The traits of the
Persian king were in marked contrast to the less sophisticated and
more rustic manners of Alexander. Alexander was younger, shorter,
and more exuberant than Darius. Their complexions were as opposite as were their temperaments. While Darius was dark and reserved,
Alexander was fair with a temperament that was often a volatile mixture of self-centered adolescent exuberance and feminine hysteria.

The verdict by historians on Darius as both a king and a man is
mixed, while opinions of Alexander are overwhelmingly positive. But
that is to be expected, since scholars traditionally tend to focus on the
winners and view them in a positive light because of their accomplishments. The losers, such as Darius, have been neglected and rel-
egated to the footnotes of history. The ancient sources, which are
based mostly on Greek references, portray Darius as a man who, with
regard to things military, was surpassingly fainthearted and irrational.
What emerges from the pages of the manuscripts is a man characterized as a chronic coward who showed little bravery or sense when it
came to war and whose life could be summed up as "a series of dis-
asters."[3] Darius is portrayed as a pathetic character who in the end
is a fugitive in his own empire and eventually murdered by those
upon whom he depended for his safety.

In examining the behavior of Darius in the two major battles of
his war with Alexander, this characterization becomes unavoidable

and on the surface seems appropriate. According to the Greek renditions of those battles, Darius lost his nerve during the fighting,[4] first
at Issus and a second time at Gaugamela. In both battles, the Persian
forces were numerically superior to Alexander's army. Darius, having
chosen the site for battle and holding a defensive position, had the
tactical advantage in each instance. At Issus, the Pesian king had
caught Alexander by surprise, yet he failed to capitalize on his advantage and ended by losing the battle.

At Gaugamela, two years later, the two kings met again on the
field of battle. This time, the sight of the advancing Persian army, with
its vast waves of infantry and rows of lethal scythe-mounted chariots, struck such fear into Alexander and his men that they came close
to panic.[5] Alexander, having never been more alarmed, was on the
verge of losing his nerve. Several nights before the battle, there had
been an eclipse of the moon—an ominous sign that coupled with the
anticipation of the forthcoming battle sent the superstitious Greeks
and Macedonians into turmoil. Their fear and general discontent
with the war were driving them toward mutiny.[6] Soldiers began complaining openly that Alexander was dragging them to the ends of
the earth just to gratify his own vanity. They complained about the
oppressive and incessant heat, the vast desert wastelands, and the lack
of decent food and potable water. They were critical of Alexander's
pretensions of divinity. They did not want to fight; they wanted to
go home.

Even the normally self-confident Alexander was filled with apprehension and doubt about whether he could hold his army together
and prevail against Darius. Throughout much of the night before the
battle, he surrounded himself with priests and sacrificed to suppress
"the god of fear."[7] Had even a fraction of Darius's huge army caught
Alexander's forces in such a state, the Persians might well have won
the battle before it started.

Darius held a better than even chance of defeating Alexander at
the opening of each of these two decisive battles. If the Persian king
had kept his composure when the fighting began and focused on directing his army through the effective use of his commanders, he
might well have won the day and probably changed the course of history. Darius had experienced and competent commanders advising

him each time he faced Alexander on the field of battle. His Persian infantry were strengthened through the placement of experienced Greek mercenaries at their center. The Greek mercenaries in the service of Darius were equal in military effectiveness to their countrymen who were allied with Alexander. One of the little-known facts in the history of the war is that Darius had more Greeks in his service than Alexander had in his entire army.[8] The Persian cavalry was easily the equal to the Companion cavalry of Alexander, and the Bactrian and Scythian cavalry contingents from Central Asia with their "huge bodies, shaggy faces and unshorn hair"[9] terrified the Greeks and Macedonians. Yet in spite of these advantages, in both instances the Persian king had fled shortly after the combat had intensified and before the issue of victory or defeat had been decided.[10] At Gaugamela, he had fled the battlefield, leaving behind one of the biggest armies the ancient world had seen.

Outside the military sphere, some of the ancient sources are slightly more charitable toward Darius as a man and as a king. They characterize him as a man who was by nature "trusting and mild." He came to the throne through treachery at a time when there was discontent at the Persian court. The royal eunuch had been a powerful force behind the Persian throne for some time, and it is generally agreed by scholars that he poisoned Artaxerxes III and then selected Darius as the new ruler. In this regard, Alexander and Darius were similar. They had both taken their places upon their respective thrones within months of each other (336 B.C.) and under similar suspicions that they had been involved in the assassinations of their predecessors. Scholars have always speculated that Alexander and his mother Olympias were involved in the stabbing death of Philip and that Darius was party to the poisoning of Artaxerxes.

The characterization of Darius as an incompetent and cowardly ruler is not completely justified. Shortly after he had established himself on the throne, there was a dramatic turn of events in the Persian court. The man chosen to become king because of his weak character and malleability asserted himself, and the eunuch was executed by royal order. Darius became his own man. In the first two years of his reign, he is credited with having shown considerable ability in consolidating power within the vast Persian Empire. Darius suppressed an insurrection against Persian rule that had begun in Egypt upon the death of Artaxerxes and had spread to Cyprus and Phoenicia. The repression by the Persians that accompanied the suppression of these insurrections probably explains in part the cooperation Alexander received when he entered Phoenicia and Egypt in 332 B.C.

Both Darius and Alexander were kings who had short reigns and violent endings. Darius ruled the Persian Empire for only six years, while Alexander ruled for thirteen. Darius's accession to the throne is dated from the summer of 336 B.C., shortly after the death of Artaxerxes III and a few months before the murder of Philip in Macedonia. Darius died a violent death in the summer of 330. He was murdered by those he trusted and thought were closest to him.

Alexander projected an intense public hatred of Darius, although privately that might not have been the case. He maintained, perhaps as a way of diverting suspicion from himself, that Darius had played a part in the assassination of Philip and for that treachery he could never be forgiven. The evidence for the complicity of Darius in the murder of Alexander's father is weak and rests mainly on speculation that several of the Macedonians implicated in the plot had fled to the Persian court for safety. Alexander also accused Darius of trying to have him assassinated as well. When Darius was trying desperately to sue for peace before the battle of Gaugamela, Alexander produced letters to show his officers that the Persian king was actively soliciting among the Greek allies for someone to murder him. These letters, which promised significant rewards for anyone in Alexander's camp who would assassinate him, became one of the more public reasons Alexander used to justify his refusal to end the war on the terms that had been offered by Darius.

The biggest mistake Darius made in dealing with Alexander was in failing to assess the danger to his empire early on when the first Macedonian expeditionary force landed in Asia Minor in the spring of 336 B.C. and to react appropriately. Philip had sent an advance force under the command of his trusted advisor Parmenio to prepare for the larger invasion to come. Parmenio was to secure the northwestern coast of Asia Minor and to elicit support among the Greek cities for the war with Persia. Initially, the armies of the western satraps of the empire, reinforced by a considerable number of experienced and skilled Greek mercenaries, kept Parmenio and his Macedonians contained to the coastal areas of northwestern Asia Minor. From 336 B.C. until Alexander crossed the Hellespont in the spring of 334 B.C. with a larger force, Darius seemed to be dismissing the war with the Macedonians and Greeks as a relatively minor matter.

The Persian king did not take effective measures to formulate a strategy to deal with the invasion. Instead, he left the early containment of Alexander to his satraps in the west. What Darius should have done was mobilize the entire Persian army and deal with the threat decisively. By the time Darius mobilized a large enough army to stop Alexander, two years had lapsed and the Macedonian king had already conquered nearly a third of the Persian Empire. Alexander had built the momentum that would carry him successfully all the way to Persepolis.

While Darius wintered at Ecbatana, he was receiving information about Alexander's actions in Persepolis and political developments in Greece. What was happening at Persepolis gave Darius little reason to hope that Alexander would not move against him in the spring, but events transpiring in southern Greece did give rise to the hope that the Macedonian king might be forced to stop the war and return to Greece. The Greeks had always been restless under Alexander's rule. Now the Spartans, led by Agis, one of their kings, had challenged the authority of Antipater, Alexander's regent in Greece.

The Spartans had never accepted Alexander as hegemon, and they had refused to join the Corinthian League that formed the alliance system under which the expedition to Persia had been sanctioned. Alexander had not forced the issue with the Spartans but, rather, left them alone while he turned his attentions toward Asia. The Spartans knew that it would only be a matter of time before Alexander would return to Greece and they would have to deal with him. So, in 331 B.C. King Agis made his move while Alexander was far away in Persia and put an army in the field to challenge Antipater.

Darius hoped that the Spartans might put enough pressure on Alexander to force him to return to Greece to reassert his control. Darius was willing to provide the money to aid the Spartans. Persian gold had played a significant role in Spartan politics for decades. It had helped the Spartans defeat Athens during the Peloponnesian Wars nearly eighty years before, and it had helped make Sparta the preeminent power on the Greek mainland for years afterward. Since the close of the fifth century, considerable numbers of not only Spartans but also other Greeks had found employment as mercenaries in the service of the Persian kings. Darius was willing to commit as much gold as it would take to disrupt Alexander's hold over the Greek mainland. Spartan and Athenian ambassadors had come to Darius with requests for money and ships since Alexander first invaded Asia Minor.

If the Spartans were successful against Antipater, Darius hoped that more of the Greek city-states might be encouraged to rise up against Macedonian rule. The Spartan insurrection could develop into a major uprising and spread throughout Greece. Major dislocations on the Greek mainland coupled with discontent among some of the most senior officers at Persepolis might be just enough pressure to force Alexander to break off the war in Persia and return to Greece.

What Darius was hoping for would never happen. Communications were so slow between Greece and Persia and the distances so great that just as Darius was learning of the insurrection by the Spartans and raising his hopes, the Spartans were being defeated by Antipater's army in a decisive battle in the Peloponnesus four thousand kilometers away. Persian gold had once again played a significant factor in Greek politics. But this time the money did not come from a Persian king—it came from Alexander, who had sent Antipater vast sums taken from the captured Persian treasuries. That gold enabled Antipater to finance the necessary military resources and secure the alliances he needed to put down the Spartan revolt. King Agis was cornered and killed on the field of battle at Megalopolis in 331 B.C., and Greece remained securely under Alexander's control.

As to what was happening at Persepolis, there can be little doubt that Darius was well informed on the discontent that was developing among some of Alexander's commanders. The distance between Persepolis and Ecbatana is relatively short, approximately one thousand kilometers. The information probably came to Darius through the remnants of the intelligence network that prior Persian kings had established throughout the empire. This network had been in place for decades and was known as the "royal eyes and ears." It was an extensive network of informants who had been strategically placed and maintained at satrapies throughout the empire to spy on the satraps and send information to the king regarding who was loyal and who was not. This network must certainly have been in place when Alexander took Persepolis, and some of the spies, given their place in the royal hierarchy, must have survived the massacre that followed and worked their way into the circle of Persians who collaborated with Alexander's army. These spies were probably able to send word on a fairly regular basis to Darius regarding the discontent among Alexander's officers and their desire to return home.

Darius was desperate to end the war with Alexander. More than anything, he wanted the return of his family; he had sent letters to Alexander on three occasions with offers of gold and territory for their ransom. If Alexander would cease his pursuit and end the war, Darius promised to concede significant sections of his empire. Darius had sent letters to Alexander shortly before the battle of Gaugamela. It was there that Darius had learned of his wife's death in the Greek camp. He had offered Alexander all of his empire west of the Euphrates River in ransom for his mother and children and an end to the war. When Alexander assembled his officers and read these letters from Darius, they urged him to accept the terms. Most of the pressure came from his most senior general and political advisor, Parmenio. Concern was rising among many of the senior officers about just how far east Alexander was willing to drag them and how long this war would continue. Many of those officers, both Greek and Macedonian, had become convinced that the war against Darius was no longer being fought to avenge Greece but for the glory and vanity of Alexander, the new "lord of Asia." Most of them were anxious to return home with the considerable fortunes they had amassed fighting Alexander's war.

This concern about Alexander's motives for waging the war and how long it would go on had surfaced during the Egyptian campaign two years earlier. Coupled with a natural tendency among soldiers to want to return home after so many years of fighting, it became an issue that bolstered Darius in the hope that he could save at least a fragment of his empire. Yet this too, like the Spartan insurrection, was a false hope. Alexander had rejected the offer and demeaned Parmenio for suggesting that he accept it.[11] Alexander was firmly in control of his officers. He had been so at Gaugamela, and he was equally so at Persepolis. No matter how much some of them longed to return home and might complain openly, Alexander was following his own vision. He would tolerate their criticism for only so long, for he was bringing into play his own methods for dealing with their discontent.

When word reached Darius in late May or early June of 330 B.C. that Alexander and his army had burned Persepolis and were moving north toward Ecbatana, he knew there was no longer any hope that either events in Greece or discontent among Alexander's officers would bring the war in Persia to an end. Darius was forced to consider his options and make a decision. Either he could remain at the summer palace at Ecbatana and fight another battle with Alexander or he could retreat to the safety of the unconquered satrapies in the east and rebuild his forces. The latter plan seemed best since in the east, in the most remote corners of his empire that today constitutes Afghanistan and Pakistan, Darius believed he could reorganize his existing forces and replenish their numbers from fresh levies of conscripts. Alexander would have to come to him, marching over vast expanses of territory and further depleting his own reserves. To make it as difficult as he could for Alexander to follow, Darius planned to burn everything behind him as he moved east.[12]

What Darius failed to comprehend was that it was not numbers that mattered in his conflict with Alexander but, rather, his ability to lead his soldiers effectively. He had to be able to inspire men to fight for him and for his empire. The commanders of the Persian army, now mostly men from the eastern provinces, had come to doubt his ability. For Darius it was sufficient that he was the king of kings, and because of that he expected unquestioning obedience regardless of his incompetence as a commander.

After the disastrous defeat at Gaugamela eight months before, Darius still commanded a formidable force at Ecbatana. There were some thirty thousand infantry, four thousand archers, and the remnants of his personal bodyguard. The most effective contingents in this force were the three thousand skilled horsemen from Central Asia and several thousand Greek mercenaries.[13] The cavalry were under the command of Bessus, the satrap of Bactria. Bessus was a distant relative of Darius and had commanded the Bactrian cavalry at Gaugamela. The contingent of Greek mercenaries was under the command of an officer named Patron.[14] He had come from the region of central Greece called Phocia to enter the service of the Persian king several years before. These mercenaries were all that remained from the original fifty thousand Greek infantry who had been in the service of Darius when the war with Alexander began.[15] Many of the original number had been killed in combat; more had probably deserted or returned to Greece to join the Spartans in their fight against Antipater. These men, the last of the mercenaries who remained with Darius, were loyal to him not because he paid their wages but because he was the only hope they had left for a future. Like so many others before them, these men had left the poverty of Greece to seek a better life in Persian service.

As Patron and his men waited for the last act of the Persian tragedy to play out, they knew that when the end came there would be no quarter for them from Alexander. They already knew how he treated Greek soldiers in the service of Persia. Twenty thousand Greek mercenaries led by a skilled and experienced commander, Memnon, had faced Alexander when he first landed in Asia Minor. At the battle of the Granicus River, four years earlier, these mercenaries had put up a fierce resistance when Alexander and his forces tried to cross the river. The battle almost cost the Macedonian king not only his first defeat but his life.

When the fighting at the Granicus River was over, the remnants of the Persian army fled the battlefield. The Greek mercenaries did not run; rather, they regrouped and took up a defensive position. Through their officers they asked Alexander for quarter. He refused their request and personally led the assault against them. In Alexander's eyes, they were traitors who had been condemned by the League of Corinth for having taken service with the Persian king. For Alexander, these were men who had chosen to fight against their fellow Greeks and for them there would be no mercy shown that day.

Most of the mercenaries at the Granicus were slaughtered, and the few who survived were sent back to Greece in chains to work as slaves in the quarries. There was no reason for Patron to think that

Alexander had tempered his feelings since then toward Greeks in Persian service. With Alexander now in control of their country, they could not return home except under penalty of slavery or death. They had no choice but to remain with Darius until the end.

Darius made the decision not to remain at Ecbatana and fight. Ecbatana is in the mountains of Iran, and in that setting Darius would not have been able to use the Bactrian cavalry or the Greek mercenaries to their fullest advantage against Alexander. It would have been siege warfare, and in the end he knew he would lose. So Darius sent the women along with the baggage and carts loaded with what remained in gold from the royal treasury east. They followed the main road leading toward a series of passes in the Elburz Mountains known as the Caspian Gates. The Caspian Gates were part of a Persian strategic highway system that crossed over a number of mountain passes, providing natural defenses that could be used to slow the advance of a hostile army. Darius intended that his army would provide a rear guard for the slower-moving baggage train.

The scant descriptions in the ancient sources make it difficult to locate precisely where the Caspian Gates are today. In all probability, the term refers to an entire complex of defiles about one hundred kilometers east of modern Tehran and the ancient city of Rhagae.[16] Once through the Caspian Gates, Darius intended to lead his army along the Great East Road until they reached the remote province of Bactria in what is today northern Afghanistan. Bactria was an important satrapy of the empire, and in its history it had been governed by the son and then the brother of Xerxes.[17]

Beyond the Caspian Gates and out of the mountains, the terrain of Iran changes and becomes flatter and wider. The vast plains and deserts are conducive to large-scale cavalry and infantry operations. The Bactrian cavalry were skilled fighters who had already proved their effectiveness against Alexander at Gaugamela. Darius may have had the advantage over Alexander a third time if he had chosen to stand and fight. Instead, his old nemesis—fear—incapacitated him again, and he abandoned the idea of a fixed battle and continued moving east. His intent was to distance himself as much as possible from a pursuing Alexander and reach the safety of Bactria before he was overtaken. The effect of his failure to stand and face Alexander at the Caspian Gates was to demoralize his army. When it became obvious to the Persian soldiers that they were running from Alexander, discipline and morale began to break down in the ranks. There was talk among the senior officers about the need for a new king. Darius had overestimated Alexander's capability.

Alexander left Persepolis toward the end of May or early June with a force of nearly fifty thousand soldiers and headed north toward Ecbatana. There he intended to confront Darius in what he anticipated would be their final battle. Along the way Alexander was joined by reinforcements from Asia Minor. The long and heavily burdened column, laden with the treasure of Persepolis, moved north and followed along the eastern side of the Zagros Mountains. The column passed by the sites of the modern-day Iranian cities of Isfahan and Qom, covering nearly seven hundred kilometers since it left Persepolis.

Three days' march from Ecbatana, Alexander encountered Bisthanes, the son of the former Persian king Artaxerxes III. Bisthanes had no love for Darius, whom he blamed for the murder of his father. He informed Alexander that Darius had left Ecbatana just a few days earlier and was heading east toward Bactria with the remainder of the royal treasury and the remnants of his army. This information caused Alexander to modify his plans and increase the intensity of his pursuit.

At this point in the story the ancient sources contradict each other. Once source makes it clear that Alexander reached Ecbatana, where he made a number of important decisions before setting out in pursuit of Darius.[18] The second source, equally credible, states that Alexander, once he heard that Darius was fleeing east, divided his forces in the area near the modern-day Iranian city of Qom.[19] Parmenio, with the bulk of the infantry and the baggage train carrying the treasure, continued the slow march northwest to Ecbatana. Alexander, with a smaller but more mobile force, diverted to the northeast to overtake Darius before he reached the Caspian Gates. The pursuit from the area of Qom to the location where Alexander eventually overtook Darius on the outskirts of the great Iranian desert covered nearly five hundred kilometers and took slightly more than three weeks to accomplish. The probable route Alexander followed skirted the Dasht-e-Kavir—one of the great salt deserts of the world—and then headed north directly for the Caspian Gates.

Speculation is that Alexander may have been pressured by the Greek and Macedonian contingents into breaking off the pursuit of Darius and marching to Ecbatana. Hunting down Darius had become a personal matter for Alexander and was not as much of a concern to the Greeks and many of the Macedonians who were anxious to return home. In the view that maintains Alexander reached Ecbatana, it is important to note that when he arrived in the capital he dismissed the Thessalian cavalry and the "rest of the allies."[20] These soldiers were paid generous bonuses and sent home to Greece. Alexander asked those soldiers who wished to remain in his service and pursue Darius to do so as mercenaries. This changed the entire character of the campaign and the complexion of the army. It was no longer the Greek war of revenge on Persia. It was now Alexander's personal war, and the motives for what he was seeking to accomplish were not entirely clear.

When Darius left Ecbatana, he and Alexander were probably only a few days' march apart. The Persian column was moving almost due east from Ecbatana toward the town of Rhagae and the mountains beyond, while Alexander was moving north toward Ecbatana. Rhagae survives today as Rey, a small city located about twelve kilometers southeast of Tehran and approximately eighty kilometers from the probable location of the Caspian Gates. At Qom, Alexander likely divided his forces and set out in pursuit of Darius, intending to intercept the Persian column somewhere between Rhagae and the Caspian Gates. Given the geography of the area and the direction in which Darius was heading, it seems pointless for Alexander to have wasted time by diverting to Ecbatana and missing the opportunity to capture Darius, his primary objective. Once past the Caspian Gates, the Persians could easily have disappeared into the vast territories of the eastern provinces of the empire. Pursuing them at that point would have been far more difficult than catching them at the Caspian Gates.

As Alexander and his army moved closer to the Caspian Gates, they began encountering deserters from the long Persian column ahead. Most of these men were ordinary soldiers who had lost their heart

for fighting and only wanted to return home. Alexander's men found
hidden among the deserters some highly placed Persian nobles who
proved eager to trade valuable information on Darius in exchange for
their lives.

Alexander received from the deserters several crucial pieces of
information about events in the Persian camp and the movements
of the column. The first piece of news he received was that Darius
was in danger of being arrested or even murdered by a cabal of his
commanders.[21] Alarmed by what he had learned and anxious to
capture Darius alive, Alexander divided his forces a second time. He
took with him only his elite cavalry, called the Companions, as well
as a group of mounted scouts called the prodromoi, and the lightest
of his infantry. These men were burdened only with their weapons
and a meager supply of food and water so that they could travel as
lightly and quickly as possible. Craterus, one of Alexander's senior
Macedonian commanders, was put in command of the rest of the
column and ordered to follow as quickly as he could.

Alexander and his men set out after dusk and traveled all that
night. They continued for a few hours into the next day until the
intense heat and glaring sun forced them to seek shelter and rest both
themselves and the exhausted horses. They resumed the pursuit at
dusk when the heat had subsided, and after traveling through the next
night they came to an oasis called Thara.[22] There was evidence that
the Persians had passed through there just a few days before. Alexander's soldiers found a number of deserters from the Persian column,
and one of them was Darius's Greek interpreter. The Persian column had left him behind because he had become too sick to travel.
At first he tried to disguise his identity from Alexander, but when
aggressively interrogated he quickly admitted who he was. In an effort
to save his life, he told Alexander all of what had transpired in the
Persian camp in the last few days.

The interpreter recounted that Darius had been arrested by a group
of his commanders and bound in chains. The king was being transported with the column in a cart. Bessus had taken command of the
army and was leading them toward Bactria. Artabazus and the Greek
mercenaries, reluctant to intervene when the king was seized because
they were vastly outnumbered, had split off from the column and

were heading north into the Elburz Mountains and the province of Hyrcania on the Caspian Sea. The interpreter explained that Bessus was leading the column toward Bactria, where he intended to raise a large army and await Alexander on more favorable terrain.

Alexander now became even more anxious to rescue Darius, for he believed, as he told his soldiers, that "on that body of his depends our victory."[23] What Alexander really meant was that he needed Darius alive to abdicate the throne in his favor. Darius dead was of no use to him. The last and perhaps most crucial piece of information to come to Alexander from the deserters was that a shortcut existed by which he could overtake the Persian column and rescue Darius. The sources are at variance with each other as to exactly which of the deserters provided this information. According to one source, local villagers guided Alexander and his men along the shortcut to overtake the Persian column,[24] while the second source relates that two Persian nobles[25] showed Alexander the shorter route. In either case, Alexander learned that the Persian column was less than one hundred kilometers ahead of him. Alexander further reduced the size of his forces to only the cavalry, leaving the infantry contingents behind to follow at a slower pace.

When Alexander had covered about half the distance, his men came upon another deserter. Brochubelus was the son of Mazaeus, whom Alexander had appointed satrap of Babylon. Brochubelus informed Alexander that the Persian column was now less than fifty kilometers ahead of him and moving east in complete disorder.[26] Darius, he reported, was still alive. Alexander was anxious to push on, but it was now mid- to late August and the heat during the day must have been brutally oppressive. This is the hottest and driest period of the year in Iran. Temperatures routinely climb to well over a hundred degrees, and travel on foot, by horse, or by camel, at that time of the year must have been, as it is even today, nearly unbearable. There is no reason to think that the sun was any less harsh to both men and animals more than two thousand years ago than it is to travelers today. In an effort to conserve their strength and water, Alexander decided that his cavalry detachment would only ride in the relative cool of the night.

The Persians also were traveling at night for the same reasons.

While travel by night was easier, the darkness also increased the level
of fear among the Persians that Alexander could fall upon them at
any moment. They would stop to make camp each morning after a
long night's march, and they hoped that Alexander would not overtake them that day. As they rested during the day, soldiers at the rear
of the long Persian column were constantly looking for dust clouds
on the horizon—a sure sign of pursuing cavalry.

This constant fear in the column coupled with the deprivations
of the march caused a general malaise to spread through the Persian
army. This in turn gave rise to more and more desertions as men fell
out of the line of march during the night and then simply faded away
into the mountains. Others turned back on the road and walked west
to surrender to Alexander in an effort to save their lives.

Artabazus had remained by Darius, his king and friend. If necessary, he was prepared to follow Darius into battle against Alexander
in the deserts of Iran and die fighting for the king he had served.
Bessus and the others had less gallant and more self-serving ideas.
They saw that Darius was useless to them either as a king or commander, so they conspired to seize him. The conspirators had formulated two contingency plans. If they were overtaken by Alexander, they would bargain the king's life in return for their freedom and
perhaps a place in Alexander's new administration. If Alexander did
not overtake them, then they planned to kill Darius and escape into
Bactria to reorganize and if necessary resist Alexander.

The conspirators constituted an important group of men in the
hierarchy. Some of them, most notably Bessus, commanded considerable military resources in a portion of the empire that had not fallen
under Alexander's control. Bactria contained a vast untapped source
of manpower and resources. It is estimated that the potential of this
satrapy in terms of manpower surpassed the numbers of soldiers
that Darius had lost in his long war with Alexander.[27] Nabarzanes,
another conspirator, was a chiliarch, or commander of a thousand
in the ancient Greek. But this title meant much more than a commander of the royal cavalry. As chiliarch Nabarzanes had charge of
the palace guard and managed all audiences with the king. He was
probably the most powerful figure in the king's entourage.[28] The
remaining conspirators were also satraps from the eastern provinces.

They were Satibarzanes, the satrap of Aria, and Barsaentes, the satrap of the Arachosians and Drangians.

Nabarzanes approached Darius in his tent and urged the king to relinquish his throne to Bessus. He maintained that there was a need among the subjects of the empire for a new beginning.[29] To confront Alexander in battle in their present condition, Nabarzanes contended, was a waste of resources and a needless death for all of them. As Nabarzanes had no desire to go to his death prematurely or needlessly, he proposed to Darius that they abandon any idea of a set battle with Alexander and instead take refuge in Bactria where they could regroup under a new leader. This new leader, Nabarzanes suggested, should be Bessus. Once they were safely in Bactria, they could draw upon fresh resources of soldiers not only from the satrapy of Bessus but also from Sogdiana and India as well as farther north from among the fierce nomadic peoples called the Scythians. When the threat had passed and Alexander was either killed or forced to return to Greece, the Persian throne, held in trust by Bessus, would be restored to Darius and the empire would carry on as before.

Darius might have been mild and trusting, but he was no fool. When he heard these words, the king could not restrain his anger. He rose from his couch and drew his sword against Nabarzanes. But Darius was quickly surrounded by Bessus and his soldiers, who gently but firmly prevailed upon the king to ignore these treasonous words and sheathe his sword.

Outside the royal tent, Nabarzanes and Bessus conferred. The king's angry response to their suggestion sealed his fate. They would await the right moment and seize Darius. The men ordered their troops to withdraw a short distance from the main camp and to remain there, conspicuously detached from the main body of the royal army. Inside the royal tent, Artabazus consoled Darius. He counseled his king to bear Nabarzanes' words with patience, as he could ill afford to risk a confrontation with Alexander so close behind. He pointed out that the king was dependent on the troops of Bessus and Nabarzanes if Alexander suddenly fell upon them. Reluctantly, Darius accepted the advice of his friend but isolated himself in the confines of his tent to sulk. The king refused to admit anyone into his presence except his closest attendants. Following the confrontation with

Nabarzanes, matters deteriorated. Darius stopped giving orders to his commanders. He refused food and remained isolated in the confines of the royal tent, lapsing into a period of severe depression.

The Persian army was coming apart. Soldiers became less disciplined and more concerned with stealing from one another and the desperate civilians who accompanied them rather than attending to their duties. More of the common soldiers, as well as officers, began to desert. There was no longer a sense of purpose or any faith in the ability of Darius to lead them. After a time, it became evident that the king was no longer in charge. In fact, no one seemed to be in charge. The Persian camp became a collection of desperate, frightened people, soldiers and civilians terrified by the specter of Alexander looming over them, larger than life and blacker than death.

Nabarzanes, Bessus, and the other conspirators were men who were seeking to fill the void created by the inability of Darius to conduct a successful war against Alexander. They had given up on him and needed to fill the vacuum that was rapidly developing due to the king's loss of will and ability to command.[30] Darius had to be removed if there was any chance of stopping Alexander and saving at least a part of the empire. But although the conspirators viewed Darius as weak and inept, they also feared him. As king of Persia, he was still a powerful symbol to the soldiers of the army. The majesty of his person commanded respect, and the conspirators feared that if they seized him the army could break up into warring factions.

For the conspirators, there was also the problem of the Greek mercenaries who surrounded the king. They were a well-disciplined, experienced group of professional soldiers who were loyal to Darius. Although outnumbered, they would be a formidable obstacle to overcome if they chose to defend the king. Tensions in the camp were high, and it was becoming increasingly unclear who was in command. Patron ordered the Greek mercenaries to remain together, armed, and on alert. As the situation in the Persian camp became more confused, Patron warned his men that they had to be prepared to respond to his orders at a moment's notice.

That night Bessus sent his agents into the main camp to talk with the Persian soldiers and encourage them to turn against the king. The agents explained to the common soldiers that their situation under

Darius was hopeless. The king had lost his will to fight and was incapable of ruling effectively. Unless they took matters into their own hands, they would all perish in the desert when Alexander descended on them. In spite of these efforts, many of the Persians, officers and soldiers alike, were reluctant to turn on their king, weak as he was. The persona of the Persian king remained strong even if the man himself was weak.

When Artabazus learned what the agents of Bessus were doing, he went out among the Persian rank and file himself as the king's representative and encouraged the soldiers to remain loyal. He reassured them that the king was strong and was prepared to lead them to the eastern provinces, where they would regroup in safety and confront Alexander on the field of battle when conditions were favorable. Then Artabazus returned to the royal tent and tended to his friend. He urged Darius to eat and encouraged him to pull himself out of his depression and fulfill his role as commander of the army.

By this point Bessus and Nabarzanes had decided that they could no longer remain in camp and wait for Alexander to catch them. Because the conspirators feared Patron and the Greek mercenaries, they formulated a plan to neutralize the Greeks by deception. Their plan was to regain the confidence of the king and then isolate him from the Greeks. Bessus and Nabarzanes approached Darius as he lay sulking in his tent. They prostrated themselves before him in the most traditional mark of respect to the royal person. Feigning contrition for their earlier words of disloyalty, they shed tears as they begged for his forgiveness. Darius was deceived by their words and saw in their tears a sincerity that moved his trusting soul to compassion. The king was taken in by the deception and even moved to shed tears of joy himself over their reconciliation. His spirits were uplifted, and he was confident that his only problem now was Alexander. He discussed with Nabarzanes and Bessus plans to continue moving east and how they would draw upon the vast resources of manpower in Bactria and India to form an army greater than any the world had ever seen. Alexander and his army would be destroyed on the vast plains of Central Asia, and the victorious Persian army would move west to regain the conquered lands. Persepolis would be rebuilt, and the Persian Empire would be greater and more glorious than before. Darius raised himself from his despondency and once more took up his role as commander of the Persian army. The king mounted his chariot and rode out among his soldiers to renew their confidence in him and uplift their spirits.

That night, Darius gave the order to break camp and the Persian army once more slowly moved east along the main road. Darius took the lead position in his chariot, and Bessus with his cavalry stayed close by him as a guard. As the column set out into the star-filled desert night, many were still apprehensive. The king's newfound confidence did little to lessen their fear of Alexander. Soldiers continuously looked over their shoulders in the direction from which they feared the Macedonians and Greeks were following them.

Patron had watched what transpired, and the false contrition of Bessus and Nabarzanes sickened him. He distrusted both men, and all that night as the column moved through the darkness he tried to approach Darius to have a word with him. But Bessus and his guards surrounded the king, posing as his trusted companions and loyal protectors. In reality they were isolating him from the only venue of help left and waiting for a favorable moment to seize him.

Finally, when the column stopped for rest, Darius noticed that Patron had been following his chariot and summoned the Greek commander to approach. Patron asked permission to speak to the king alone, without an interpreter or any others present.[31] The two men moved away from the column to speak privately, but Bessus remained close by. He was suspicious of Patron and fearful of letting the king out of his sight. Bessus remained as close to the king as he could and watched attentively as the two men spoke.

Patron was direct with the king. He disclosed his fear that a coup was imminent and named Bessus and Nabarzanes as the principal conspirators. He warned the king that the conspirators were plotting his assassination. Patron implored Darius to separate himself from Bessus and Nabarzanes and allow the Greek contingent to serve as his bodyguard. The mercenary commander explained that the king could have confidence in the loyalty of the Greeks since their only hope for a future lay with him. There was no going home for them, and surrender to Alexander was out of the question. These factors were the king's guarantee that the Greeks were trustworthy and loyal.

Darius listened to Patron's words calmly and with little show of surprise. He remained reserved in his demeanor, and after Patron finished he praised the Greek commander for his loyalty and his concern. Darius wanted more than anything to believe that Bessus and Nabarzanes were loyal to him, although deep within he must have known otherwise. He refused Patron's offer for protection and explained that as the king he could never accept a Greek bodyguard in place of Persians. It was not from lack of trust that he refused the Greek offer but because of what it would symbolize to the Persian soldiers who were loyal to him. It would send a message that Darius did not trust his own people and felt more secure under the protection of strangers. He thanked Patron for his concern and decided that he would take his chances and see how fate would play out its hand.[32]

As Bessus watched the two men speaking, he became more and more apprehensive. The longer they talked, the more his anxiety increased. Finally, anxiety gave way to impatience and then to agitation. Bessus sensed that Patron was revealing the plot to Darius, and he was seized by an impulse to strike at the king immediately. Nabarzanes came over and restrained him. His co-conspirator reminded him that if Alexander overtook them, Darius alive might be worth more to them than Darius dead. The Persian king could become a valuable commodity when negotiating with the Macedonian. Bessus accepted his friend's advice and restrained himself.

When Darius had finished speaking with Patron, he summoned Bessus. In front of the Greek commander he confronted the Bactrian satrap with the accusation of his treachery. Bessus, controlling his impulse to kill Darius, asserted his innocence. He implored the king not to take the word of a mercenary, a man who would serve only those who paid him, over the word of his kinsman and loyal satrap. Once more Darius allowed himself to be swayed more by what he wanted to believe than by what he suspected to be true. He accepted the assurances of the wailing Bessus, though in his heart Darius must have known by this point that what Patron had told him was true.

Darius in all probability realized that the situation had become so dangerous for him that he had no choice but to pretend to accept the assurances of Bessus and thus maintain a necessary facade of cooperation and amicable relations. Darius did not know how many of his soldiers might follow Bessus if it came to a rupture in their relations. At best, the camp would be divided into two hostile groups and fighting was sure to break out. If he accepted the Greeks as guards, he gave his enemies the perfect excuse to turn on him. There were only a few thousand Greeks to protect him in a camp of more than thirty thousand armed men. As skilled and disciplined as they were in combat, the mercenaries were sure to be overwhelmed by the greater numbers of Persians and Bactrians. So Darius accepted the assurances of Bessus a second time, and the uneasy and delicate truce between the king and those who were about to murder him continued for the time being.

When dawn came the Persian soldiers settled down to rest from their march of the night before. They put aside their weapons and began to prepare their meals. They stayed in camp all that day and waited for the order to resume the march that night. No order came. Bessus kept his men armed and about him all that day and into the night. Darius was disturbed by what he saw, and that night he summoned Artabazus to his tent. There he quietly confided in his friend his fear that he was about to be assassinated.

Artabazus advised his king to surround himself with the Greeks as quickly as possible. Darius refused. He was tired and despondent. He had reconciled himself to his impending death and had no fight left in him. He was a worn and tired man. He would not die at the hands of Alexander; he would die at the hands of Bessus and be done with it. Darius no longer had the will to fight, and he was too tired to continue running. He had given up hope and now thought only to join his wife in death. He embraced his friend, and the two cried together over what they both knew was about to happen and what neither was able to prevent. The aged Artabazus offered to remain by his king and friend to the end, but Darius ordered him to take the opportunity and escape. Reluctantly, Artabazus took his leave.

Now alone in his tent, Darius, the last king of Persia, lay upon his royal couch and wept. He cried for his family, and he cried for Persia. His bodyguards, sensing the end was near, began to think only of their own safety. One by one they quietly deserted their posts and disappeared into the night. Darius was unguarded. An eerie silence descended on the royal tent. Then a few of the eunuchs who had remained just outside the entrance to the tent because they had nowhere else to go began a slow and quiet lament for their king. It was the requiem for Darius, the last king of Persia.

While Darius lay upon the royal couch and listlessly awaited his fate, Alexander was closing in on the Persians from the west. He knew Darius was close, and he pressed his cavalry to reach the camp and prevent the murder. Alexander's force was down to six thousand of his best cavalrymen. For Alexander, the most important factor was that his men could move quickly and would require very little to sustain them. So once again he cut his force in half. Alexander, although he was dangerously outnumbered,[33] intended to attack the Persian camp.

Nicanor and Attalus, two of the senior Macedonian commanders, were ordered to follow as quickly as possible with the remainder of the cavalry and with a minimum of equipment. Alexander intended to surprise the Persian column, rescue Darius, and then hold out until Nicanor and Attalus arrived with reinforcements. They would stay there until the main force of the army under Craterus arrived. Craterus was still two or three days behind. It was a risky plan, considering that Alexander was attacking a Persian column of more than thirty thousand armed men with a force of only three thousand horsemen. But it was typical of Alexander to reject the odds when he had his mind set on an objective.

Bessus and Nabarzanes remained near the royal tent. When they heard the wailing of the eunuchs, they feared that Darius had taken his own life. They rushed into the royal tent with their swords drawn. This time there were no guards posted at the entrance—they did not have to ask permission to enter. No one prostrated himself before the king; instead, they fell upon Darius. With a cruel twist they bound the Persian king in golden chains. He did not resist but submitted complacently to his fate. They pulled him from the tent and threw him into a wagon pulled by mules. To conceal what they had done, they covered Darius with the skins of oxen and placed a guard around the wagon. Then they returned to the royal tent and took the time to loot the king's personal possessions.[34]

Artabazus and the Greek mercenaries did not intervene. Instead, along with some units of the Persian army loyal to Artabazus, they left the main column and turned north away from the main road.

They set out to cross the mountains and reach the Caspian Sea beyond. Bessus now ordered the column to move out along the road. The Persian army was unaware of what had happened to the king and complied with his order. Bessus and the other conspirators were nervous at the prospect of fighting Alexander. Even though they had faced Alexander on the field of battle at Gaugamela and the Bactrian cavalry had proved itself the equal to the Macedonian cavalry, two years had passed and the reputation of the Macedonian king had grown out of all proportion to his accomplishments. He seemed invincible to them—a warrior king larger than life—and it was his reputation that intimidated them more than the man who was pursuing them.

The thought that Alexander was close behind and pursuing them proved more terrifying and unnerving to the Persians than the reality of the situation. In fact, Alexander had only a small force of cavalry with him,[35] and Bessus had command of nearly thirty thousand Persians plus his own cavalry. Even if the masses of Persian infantry were not the most reliable and skilled, they could have overwhelmed Alexander's small force by their sheer numbers alone. The Bactrian cavalry were among the best in the ancient world and a match for Alexander's Companions. They were motivated and willing to stand and fight. If Bessus and Nabarzanes had laid an ambush for Alexander or even taken him head-on, they could easily have defeated the Macedonians, saved their own lives, and changed the course of history. But the specter of Alexander so terrified the conspirators that it clouded their judgment as commanders and caused them to run rather than stand and fight.

The pace of the Persian column became increasingly slower as dehydration, shortages of rations, and despondency took their toll. The column was moving too slowly for Bessus, so he decided to leave it behind to slow Alexander while he moved ahead. With his Bactrian horsemen, Bessus rode to the cart where Darius lay and ordered him unchained and mounted on a horse. Darius refused to cooperate. He lay in the cart depressed and defiant toward his captors. He was covered only in animal hides that contrasted ironically with the golden chains that bound him. Bessus and the conspirators dismounted from their horses and approached the cart. Bessus ordered the two slaves who drove the cart to unchain the king, but Darius refused to allow anyone to touch him. The slaves, in confusion and fear, could only cower.

Suddenly there was shouting—an alarm spread forward from the rear of the column. Horsemen had been spotted bearing down on them. The word spread that Alexander was upon them, and there was general panic throughout the Persian army. Darius cried out in joy that his avenger had come. He raved like a madman that now the gods would ensure that Bessus and the conspirators would pay for their crimes. Bessus, agitated and near panic at the prospect of fighting Alexander, lost patience with the king and drew his sword. Two of his fellow commanders, Satibarzanes and Barsaentes, seeing this as a sign from Bessus to execute Darius, hurled their javelins at the king as he lay chained to the cart.[36] Following their lead, each of the other conspirators in turn hurled his javelin into the king in a grotesque and ritualistic slaying that served to bind them together in their nefarious deed. It was over in an instant, and they left Darius dying in the wagon. One of the assassins led the harnessed animals that drew the cart off the main road and onto a secluded path, where he crippled each animal with his sword. Then the group mounted their horses and set out in different directions in an attempt to elude capture. Bessus and Satibarznes moved east along the direct road to Bactria, Barsaentes moved south to Arachosia, while Nabarzanes and some of the others moved to the north toward the Caspian Sea.

Darius was left, dying and alone on a dusty desert road, chained to the cart. Bleeding from his wounds, the last king of the Persian Empire was pulled along a deserted path in the Iranian desert by a pair of wounded mules desperate to find water and impervious to the sufferings of the dying man in the cart behind them.

Alexander and his cavalry had first caught sight of the Persian column shortly after dawn. They had ridden through the night, and as first light broke over the desert they could see the dust from the retreating Persians. Then as they came closer they could make out the din of the long column as it snaked its way along the road. Alexander held his men back until the dust began to settle and they had a clearer view of just how the enemy was dispersed. The Persian rear guard saw Alexander's cavalry and sounded the alarm. Alexander ordered an attack, and his cavalry bore down on the Persian column.

They attacked the Persian column from the rear where the panic was greatest. The Persian rear guard offered no resistance. They either surrendered or fled. Alexander and his men rode past hundreds of wagons filled with gold and silver that had been deserted by their drivers. There were wagons filled with women and children, slaves and civilians, who cried out to them for mercy. Alexander and his cavalry rode along the column heading for the front where they expected to find Darius.

All of the ancient sources relate that Alexander had very few men with him when he attacked the Persian column that morning. If Bessus and his commanders had not panicked and chosen to run but had organized themselves to meet Alexander's attack, they would certainly have prevailed. Alexander was vastly outnumbered, and his men were tired from riding all the night before. The Persians could easily have overwhelmed them just by the sheer force of their numbers. The attack on the column was impetuous and typical of Alexander when he was determined to accomplish his objective at any cost. But it worked. The reputation of Alexander had so cowed the Persians that resistance was nonexistent. So many Persians surrendered that morning that Alexander's cavalry could not contain them all; the Persians were simply allowed to remain free until the Macedonian infantry following behind arrived to take charge of them. The number of Persian prisoners who surrendered that day far exceeded Alexander's forces.

Exactly where the last king of Persia died remains controversial even to this day. While the general area in Iran where Darius was murdered is undisputed, the specific location of his death is debatable. He was assassinated somewhere in an area that begins approximately two hundred kilometers east of modern-day Tehran and ends at the ruins of the ancient city of Hecatompylus at Shahr-I-Qumis. It is here that the Elburz Mountains come down to touch the edge of one of the world's great deserts, the Dasht-e Kavir. The road stretches from Tehran east toward Afghanistan and is doubtless the same route that was used by the Persian column fleeing Alexander. The road has been in continuous use since ancient times and formed part of the network of royal highways that covered the empire. It was the principal route from the main Persian administrative centers—Babylon,

Susa, and Ecbatana—east to the satrapy of Bactria and beyond to India. The place where Darius died would be impossible to locate today. Among the strongest possibilities is the modern village of Lasjerd. The village lies by the side of the road along a two hundred-kilometer stretch of flat arid land. Even today travelers on this stretch of the road need to be self-sufficient, as resources are scarce and water precious.

Another location is Thara,[37] an oasis a few kilometers farther west than Lasjerd. A third possibility is the small town of Damghan[38] some one hundred kilometers farther east than Thara. The oldest view has the location still farther east, in the vicinity of the town of Shahrud.

The ancient sources are not in agreement about whether Darius was already dead when Alexander reached him.[39] There are romantic stories that have circulated over the centuries about the death of the Persian king. One of the more dramatic renditions has a Macedonian soldier, Polystratus, searching for water when he comes upon Darius lying in the cart and very near death. The Macedonian found some water for the king to quench his thirst and comforted him as he lay dying. Darius asked Polystratus to thank Alexander for his kind treatment of the royal family and bestowed upon Polystratus his blessing. Then the Persian king held the right hand of the Macedonian soldier and expired. By the time Alexander rode up, Darius was dead. As Alexander looked at Darius lying in the cart he was moved by pity. After all these years, this was the first time he had seen his adversary face to face. Alexander took off his own cloak and covered the Persian king.

In the most romantic version of all, it was Alexander who found Darius still alive.[40] The Macedonian king compassionately consoled the dying Persian in his last moments, and in return Darius gave Alexander his blessing and designated him heir to the throne of Persia. It is this version, for obvious reasons, that has found the most favor throughout history. Yet modern scholars are nearly unanimous in dismissing the story as highly unlikely, but it plays well to audiences enamored with the romance of the Alexander mystique.

Alexander sent the body of Darius to Persepolis for burial in accordance with the Persian royal traditions.[41] It was a noble and gracious gesture by the conqueror toward his defeated enemy. Darius was brought home, where his mother and daughters were allowed to prepare his body and lay him to rest in one of the royal tombs cut into the rock face of a low promontory of the mountain that lies just to the southeast of the palace terrace.

CHAPTER 3

FROM PARTHIA
TO BACTRIA

FROM THE OASIS WHERE DARIUS HAD DIED ALEXANDER moved his forces a few kilometers farther east to Hecatompylus,[1] a prosperous city that had a reputation in the ancient world for offering every vice and pleasure for which the Orient had ever been known.[2] It was the ideal place for Alexander to quarter his soldiers while he planned and organized the next phase of his campaign. At Hecatompylus, Alexander allowed his troops to stand down and enjoy the pleasures the city had to offer while he awaited the arrival of Craterus with the slower-moving infantry units and the baggage train that he had left behind several days before. When the last units of the column finally arrived, they included a contingent of fresh reinforcements that had been sent from Asia Minor. By the time the last stragglers arrived in the city, Alexander had assembled a considerable force, perhaps as many as forty thousand soldiers.

Now that Darius was dead, the Macedonians and the Greeks expected that Alexander would declare an end to the war and lead them home. They were anxious to see their families, and they wanted to rest and enjoy some of the wealth they had amassed during their years of campaigning. But as the days passed at Hecatompylus, Alexander made no mention of going home. He proceeded to reward his men, both officers and enlisted men alike, with generous dispensations from the treasure that had been taken from the Persian column. There was a considerable amount of gold and silver that was distributed among the soldiers as well as all sorts of luxurious commodities that had once belonged to Darius and his nobles.[3] With gifts and bonuses, the activities in the brothels, and the flowing wine, the king was able to divert the minds of his soldiers, temporarily at least, from any thoughts of going home.

But as the novelty of the whoring and the drinking began to diminish over the next several days, the thoughts the soldiers once more turned to home. Pressure began to build within the army. With idleness came discontent followed by gossip. The first word spread through the camp was that the king was sending home the Greek contingents, a rumor that subsequently proved to be true. Then a second rumor circulated that Alexander had decided to send the entire army home. This was followed by another rumor that the order had been given for the army to break camp and prepare for the long journey home. With the last rumor, pandemonium broke loose among the soldiers.

Alexander had, in fact, ordered the Greek contingents to be paid off and sent home. With Darius dead and the war of vengeance over, he had no need of his Greek allies any longer and was probably glad to be rid of them. But that was as far as the demobilization order went. However, once word of the Greek dismissal began to spread through the camp, the rest of the soldiers believed that they were going home as well. Men, especially unhappy, discontented men, are prone to believe what they want to believe, not necessarily what is true.

Once started, the rumor that they were going home could not be contained. It spread through the brothels and emptied the taverns as men returned to their units and began packing their belongings. Tents were being dismantled and carts loaded, yet no order had been given.[4] Many of the junior officers joined with the enlisted men, while others stood by confused, not knowing what to make of the madness that had come over the army. The frenzy indicated just how tired these soldiers had become of this long war and how strong was their desire to return to their homes. Everyone—even the newly arrived reinforcements—was caught up in the euphoria over the prospect that the long campaign had ended.

Yet returning home was the furthest thing from Alexander's mind. For him the campaign was far from over, since his goals had not been realized. Although Alexander was intent on catching Bessus and the other conspirators, he was more interested in leading his army to the limits of the known world. He believed that there were distant lands of incredible wealth to conquer and greater treasurers to plunder. For Alexander, it was about conquest and ego—the gold was a way to pay for it. Alexander longed to see India and the farthest reaches of the Orient. His tutor Aristotle had taught him as a young boy that beyond India lay a great Ocean, and Alexander wanted to see it.

When word reached Alexander about what was happening in the camp, he summoned his senior officers to a meeting. At first he spoke to them about disloyalty, then with tears in his eyes he pleaded with them not to allow the campaign to end. The madness that had taken hold of the soldiers was the work of the gods. The gods were envious of all the army had accomplished and had sent this madness down from heaven to take hold of the soldiers in an attempt to stop them from achieving even greater glory. This desire to return home and see their wives and children was normal for all of them, and it was to be expected. They would all return home, Alexander promised them, but now was not the time. They could return home when they had brought those who had murdered Darius to justice and secured the Hellenic world from any future threat of barbarian invasions. This last argument played into Alexander's personal agenda. For by explaining to his officers the necessity of suppressing all potential threats to Greece and Macedonia, his justification allowed him to continue pushing east because there would always be more enemies to subdue, real and imagined. Alexander implored his officers to be patient and put their trust in him.

Alexander's words worked their magic. He was the consummate alchemist of emotions. He used his special mixture of charisma, flattery, and intimidation on his officers, especially on the younger ones. He manipulated them to do his bidding through an age-old combination that leaders have used throughout time to motivate their followers: fear and self-interest. The assembled officers pledged their loyalty to Alexander and vowed to carry out his commands. They promised to follow him to the ends of the earth and only asked in return that he might address the soldiers in assembly and inspire them with his vision. Alexander agreed but shrewdly required that his officers first go out among the common soldiers to "prepare their ears" for what he had to say.[5]

That next morning Alexander stood upon a dais before the assembled army. Heralds were placed at intervals to carry his words to those farthest from the speaker. Alexander began by recounting all they had accomplished together over the past several years. He recited the list of all the lands and cities they had conquered, the mountains they had climbed, the rivers they had crossed, the cities they had pillaged, and the armies they had fought. All this they had done together, he argued, to bring freedom to those in bondage and to avenge the sacrilege of the Persians who had pillaged and burned the temple of Athena at Athens. Then Alexander softened his tone and began to speak to the soldiers of their homes. He knew it had been years now since many of them had last seen their wives and children. He too felt a longing to see his native Macedonia and to embrace his mother and sister. More than any of them he wished to return to his homeland and enjoy the benefits of peace and the fruits of their valor.

But, Alexander went on, their work was not done, and labors lay ahead of them that had to be finished. The army still had to subdue the barbarian nations that lay farther to the east. Men such as Bessus and Nabarzanes, Satibarzanes and Barsaentes, might one day lead the barbarian hordes west and retake what the Greeks and Macedonians had come so far and fought so hard to conquer. Barbarian hordes might one day sweep across the plains of Asia Minor and lay waste to the Greek cities of the coast. A day could come when they might even launch their ships against Greece. The barbarian nations of the East had to be subdued. Only when that had been accomplished could Alexander lead them home, secure in the knowledge that they had secured the safety of Greece and Macedonia for all time.

Final victory was close, Alexander assured his men. Only "four days more of marching" through "country that is level and easy" was left. It would not be a difficult campaign, as they were chasing nothing more than "a few runaways and slayers of their master."[6] They would not be fighting an army of disciplined soldiers but, rather, barbarians who had lost the will to resist. Alexander made it sound as if upon them depended the future survival of the Western world. What Alexander warned against—barbarian invasions of the West—would eventually come to pass, but it would be centuries before Attila (A.D. 451), Genghis Khan (A.D. 1200), and Tamerlane

(A.D. 1450) would ride out of the East to ravage and plunder Hellenic civilization.

Alexander was preparing his men to wage a new war in the East but for different reasons than the war had been fought in Persia. This would no longer be a crusade to avenge Greece for the wrongs done by the Persians; now Alexander was asking his army to avenge the brutal murder of an enemy king and to secure the safety of Greece and Macedonia for their children and grandchildren. This campaign was sure to earn them a reputation for righteousness throughout the ancient world. They were destined to be numbered among the greatest and most glorious of the heroes and certain to be blessed by the gods.

Probably no general in history has ever told greater lies to his men about where and why they were going to fight than Alexander did to the Greeks and Macedonians that day in Hecatompylus. Nor could any general have deceived his men more about what hardships really lay ahead of them. These were soldiers who believed in Alexander and were prepared to follow him, but they had no idea to what extent they were being manipulated. It was Alexander's intent to lead the army to the very ends of the earth, not to protect Greece from the barbarians or avenge Darius of Persia but for his own glory.

The four days more of marching he promised them would turn into six years—years that would prove to be among the most difficult and deadly the army had endured and worse than anything they could have imagined. The hardships and the fighting in the years ahead would be equal to and in many cases much worse than what they had experienced in the western part of the Persian Empire. The "runaways" and "slayers of their master," men Alexander had characterized as cowards and dismissed with such contempt, would prove to be among the most skilled, resourceful, and tenacious adversaries that the Greeks and Macedonians had ever engaged on the field of battle.

As Alexander and his army moved to the east they would bring untold suffering and misery to a world that at the moment was only beginning to realize they existed. Villages, towns, and cities from what is today Afghanistan all the way to India would be devastated and their people massacred. Alexander and his army would suffer as well as they marched through some of the most inhospitable and desolate land on the face of the earth. The elements of nature—the heat and the cold, the snow and the rains, the thirst and the hunger—would all extract more casualties than the enemy they were fighting. In the years ahead they would climb some of the highest, coldest, and most treacherous mountains in the world and cross some of the driest and hottest deserts for no perceptible reason other than simply to pillage the lands they invaded and add to the glory of a man who would never be content with his accomplishments. They were about to enter a part of the world that today is still considered to be one of the poorest and most dangerous areas on the face of the earth—Central Asia from Afghanistan to India.

Alexander's soldiers were swept up by his words. They responded with enthusiasm and never comprehended the extent of the misery that lay ahead of them. They roared their mindless acceptance of his words and pledged to follow him wherever he might lead, little realizing that most of them would never return. Many would be killed at the hands of an enemy they had as yet not seen. Some of them would be taken by the hardships along the long and arduous route; still more would fall from disease. Others would be involuntarily resettled in colonies and outposts and then abandoned to fend for themselves in desolate and remote areas. There they would be left by Alexander to live out the remainder of their years as colonial masters oppressing a hostile native population.

Some of the men who listened to Alexander's words that day were destined to die at his own hands, the hands of the leader they now so revered. For the moment, however, the soldiers put aside thoughts of home and reveled in the excitement of the new adventure they were about to undertake. Alexander had taken their discontent and transformed it into enthusiasm. When the assembly was over, the soldiers returned to the taverns and brothels where they repeated Alexander's words to the bored prostitutes and boasted of their prior exploits to the ever-solicitous tavern keepers.

Within a few days the army was ready to move. Most of the Greeks had been released from service, paid their wages, and given a generous bonus to ensure that when they reached home they would only speak well of Alexander. They were sent on their way west across the deserts and mountains of Iran through Iraq and Syria and finally to the Mediterranean Sea, which would carry them home. It would be six months at best before any of them would touch Greek soil.

The army that moved east with Alexander was lighter armed and composed of greater numbers of cavalry due to the changed nature of the fighting. While Alexander retained his core of infantry known as the phalanx, as well as his Companion and Thracian cavalry units, he added the elite Persian cavalry of Darius. The Persians who joined Alexander did so as common soldiers, officers, and administrators. Many had been princes and nobles from old Iranian families. They were proud men, hopeful of opportunities in Alexander's new world. Many had demonstrated ability and experience both in the political and military realms, and Alexander needed their skills as he sought to rule the lands he was so quickly conquering. They often knew the dialect spoken by the people, and they were able to put into place a system by which the conquered territory could be administered.

Over the next few years, Alexander would bring the Persians not only into his army but also into his inner circle of confidants and intimates. Their presence and their appointments to military and civil positions in the new empire became a focal point for the discontent that would grow among his Greek and Macedonian officers. Alexander came to rely on the Persians, who often knew the local dialects as well as the customs of the people, to act as his advisors and also his administrators. In addition, the Persians were accustomed to treating their kings as divinities, and this pleased Alexander. As the years wore on and the army moved farther into the East, Alexander would become closer to the people he had conquered than he was to his own countrymen.

It was the start of autumn when Alexander and his army left Hecatompylus. They did not move east to follow Bessus and the other conspirators into Bactria but moved due north, over the Elburz Mountains and then down into a narrow and lush semitropical area called Hyrcania, wedged between the mountains and the Caspian Sea. Hyrcania was part of a larger Persian satrapy called Parthia and under the control of Phrataphernes, a Persian commander who had been present at the battle of Gaugamela.

Alexander had decided, for the moment at least, not to pursue the murderers of Darius. Instead, he was moving into Hyrcania to neutralize a more immediate threat to the security of his army in the form of the remnants from the Persian column. A sizable force of Persian infantry under the command of Artabazus had left the main column when Darius was seized. The Greek mercenaries under Patron had joined Artabazus, and their column had retreated north across the mountains to take refuge in Hyrcania. Phrataphernes and his soldiers were also in Hyrcania, and Alexander feared that the combined forces of these Persians and Greeks, experienced soldiers under the command of competent officers who had been fiercely loyal to Darius, could pose a threat by disrupting his communication and supply lines to the west. They could present security problems as well if the time came when Alexander needed to retreat from Bactria and return to Iran.

Alexander probably crossed over the Elburz Mountains by the Shamshirbun Pass, which historically has been the easiest and safest route to the Caspian Sea from the Iranian city of Damghan. This pass would have brought Alexander to the upper reaches of the Dorudbar River, and from there it would have been an easy matter for his army to follow the course of the river down to the shores of the Caspian Sea and the ancient city that was known as Zadracarta.[7]

In the entourage of the king, riding as a privileged member of the elite Companion cavalry, was Oxathres, the brother of Darius. A few weeks earlier he had been discovered among the prisoners taken from the Persian column.[8] Hephaestion, Alexander's close friend and lover, had come across Oxathres while interrogating a group of prisoners who were suspected of being Persian nobles. Alexander welcomed Oxathres into the Companions, his elite cavalry, because the brother of Darius could serve as a symbol. His presence was visible proof for the entire world to see that Alexander the Great had forgiven the Persians and sought to integrate them into his new empire.

Shortly before reaching Zadracarta, Alexander received a letter from Nabarzanes and several other Persian officers. They had taken refuge in Hyrcania thinking they would be safe as Alexander passed them by in pursuit of Bessus. They did not count on Alexander's making an unexpected turn to the north. It became evident to them that sooner or later they would be caught up in his net as Alexander swept the province of Hyrcania. They thought it best to try to come to terms with the Macedonian conqueror before he cornered them.

In the letter carried by his emissary, Nabarzanes attempted to justify his role in the murder of Darius. He pleaded to Alexander that killing Darius had been a matter of self-defense. Nabarzanes explained that, he, like the other Persian nobles, feared that Darius was about to place himself under the protection of the Greek mercenaries—a move that would have been an affront to the loyalty of the Persian officers who guarded the king and gone against more than two hundred years of Persian tradition. Darius, Nabarzanes argued, had been killed because the nobles around him feared that he would have turned his Greeks against them. He asked for Alexander's pardon and offered to surrender. It was a pathetic excuse, but Alexander chose to accept it and sent word to Nabarzanes that if he and his companions surrendered their safety would be guaranteed.

When they received Alex's response, Nabarzanes, Phrataphernes, and a number of other Persian nobles and officers came down from the mountains and surrendered. Among the gifts that Nabarzanes brought Alexander that day was a young eunuch of exceptional beauty named Bagoas. Bagoas was, in the words of the ancient manuscripts, "in the very flower of boyhood." He had been "loved by Darius and now would be loved by Alexander."[9] Over time Bagoas would become a favorite of Alexander's and exercise considerable influence over the king throughout his travels in the East and at Babylon.

Not long after the surrender of Nabarzanes, Artabazus and the Greek mercenaries sent emissaries to Alexander asking for pardon and terms of surrender. Artabazus was the grandson of a Persian king and the father of Alexander's current mistress Barsine. He had been a respected figure in the Persian nobility and venerated both because of his age (ninety-four) and his closeness to the royal family. Alexander was anxious to add Artabazus, along with Oxathres, to his collection of Iranian nobles.[10] Riding with Artabazus into Alexander's camp were his nine sons "all born of the same mother."[11] When Artabazus descended his mount, Alexander extended his right hand and welcomed the Persian noble as he would welcome an old friend. That night the men dined together in the royal tent and, like old

friends reunited after an absence of many years, delighted in reliving
the days when Artabazus had been a guest in the palace of Philip. Alexander respected Artabazus for the loyalty he had shown to Darius,
and Alexander showed considerable respect toward the Persian noble
because of his age. Artabazus was given a place of honor in the entourage of Alexander, the new Asian king, and his sons were accepted
into the army as officers.

The Greek mercenaries had a more difficult time than the Persians
obtaining a pardon from Alexander.[12] While Alexander could easily
forgive barbarians, he could not always forgive the Greeks in their
service. The Greeks did not accompany Artabazus into Alexander's
camp. Rather, they remained outside the camp and asked for terms
through their emissaries. Alexander could not bring himself to forgive them for having fought against Greeks, and he condemned them
as guilty of "grave wrongs."[13] The only terms the Greek mercenaries
could extract from Alexander that day were unconditional surrender,
or they could take their chances in the mountains.

The mercenaries elected to surrender under a promise of safe
conduct and take their chances with Alexander. When they arrived
in the camp, there were only fifteen hundred of them left. They were
led by a new commander, Andronicus, an officer from Macedonia.
The mercenaries had changed commanders, perhaps in the hope that
Alexander might be more favorably disposed toward them if they
were led by a Macedonian rather than a Greek. There is no indication in the ancient sources of what eventually became of Patron,
the former leader, and the other mercenaries. Whether they chose to
remain fugitives in the mountains behind Hyrcania or managed to
escape and eventually return home to Greece is something that will
never be known.

Alexander ordered that those mercenaries who had entered the
service of the Persian king before the alliance between the Greek city-
states and Macedonia were to be released and allowed to join regular
units in the army for full pay. The mercenaries who had entered
Persian service after the alliance were to remain prisoners. Hidden
among the mercenaries, Alexander's soldiers discovered a number of
Spartans and Athenians who had been ambassadors to the Persian
court. These men had been sent to Ecbatana months before in an

effort to solicit money from Darius to help finance resistance against Alexander's regent in Greece. When Alexander had moved north toward Ecbatana in pursuit of Darius, their route home had been cut off and they had been forced to join the retreating Persian column moving east. Alexander ordered these men held as prisoners. This was the second time he had found Greek ambassadors colluding with the Persians. The first time had been after the battle of Issus nearly three years earlier, when ambassadors had been discovered in the camp of Darius. Collusion between Alexander's Greek allies and the Persians had been an ongoing problem for him since the war began and showed just how tenuous was his hold over the mainland Greeks.

When Alexander reached Zadracarta a few days later, he moved into one of the palaces of Darius. He was joined by two of his senior commanders, Craterus and Erigyius, who arrived with additional reinforcements and supplies. Alexander remained at Zadracarta for several weeks, and during that period the Amazon queen, Thalestris,[14] arrived with her entourage for a visit. She had come from Thermodon, an area she ruled on the southeastern coast of the Black Sea.[15] Thalestris was a woman of exceptional beauty and remarkable size. Her athletic prowess and bravery in combat made her legendary among her people.

Alexander was awed by the queen and her escort of three hundred heavily armed Amazon women. When the queen dismounted, Alexander was impressed by her form and size. Her clothing, like that of all the Amazon women, did not entirely cover her body. Her left side was exposed to the breast, while the right was veiled. The folds of her garment, which gathered in a knot slightly above her knees, rested upon firm athletic thighs. One breast had been removed so that she might more easily draw back her bowstring, while the other had been left intact to nourish female children.

When Thalestris saw Alexander, the Amazon queen could hardly mask her disappointment at his less than majestic presence. While Alexander was short for a man, he was not unattractive. His face was fair and clean-shaven. The pose of his neck was odd in that it was slightly bent to the left, while bright golden locks of wavy hair lay touching his shoulders. He was fair complexioned, and it has been written that his physical characteristics coupled with his youth caused all who saw him to refer to the young king as beautiful. Alexander was a man continually torn between the passionate, emotional nature inherited from his mother Olympias and the focused mind and alcoholic predisposition he inherited from his father Philip.

However, like all barbarians, Thalestris that believed only those men "adorned by nature with extraordinary size and physical attractiveness were capable of great deeds."[16] So in that regard Alexander was a disappointment to her. Nor was Thalestris the first queen to have been disappointed in her physical expectations of Alexander. Sisigambis, the mother of Darius, in an embarrassing faux pas, mistook the taller Hephaestion for Alexander when she first laid eyes on the pair in the royal tent following the battle of Issus.[17]

Alexander's manner charmed the Amazon queen just as he was able to charm most men and women. With a voice that flowed on tenor chords in moments of calm, he was able to seduce and draw obedience, love, and admiration from the most jaundiced of his veterans. While often impetuous and violent in some matters, Alexander could be restrained, moderate, and even tender in others. His physical appearance could be deceptive, for within this young man of diminutive size was an unyielding nature. Alexander was a man who resisted compulsion but often, in the beginning at least, could be easily moved by emotion. He was sometimes influenced more by anger, and in certain circumstances he could act more like a "frenzied and foolish commander than a wise one."[18]

Alexander was a man driven by his own internal demons, and those demons compelled him to excel in everything and continue to push the limits of human endurance and patience. He was driven to expose himself to personal danger, and while this was a component of his complex personality, it was also characteristic of an earlier period in Greek history. At the time of the Trojan War kings were expected to be in the forefront of combat and to exceed all others in bravery, cunning, and skill. Alexander was driven to emulate the characteristics of the exploits of his childhood heroes, men such as Achilles and Heracles who excelled in hand-to-hand combat.

Ironically, Alexander held a marked aversion to competitive athletics such as boxing and a love of literature, music, and poetry. As king he sponsored competitions for poets and musicians, and his favorite literary piece was the *Iliad*. Throughout the long campaigns, he carried a copy of the classic work revised for him by Callisthenes. Alexander often referred to it as his most treasured possession, for it carried within its pages the story of the exploits of his hero Achilles. Alexander claimed heroes such as Achilles and Heracles as his ancestors. He sacrificed to the god Dionysus because he had been born of a mortal mother and a divine father. All these emotional forces Alexander held together, at least in the beginning, within a firm wrapping of personal discipline.[19] He had that combination of boyish vulnerability and masculinity that women often find so irresistible.

Thalestris recovered from her initial disappointment and eventually found herself attracted to the young king. She explained why she had come so far to find him. Thalestris considered Alexander the greatest of all warriors in her age, and she considered herself the strongest and bravest of all women. Because of their unique characteristics, she thought they should have a child together. It was certain to her that any child who would come forth from their union would surpass all other mortals in strength, courage, and intelligence. If a female child was born of their union, she would remain with Thalestris to be raised as the heir to the Amazon throne. If a male child was born to her, she proposed that the infant would be sent to Macedonia to be raised by Alexander's family and become heir to his empire.

The young king spent thirteen days and nights tending to the needs of the Amazon queen.[20] The diminutive Macedonian and the one-breasted Amazon made love while the army shook its collective head in disbelief. Scholars have tended to be skeptical of this story, and at least one credible source termed it nothing more than "a fiction."[21]

Completing his amorous interlude with the Amazon queen, Alexander moved his forces east out of Hyrcania and into the satrapy of Aria. Aria is now part of the deserts and wastelands that comprise the easternmost limits of Iran and western Afghanistan. It was now the autumn of 330 B.C., and there were signs of change not only in the weather but in Alexander himself that foretold the coming of a darker time.

The army that followed Alexander into Asia had changed from the

one he had led through Asia Minor and Persia. This was now an army
of men who either fought with him for pay or loved him so deeply
that they would follow wherever he led. Among his closest officers
were some of his childhood friends and men who had served with his
father years before. There was a new component—large numbers of
Persian nobles who had joined the army seeking opportunities in
Alexander's new administration.

Large numbers of people followed Alexander's army and earned
their living from it. There were slaves, prisoners, merchants, men
who drove the supply wagons, and those who transported the looted
treasures of the fallen empire. A host of craftsmen and artisans as
well as prostitutes and wives followed to tend to the needs of the
army, some by choice and others by force. The army of Alexander did
not travel lightly, nor did it move quickly.

As the army approached the borders of Aria, Satibarzanes, the
satrap of the territory, offered to surrender. He was a friend of Bessus
and one of those who had helped to murder Darius. The exact circumstances and conditions of his surrender are not known. All that
is known is that Alexander, for whatever reason, spared his life and
allowed him to retain his position as satrap of Aria.[22] When the army
moved on, Alexander left behind a member of his Companion cavalry, Anaxippus, with a small detachment of Macedonian horsemen.
Anaxippus and the Macedonians were left behind presumably to
ensure the continued compliance of Satibarzanes as an ally, but the
very small size of the contingent indicates that Alexander must
have felt confident that Satibarzanes would prove to be loyal. This
would shortly prove to be a costly error in Alexander's judgment of
character.

It was during the period when Alexander left the Amazon queen
at Zadracarta and his entry into the ancient city of Susia[23] that he
began to succumb to the extravagance of Persian luxury. Alexander's
previous simplicity and continence now began to transform itself into
arrogance and dissipation. Alexander began to ape the Persian royalty
and became enamored with the quasi-divine status it bestowed upon
its kings.[24] More and more he emulated the loftiness of the Persian
kings and began to exhibit an insolence of spirit in dealing with those
in his company.

Alexander began to reject the customs of the Macedonian kings because he found them to be unsuitable for his new image of himself as king of Asia. He began to wear Persian clothes in place of his simpler Macedonian vestments. Alexander encircled his brow with a purple diadem, the kitharas, similar to the one Darius had worn, instead of the traditional Macedonian crown. He began to wear the robes of the king he had conquered. At first he wore the elaborate robes of the Persian royalty only when he met with the barbarians or in the privacy of his quarters, but later he enjoyed wearing the vestments when he went out among his soldiers.

When Alexander wrote letters of instruction to his regent Antipater in Macedonia or corresponded with his allies in Greece, he sealed each letter with his own ring. But when he wrote instructions and decrees for his new empire, he sealed them with the signet ring he had taken from the finger of Darius. When those around him questioned his actions, he excused them by saying that he was adapting to the native customs and making those he had just conquered feel more comfortable with his rule.

Alexander's adoption of Persian dress, manners, and affectations would increase the farther the army moved into the East and exacerbate the resentment and dissatisfaction among many of his Greek and Macedonian soldiers. In the beginning, they tolerated Alexander's Persian affectations because he had told them they were necessary to ensure harmony with the defeated barbarians and to facilitate their greater cooperation and acceptance of his rule. As the influence of the Persians increased, it was difficult for the Greeks and Macedonians to comprehend why they, as victors, had to have harmonious relations with the vanquished.

As Alexander began to include more Persians in his personal entourage—distinguished persons from among the nobles such as Oxathres, the brother of Darius, and Artabazus. This offended many of the Macedonians and Greeks. Alexander imposed on many of his friends and those in the Companion cavalry to wear Persian dress, and this caused resentment. Because many of these men were close to Alexander and loved him as a friend, and because they admired his other qualities, at first they accepted the Persian dress as necessary to please him.[25] The Companions were issued Persian cloaks with purple borders, and their horses were fitted out in elaborate Persian harness. The resentment built as the army moved east.

It was the tradition in Iran and in the eastern satrapies for the subjects of the Persian king to prostrate themselves in his presence. The Persians and other barbarians who came before Alexander in his new role as king of Asia had a natural tendency to follow their old habits. They would not only bow before Alexander but would prostrate themselves with their chins to the floor and arms outstretched. Alexander had initially tolerated the practice, certainly since he had entered Babylon and Susa. Now he came to enjoy it and eventually require that all those he had conquered prostrate themselves before him. Eventually, he would attempt to extend the custom to the Macedonians and Greeks in his army with disastrous results.

Alexander gave loose rein to his passions as well during this period. He added more than three hundred concubines to his retinue in the manner of Darius, along with large numbers of eunuchs, young men who were also accustomed to prostituting themselves for the pleasure of the king and his companions. The eunuchs and concubines would parade around Alexander's couch after dinner so that he might select the ones with whom he would lay that night. Drinking and feasting became the accepted standard of life for Alexander and those closest to him.

The more Alexander turned away from the simpler elements of Macedonian life and tradition, the more his lifestyle disturbed the more conservative Greeks and Macedonians in his command. What disturbed these men the most was Alexander's rejection of a fundamental premise of Greek and Macedonian political life—that all citizens were equal.[26] Alexander was now living in a time and place where he was increasingly being worshiped as a god-king by those he had conquered, and he came to enjoy it. He had no desire to return to the simple life in Macedonia and to rule over people such as the Greeks—contentious subjects who regarded him at best as no more than the first among equals.

The Macedonians and Greeks around Alexander were divided in their reaction to the king's behavior and to what was happening around him. Most were unaccustomed to this type of life and had never seen either such a degree of wealth or such obsequiousness.

Certain of Alexander's officers and friends, mostly the younger ones, embraced the new lifestyle of the king and willingly participated in the excesses of the royal entourage. Yet the older officers disapproved and over time became increasingly more critical of the king. These officers began to speak openly in the camp against the king's lifestyle and voiced the opinion that more had been lost by victory than had been gained by war. The feeling was spreading among the Greeks and Macedonians in the army that while Alexander had been victorious on the battlefields of Persia, he was being corrupted by the excesses of the barbarians.

At first Alexander tried to placate his critics and win back their favor. He attempted to silence them with generous gifts of money from the looted Persian treasury, but that tactic only provided a temporary solution to the problem. Discontent and criticism regarding his lifestyle continued to resurface.[27] The situation soon began to deteriorate to the point where Alexander became concerned that certain units might mutiny. Common soldiers openly began to refer to him pejoratively as the Satrap of Darius. Clearly, the situation was becoming unstable as larger numbers of officers and common soldiers no longer saw any purpose to what they were doing or where they were going. The army was now barely moving and seemed to exist for the sole purpose of transporting and protecting the king's luxurious entourage of concubines, catamites, and treasure.

Nowhere on Alexander's general staff was this difference of opinion about the king's lifestyle more evident than between his two closest friends, Hephaestion and Craterus. The rift eventually became so wide that it brought the men to draw their swords against each other.[28] Alexander was forced to intervene, but he was never able to close the gap. Yet he valued both men and would often comment that while Hephaestion was a friend to Alexander, Craterus was a friend to the king.

Hephaestion was Alexander's closest companion and lover. They were close in years, and Hephaestion openly embraced Alexander's new mode of life. He willingly participated in all its excesses. Hephaestion lived to please Alexander, and their bond of friendship was that much stronger because they were lovers as well. Craterus was a professional soldier and older than Alexander. When Parmenio had been left behind at Ecbatana, Craterus eventually became Alexander's most senior commander. Throughout his years with Alexander, he remained what he had always been—a conservative Macedonian and a loyal, obedient officer. To Craterus, the Persians were the barbarian enemy. They had been conquered, and in accordance with the dictates of Greek political philosophy they were a people who should either be enslaved or exterminated. For Craterus, nothing could be more disgraceful than that Alexander's army should return home forced by their leader to wear the clothes and bear the customs of the very barbarians they had conquered. Yet in spite of his feelings, Craterus remained a loyal and obedient officer. He saw his duty as a soldier, and to the very end he carried out Alexander's orders and remained his senior commander.

Alexander must have sensed that he was sliding too far into a life of debauchery and excess. His soldiers were idle, and he needed to inspire them once again with a sense of purpose. It was at this point that Alexander learned Bessus had assumed the title of Artaxerxes IV in Bactria and was calling himself king of Asia. He was reported to be assembling an army and preparing for war. This was the moment for Alexander to inspire his army with a new sense of purpose and to move against Bessus.[29]

In some dramatic way, Alexander had to show the army that he had not forgotten his Macedonian roots and to inspire in them an enthusiasm for the war against Bessus. He assembled the army on a wide plain where he had his own possessions, which contained the best pieces looted from the Persian Empire, as well as the baggage of the soldiers collected, loaded onto wagons, and placed in a great circle. Only the weapons of the soldiers and the most essential equipment for waging war were not placed into the circle. The soldiers speculated among themselves as to why the king had assembled them and what he was about to do. Alexander ordered the animals unhitched from the wagons and led away. Then he went forward into the middle of the circle and with a torch in hand began to set fire to his own wagons. As Alexander's possessions were burning, he ordered all the remaining wagons to be set on fire.[30] The soldiers were appalled and shouted their disapproval. But as it was the king's baggage that had first been put to the torch, the soldiers accepted the destruction and returned to the camp to prepare for the march to Bactria and then war with Bessus.

As the army moved east, Alexander chose to follow a much easier but longer route to Bactria. Instead of moving along the more difficult but direct route due east and into the Hindu Kush Mountains, the army followed a route that today serves as the principal highway from Herat in western Afghanistan to Kandahar in the south and Kabul in the north. As the army began to move into Afghanistan, somewhere between Susia and Herat, Nicanor, a son of Parmenio and senior officer on Alexander's staff, became sick and died. He was a respected commander and one of Parmenio's sons, yet Alexander refused to halt the column to allow for his funeral according to Macedonian custom. There should have been several days of mourning, sacrifices, and games for Nicanor, but Alexander ordered the column to continue moving east deeper into the satrapy of Aria and toward the ancient city of Chortacana.[31] Philotas, the older brother of Nicanor and himself a senior commander of cavalry, was detached from the column along with an escort of several hundred men and allowed to remain behind to perform the funeral rites.

This was a significant episode and an indication of the rift that had developed within Alexander's staff. Alexander had failed to honor, in the proscribed tradition, the memory of one of his senior officers and a son of Parmenio. Funerals were important to the Greeks and Macedonians, and Alexander's refusal to attend the funeral of Nicanor was an indication that Parmenio and his sons were falling from Alexander's favor. Word was sent to Parmenio at Ecbatana informing him that his son had died.

As Alexander and the army moved deeper into Aria, news reached them that Satibarzanes had revolted. He had massacred the Macedonian contingent that Alexander had left behind to guarantee his loyalty. In a fury, Alexander broke off from the main column with a lighter armed infantry force and some of the cavalry. In a series of forced marches, mostly at night, he returned to western Aria and unexpectedly came upon Satibarzanes and about two thousand of his horsemen. Satibarzanes was caught unprepared and was stunned by the speed with which Alexander had closed in on him. Rather than fight, he retreated into the Hindu Kush Mountains to join Bessus in

Bactria. During the next thirty days, Alexander punished the people of Aria for the revolt of Satibarzanes. Towns and villages all over the western part of the province were burned and fortifications were demolished. Alexander took out his anger on the local people and brought the satrapy once more firmly under his control.

While Alexander was in western Aria, he received additional reinforcements of Greek and Macedonian infantry and cavalry from Antipater. With these reinforcements Alexander rejoined the main column, which by this time had moved south from Chortacana and entered the satrapy of Drangiana. This had been the satrapy of Barsaentes, another one of the conspirators who had a direct hand in the murder of Darius. Barsaentes, like Satibarzanes, chose not to fight Alexander and instead fled to India.

Drangiana was an ancient satrapy, and today it comprises the southwestern part of Afghanistan where that country's borders come together with those of Iran and Pakistan. It is still today a desolate, arid, impoverished, and troubled place as it was in Alexander's time. Alexander halted his army for several days at Phadra, the capital of Drangiana.[32] It was here that the dissension on Alexander's staff came to a head and resulted in the purges that over the next several months would decimate the ranks of his friends and officers and change the course of his rule irrevocably.

Philotas returned from the burial of his brother and resumed his role as commander of the cavalry. The events at Phadra were set in motion when a Macedonian named Dymnus, a junior officer in the entourage of Alexander, set about to impress a young boy with whom he was enamored. The young boy was named Nicomachus, and he was one of a number of catamites who were kept in the entourage of Alexander for sexual amusement. At an intimate meeting, Dymnus revealed to the boy that he was part of a plot to assassinate Alexander within the next three days. Dymnus intimated that his co-conspirators were important men around the king, and to impress the boy further he named Demetrius, one of Alexander's closest bodyguards, as well as a number of other high-ranking officers including Nicanor, the son of Parmenio who had recently died.

Nicomachus immediately told his older brother Cebalinus about the plot. Cebalinus became fearful that they could both be caught up in its aftermath. Cebalinus warned his younger brother that in order to save themselves, the plot had to be revealed to the king immediately. Neither boy was allowed to approach the king directly, but Cebalinus was allowed access to the vestibule of the royal tent where the highest-ranking officers passed through each day on their way to see Alexander. The boy hurried to the tent and waited there to try to get a message to the king.

Philotas passed through the vestibule on his way to see Alexander. The boy took the opportunity to speak to him. With confused words and excited gestures, Cebalinus revealed to Philotas the plot against the king. Why the boy would reveal a plot to Philotas that implicated his dead brother, Nicanor, is difficult to comprehend, but the sources are clear that he did. Philotas listened, commended the boy for his concern for the king's safety, and then entered the royal tent for his audience with Alexander. The next day, the anxious boy returned to the vestibule and waited. When Philotas passed through, Cebalinus stopped him and asked if Alexander had been informed. Philotas replied that he was still awaiting the right moment to bring the matter to the king's attention, and then he went in to see Alexander. The boy became increasingly apprehensive at the delay and began to suspect that Philotas could be one of the conspirators.

It was now the second day since the brothers had learned of the plot, and the assassination was planned for the third. Cebalinus feared for his own life. In desperation, he sought out another officer on Alexander's staff, Metron. When Metron heard the boy's story, he took the matter directly to Alexander. Metron was admitted to the king's chambers, and Alexander listened carefully to what he had to say. Once Metron finished, Alexander ordered his guards to arrest Dymnus and bring Cebalinus into the royal quarters for questioning. Alexander interrogated the boy intently, and when he learned that two days had passed since he had first learned of the plot Alexander became furious. He ordered the boy executed. To save himself, the boy cried out that he had told Philotas about the plot the very first day and it was Philotas who had concealed it from the king. Alexander, now in a rage, interrogated the boy over and over about Philotas. In spite of his terror, the boy stuck to his story. Alexander, now nearly hysterical and with tears streaming down his checks, screamed out, asking why he had been betrayed by one so close to him. Then Alexander ordered everyone named by the boy to be arrested.

Suspicions of disloyalty were not new in the royal entourage or on Alexander's staff. Officers and friends had increasingly been expected to agree with the king in all matters, and those who did not were regarded suspiciously. But up to this point Alexander had never taken any aggressive or punitive action against them to stifle their criticism. Alexander had long considered Philotas one of his critics.[33] Shortly after the battle of Issus in 333 B.C., Philotas had taken as his mistress a young captive named Antigone.[34] He had become attached to her emotionally as well as physically. Over the months he began to confide in Antigone as a man would in his wife. In intimate moments, or when he had too much to drink, Philatos would complain that while Alexander received all the glory it was Parmenio, Philotas, and his brothers who won the victories for him. He criticized Alexander as little more than a petty tyrant who ruled only because they allowed him to. Antigone betrayed the confidences of Philotas to a friend, who in turn told someone else until the words reached the ears of Craterus. Craterus brought the woman to Alexander, who ordered her to report to him on a regular basis everything Philotas was telling her.

Alexander received reports that Philotas was often critical, angry, and disrespectful in his words toward the king. But Alexander took no action and bided his time. He was waiting because he feared the power and standing that Parmenio and his sons held within the army. Alexander had needed them in the crucial years between the battles of Issus and Gaugamela in order to defeat Darius. Now in the remote parts of the eastern empire, two of Parmenio's sons were dead and Parmenio was far behind them at Ecbatana. Alexander now had evidence of disloyalty that went beyond angry and disrespectful words uttered to a mistress in the confines of a bedroom. The catamites had implicated one of Parmenio's sons in a plot to assassinate him, and the other son had failed to reveal the plot when it was brought to his attention. Alexander had all he needed to move against not only Philotas but Parmenio as well.

When Alexander's guards arrived to arrest Dymnus, he drew his sword and stabbed himself. Although dying, he was dragged before

Alexander where he expired before saying anything. Then Philotas was escorted by Alexander's guards to the royal tent and confronted with Cebalinus. Alexander reiterated his order that the boy be executed for his delay in reporting the plot. Philotas spoke up and admitted that Cebalinus had reported the plot to him two days before. The Macedonian went on to explain that even though he had seen the king within minutes of learning of the plot, he had not mentioned it because he did not think it was a serious matter. He had dismissed it as nothing more than a quarrel between lovers. Philotas contended that if he had brought the matter to Alexander's attention solely on the word of a catamite, he would have been laughed out of the royal tent.

Then Philotas realized the gravity of the situation. He embraced Alexander and begged the king to judge him based on long and faithful service and not condemn him because of this single misunderstanding. Alexander seemed to soften toward Philotas and offered his right hand as an indication that he accepted the explanation. But Alexander's hand in friendship masked what the king really believed.

On the following day, Alexander convened a meeting of his closest friends. Philotas was excluded. Nicomachus, the younger brother of Cebalinus, was brought before them and interrogated by Alexander as to what he had been told by Dymnus. Among those present was Craterus. Craterus was not particularly fond of Philotas. Although both men were senior in the command structure and both held similar conservative views, Craterus had warned Alexander earlier that Philotas was too arrogant for his own good. Philotas had a reputation for arrogance among the other senior officers as well as the friends of Alexander, and this had made him many enemies over the years. Craterus and some of the others present that morning saw an opportunity to destroy him under the guise of loyalty and concern for the safety of the king.

The characterization of Philotas as arrogant seems to be borne out by his description in the ancient sources. He was an arrogant, self-centered man, as were many in Alexander's entourage and on his staff. Successful men in any age tend to become arrogant and self-centered. Yet Philotas is also characterized as having been generous with his friends and fellow officers. He displayed a pride of spirit that offended many. Even Parmenio was alleged to have once warned his son to be "less of a personage."[35]

Craterus advised against accepting the explanation of Philotas for failing to report the plot and implored Alexander not to forgive him. Philotas, he warned, because of his arrogant nature would view such a royal pardon more as an insult to his character than a reprieve on a charge of treason. Then Craterus pointed out that there was Parmenio to be concerned about. Parmenio commanded a large army at Ecbatana and was in control of the bulk of the treasure that had been captured. The old general, now in his seventies, was loved by his soldiers and occupied as large a place in their hearts as did Alexander. Craterus believed that Parmenio and Philotas were men whom Alexander could not trust. The army had enemies enough in front of them; they could not afford to worry about leaving enemies behind them as well.

The others present agreed with Craterus. Many voiced the opinion that Philotas must have been involved in the conspiracy. They pointed to the fact that his brother had been implicated and that Philotas himself had failed to reveal anything about what he had learned even though he had daily contact with the king. No threat, they all agreed, no matter how trivial could be ignored when it came to the safety of their king. Alexander thanked them for their concern and advice, dismissing them with the warning that they should not speak about what they had learned.

The same night, Alexander held a banquet to which Philotas was invited. Alexander dined and conversed amiably throughout the night with the man to whom he had given public assurances of his friendship and yet had privately condemned to death. While Alexander and his guests dined, a heavily armed bodyguard surrounded the royal tent. Security throughout the camp was increased, and officers were sent out with detachments of specially picked soldiers to arrest all those who had been named by the young brothers in the plot to kill the king. As Alexander and Philotas dined, men were being arrested throughout the camp. Cavalry detachments were posted at every exit of the camp to ensure that no one might slip away and take word to Parmenio of what had happened.

Philotas was arrested in the early morning hours in his tent, where he had retired after the banquet. Aroused from a deep sleep, he was bound and his head covered with a hood. Then he was brought back to the royal tent, where he was held. That day Alexander convened an assembly of soldiers to hear the charges against Philotas. It was done in accordance with the traditional practices of the Macedonians and Greeks in matters of treason. Six thousand Macedonian soldiers were called into assembly by Alexander and asked to hear the evidence and pass judgment in a criminal matter. The king played the role of prosecutor, while the soldiers acted as jury. Alexander would follow Macedonian law and precedent in this affair and not take any chances that the matter might be dismissed or that he might be criticized because he failed to follow tradition. Alexander appeared before the assembly in his traditional Macedonian dress. There was no Persian tiara upon his head or purple robes over his shoulders on this occasion.

The first piece of evidence Alexander introduced to the jury was the corpse of Dymnus. The lifeless body was laid out on the floor before them. With a pained expression, Alexander stood before the assembly of stunned soldiers. No one knew what had happened. The friends of Alexander and his closest officers wore the same somber faces as their master. Their reticence and somber expressions conveyed to all present the gravity of the matter that would shortly be put before the assembly.

This was not a trial for those who had been named by Dymnus as conspirators; they had already been condemned by Alexander. This trial was about Parmenio and his son Philotas. This was to be the first of a number of such show trials that would characterize Alexander's reign over the next several years. This was the beginning of the purges, the removal and execution of all those who questioned or threatened the authority of Alexander of Macedonia, lord of Asia and son of Zeus.

For a long time Alexander stood motionless over the body of Dymnus and said nothing. Members of the assembly became uneasy and began nervously speaking among themselves. Then Alexander addressed the assembly. He began by telling them how he had nearly been taken from them, his beloved army and brothers in arms, by the wickedness of assassins and traitors. Alexander named Parmenio first as the mastermind of the plot and Philotas, his son, as the tool of assassination.[36] Philotas had co-conspirators, men among them whom he had infected with his father's madness, including the lifeless Dymnus who lay before them. Others who had been named in the plot to kill Alexander would presently be brought before the assembly.

The terrified brothers Nicomachus and Cebalinus were brought forward and questioned in front of the assembly. Those who had been routinely used to satisfy the sexual appetites of the officers in the retinue of Alexander were now presented by the king of Asia as credible witnesses. The terrified boys, led by Alexander, recounted to the assembly what little they knew of the plot. Most of what they had to say was hearsay from the lips of a man who now lay dead on the floor. It did not matter that Dymnus could not be cross-examined. His suicide proved to the assembly that the conspiracy was true, for no innocent man would take his own life.

The brothers never once implicated Philotas or Parmenio in their testimony. Cebalinus explained how he had brought news of the plot to Philotas, and Alexander asked the assembly rhetorically what conclusion they could draw from the failure to report this matter. Alexander reminded them that Philotas had daily contact with him and more than ample opportunity to bring up the matter. Alexander cited the example of Metron, the young officer who understood his duty and loyalty to the king. Metron thought the information of the plot so important that he disturbed the king while he was bathing.

As for motive, Alexander told the assembly that it was clear. Parmenio controlled the western part of the empire as well as the vast repository of the treasury. Both father and son had aspirations of creating a dynasty. First Parmenio and then Philotas would be king. Alexander stated that Parmenio could never have been king, for he was a man whose "aspirations far outstripped his capabilities." Then the king produced a letter, allegedly intercepted, that Parmenio had sent to his sons Nicanor and Philotas. The letter contained advice from the father to his sons to "look out for yourselves and after your own . . . then shall we accomplish what we have planned."[37] The letter, Alexander argued to the assembly, had been written in such a way that a casual and uninformed reader would regard the phrase as innocuous while the sons would understand the secret message within. The letter, Alexander maintained, was incontrovertible evidence that Parmenio and Philotas were implicated in a plot to assassinate him.

The king related to the assembly how Philotas had reacted several years before when he learned that the priests of Siwa, in the deserts of Egypt, had hailed Alexander as a son of Zeus. Philotas had congratulated Alexander on having been received into the company of the gods but commented sarcastically that he pitied those who would now have to live under him. This was evidence of a man who was jealous and envious. Alexander recounted to the assembly with all the consummate skills of a seasoned actor the pain he felt at these words. He related how he had buried deep within his heart the hurt he felt, and yet he had appointed Philotas commander of the cavalry. But now his once trusted senior commander had gone from hurtful words to evil deeds. Alexander had always, in the Macedonian fashion, turned to the army in matters of his personal safety. Yet it was an army officer who had violated that sacred trust. Now at the end of his speech, Alexander asked the assembly to protect him from those among them who would conspire against him. Philotas was condemned to die before he even appeared before the assembly.

Though no one posed it to the king, an unanswered question hung over the assembly. If Philotas was implicated in the plot, why had Dymnus never named him? Alexander offered a simple explanation to the assembly. So great was the power and authority of Parmenio and Philotas over the other conspirators that they feared to reveal his name even under torture or as they lay dying.

Then Philotas was led in with his hands bound behind his back and his head covered by a worn and dirty cloak. The tactic of trying to make Philotas look like a common criminal backfired on Alexander. Instead of engendering the anticipated hatred and condemnation from the assembly, the soldiers were first shocked and then driven to pity to see such a respected commander and the surviving son of Parmenio treated thus. Sensing that sympathy for Philotas was building, another of Alexander's senior commanders, Amyntas, rose to speak. He delivered a short and emotional speech in an attempt to turn the assembly away from sympathy. Amyntas shouted that Philotas had betrayed them all to the barbarians. If their king and leader Alexander had been assassinated, they would all have been lost. Without Alexander to lead them, they never would be able to find their way home to their wives and children in Greece and Macedonia.

The message was not well received by the assembly. All Amyntas succeeded in doing was to remind the soldiers of how much they missed their families and their native land. So instead of focusing on the guilt of Philotas, the assembly became distracted and started talking to one another about their wives and families at home. Alexander was not pleased.

Then Coenus, another senior officer and married to the sister of Philotas, tried to get the assembly back on track by delivering the most savage attack of all. He began screaming hysterically that Philotas was a traitor. Coenus picked up a rock and prepared to hurl it at the unfortunate Philotas, who was bound and kneeling on the ground before him. Coenus might have been hoping that the others in the assembly would be angered enough to follow his lead and that Philotas would be quickly killed and the matter ended. But Alexander intervened and stayed his hand. Alexander asked the assembly to give Philotas the opportunity to plead his case before them. In Macedonia, Philotas, as a noble and an officer, would have had the right to plead his case before the assembly, but here, in the lands of barbarians, Alexander was the law. And Alexander, out of respect for the traditions of the Macedonians and as a demonstration of his magnanimity, compassion, and fairness as a king, was granting Philotas the opportunity to answer the charges. Alexander was being careful to orchestrate the trial in such a manner that after Philotas was executed nobody could accuse him of having ignored the customs and lawful procedures of the Macedonians. Philotas would have his due process even if the outcome had already been decided.

Philotas was brought to his feet by the guards, and at first he was so disoriented and terrified that he was unable to find the words to speak in his defense. When he opened his mouth to speak, his eyes filled with tears and he fainted. When Philotas had been revived and his composure restored, Alexander asked if he wished to address the assembly in the Macedonian dialect or in Greek. Alexander had been speaking in Greek, and many in the assembly were Greeks or allies who did not understand the Macedonian dialect. Philotas replied that he would speak in Greek. Alexander turned to the assembly and in a fury condemned Philotas for refusing to speak in his native tongue.

The king, who wore Persian dress and had embraced Persian customs, was condemning one of the most conservative officers on his staff for rejecting his native tongue and the customs of the Macedonian people. It was the theater of the absurd. Philotas, the son of Parmenio, was condemned not on the basis of the evidence against him but for renouncing the Macedonian ways. It was an example of the ad hominem attack at its most pernicious.

As Philotas began to speak, Alexander left the assembly. By his actions Alexander made it evident that he was becoming impatient and expected a quick verdict of guilty. Slowly and haltingly, Philotas began his defense. First, he explained that he did not understand why the king who accused him now left the assembly and refused to listen to the words of a loyal veteran officer and friend. Still, Philotas went on, he would speak. Of what, he asked, was he accused? What crime had he committed that he was on trial for his life? Neither those charged as conspirators nor the boys who had brought the matter to the king's attention had named him. Yet he had been arrested and now stood before the assembly charged as the leader of the conspiracy to kill the king.

It was ill fortune that had brought him to this assembly. Had Cebalinus not come to him with the information of the plot but gone to another officer, someone else would now be standing before them condemned to die. The only accusation against him was that he failed to tell the king what Cebalinus had reported. He had explained to the king why he had not reported the matter. Alexander had accepted his explanation and even invited Philotas to dine with him as a show of friendship. What, he asked the assembly, had transpired in one night to so set the king against him? They had dined and drank together the night before. Philotas had returned to his quarters and slept soundly, the sleep of an innocent man, until soldiers roused him and placed him under arrest.

Philotas went on to explain why he did not report the matter when it was first brought to him. It was simple; he had given it no credence. It was reported by a mere boy, and it was hearsay. Furthermore,

Philotas argued, he feared alarming the king unnecessarily and possibly bringing harm to men who were innocent. Lastly, if he intended to assassinate the king, he had access to him daily. Philotas wore his sword when he met with the king, often in private. Why did he need conspirators to help him do what he could have done alone in an instant?

As to the charge that he would be king of Macedonia, Philotas argued it was preposterous. How could Alexander accuse him in one instance of aspiring to be king of Macedonia and in the next of rejecting the customs and language of the country he wanted to rule? Philotas explained that he spoke Greek because everyone spoke Greek. It had become the language of the military, diplomacy, and commerce. Macedonian had fallen out of favor many years before.[38] Was he to be condemned solely because he spoke Greek?

Yes, it was true he had been critical of Alexander for his belief that he was the son of Zeus. He spoke the truth, and he spoke it to Alexander as his friend. He had advised Alexander that if he wished to regard himself as the son of Zeus, it should be done privately, not publicly, so as to avoid ridicule. Philotas had always spoken the truth as he saw it no matter how unpopular it might be, and now he would have to pay the price for doing so.

Under Macedonian and Greek law, it was the right of those accused to bring their families before the assembly to speak on their behalf. Whom, Philotas asked, could he call? His two brothers had died in the service of Alexander. His aged father, a loyal commander and senior advisor to both Philip and Alexander, stood accused of complicity with him in this treason.[39] It was evident, Philotas told the assembly, that the entire family would be wiped out. He reminded the soldiers how years before his father had warned Alexander of an attempt against his life by the court physician that had proved false.[40] Yet Parmenio was ridiculed when he spoke out to warn the king. Now Philotas was condemned when he remained silent. Philotas finished by asking the assembly what he should do. Someone yelled back that he should not plot against his king. The assembly roared its approval, and Philotas was led away by his guards.

Then a senior Macedonian officer named Bolon rose to speak. He was a coarse and crude man who because of his bravery in combat had risen from the ranks to become a general. He was well respected, and he reminded the assembly how Philotas took pride in speaking Greek even though many of the common Macedonian soldiers, men like himself, did not understand it. He reminded them how the wagons of Philotas were always filled with greater quantities of gold and silver than any others except for the king's. He reminded them how Philotas always reserved for himself and his entourage the finest houses and palaces in each city that they took. Common Macedonian soldiers, men like himself, could not even be admitted to the neighborhood where Philotas lodged. Philotas was an officer with aristocratic airs and a man who had often mocked simple men. Again the matter of arrogance—not evidence—surfaced.

Then Bolon shifted the attack to Parmenio. He charged that even now the most senior of all Alexander's officers was plotting to use the king's money to establish his own dynasty. Bolon further inflamed the assembly, and they were now to the point where they called out for the immediate execution of Philotas. The king's bodyguards shouted out that they should be allowed to tear him to pieces with their own hands. Philotas was held just a short distance away, bound and with his head covered. He heard everything that was said, and more than anything Philotas feared not death but the manner in which he would be tortured.

Alexander returned to the assembly and dismissed it until the following day. Nearly the entire day had been spent in hearing testimony and in deliberations. It was approaching late afternoon, and all were anxious to prepare their suppers. Alexander dined with his friends that night, and they urged him to have Philotas stoned to death according to the ancient custom of the Macedonians.[41] Hephaestion, Craterus, and Coenus recommended that Philotas be tortured first and made to confess. A confession, they urged, would be important to present before the assembly and would serve to defuse any tensions within those army units where Philotas was respected and had support. The dinner guests all agreed, and Alexander appointed the three to supervise the torture. Following dinner, they went to where Philotas was being held and had the torturers lay out before the terrified man all the instruments of their cruel craft. Alexander retired to his quarters and awaited the outcome.

Philotas readily offered to confess to the crime and begged to be spared the torture. He asked only for a quick death. But the three men were not concerned with his confession. They were overseeing the torture of a man they intensely disliked, and they intended to savor the moment. At least two of them were using the torture of Philotas as a means of diverting suspicion from themselves and proving their loyalty to Alexander. The torture of Philotas was carried out by his enemies to gratify the king. It was not torture used to extract the truth but torture as punishment, and it showed how deeply were the divisions and fears that existed among the officers of Alexander's staff.

Craterus might have taken a leading hand in the torture of Philotas to prove that his loyalty was beyond question even if he was reluctant to embrace the king's new style of living. Coenus was related by marriage to Philotas, and he was equally as eager to show his loyalty to Alexander and demonstrate his hatred of his traitorous in-laws.[42] He was eager to show that his attempt to have Philotas killed quickly at the assembly had not been done to cover up his involvement in the plot. Hephaestion, the last of the three and the king's favorite, undertook the torture to please Alexander.

The sadistic manner in which the prolonged torture of Philotas was carried out by those closest to the king, and his brutal death the next day, showed the degree of anger that Alexander held toward Parmenio and his family. That Alexander offered Philotas his assurances of friendship, dined with him to make him think the matter was dismissed, and then within hours had him arrested and brutally tortured shows the degree of paranoia the king was suffering.

Philotas was tortured and killed more for who he was and what he represented than for anything Alexander believed he had done. What Philotas had to endure before he died was not lost on those around Alexander. During the torture, his body was burned and broken. Philotas begged for death and asked his fellow officers to stop the torture in return for his confession.[43] When the torture was stopped, Philotas turned to Craterus and asked what it was he wanted him to confess to. Craterus became angry because he believed that Philotas was mocking him, and the tortures began again with greater intensity.

While Philotas was being tortured, there was panic among his cavalry officers. Word spread about what was happening to him, and men who had loyally served under him for years became fearful for their own lives. Especially vulnerable to arrest and execution were those officers and civilians in the camp who were related by blood or marriage to Parmenio or any of his sons.

It was an ancient Macedonian custom that the relatives of those who were accused of plotting to take the life of the king would be executed along with the conspirators. Some of the relatives and close friends of Philotas committed suicide in their tents. Others slipped out of the camp and, evading the pickets, vanished into the mountains and deserts of Afghanistan and Iran. Many who deserted were eventually hunted down and brought back to Alexander for punishment. The panic and fear in the camp grew to such proportions that Alexander issued a proclamation to calm matters before they got out of hand. He proclaimed that the ancient law was suspended in this matter and that those related by blood or marriage to Parmenio and Philotas would not be arrested, tortured, or executed.

Eventually, Philotas told his torturers what they wanted to hear. He confessed that the conspiracy was true. He had begun to think of assassination shortly after Alexander had proclaimed himself the son of Zeus. Macedonian officers had come to Parmenio and protested "this king who disdains Philip as his father."[44] They could not endure to serve under a king who demanded that he be worshiped as a god. The plan was to murder Alexander after Darius had been captured or killed. To kill Alexander before would only serve to increase their risk of defeat by the enemy and throw the Greek and Macedonian forces into turmoil.

Craterus and the others continued torturing Philotas in an effort to customize the confession and widen the net of conspirators. They induced him to admit that the murder of Alexander had been planned because the conspirators feared that the farther Alexander moved into Bactria the farther they would be from Parmenio and the support of his army. This allowed the direct implication of Parmenio. Then Philotas was made to confess that he had decided to act now because he feared that as Parmenio was well into his seventies, he might die soon and the conspirators would lose control over the large army he commanded and the treasure he held.

The following day, what had been extracted from Philotas by torture was read before the assembly. Philotas was so badly injured from the torture that he was brought in on a stretcher and placed on the floor. Barely conscious, he nodded his ascent to everything that was read to the assembly as his confession. Then Demetrius, the bodyguard of Alexander who had been named by Dymnus, was led in. The assembly was in no mood to hear his defense. His appearance was brief. He denied that he had been part of any plot to kill the king but was all the same condemned to death. All those who had been named by Nicomachus were stoned to death, the traditional punishment of the Macedonians for treason.[45]

Following the execution of Philotas, Alexander dispatched one of the companions, Polydamas, on a secret mission to assassinate Parmenio. Polydamas had been a close friend of Parmenio, so he was deemed the perfect agent to carry out Alexander's order. His younger brothers were taken hostage to ensure his loyalty and compliance with his orders. Alexander ordered Polydamas to proceed to Ecbatana with three letters, the first for the three generals serving under Parmenio and the second and third letters for Parmenio. The first letter to Parmenio was from Alexander and was intended to distract him and relax his suspicions. The second letter was supposedly from Philotas. The letter to the generals was an order from Alexander for them to assist Polydamas in assassinating Parmenio immediately.

Polydamas changed into native Arab dress and with two local guides mounted racing camels[46] and set off by night in a northwesterly direction, across the great Parthian desert. He took the quicker but more dangerous route to Ecbatana so that he would arrive well before any news concerning the execution of Philotas could reach Parmenio. By utilizing the more dangerous route directly across the desert, Polydamas and his Arab guides covered a distance of nearly two thousand kilometers in eleven days.[47] It was an extraordinary feat of courage, endurance, and navigation by a man in fear for his life and that of his family. Polydamas arrived in Ecbatana shortly before dawn on the twelfth day and went directly to the palace of Cleander, one of the generals.

The other two generals, Sitalces and Menidas, were summoned and the letter from Alexander read to them. Shortly after dawn the four set out for the home of Parmenio, where they found him walking in his garden. Parmenio was surprised and delighted to see Polydamas and embraced him warmly. He was stabbed by Cleander as he turned away from the men to read Alexander's letter. The others followed suit and continued to stab the old commander even after he had fallen and his body was lifeless. The man who had once been a friend and advisor to Philip and mentor to Alexander was murdered. His lifetime of loyal service to the royal family counted for nothing. He was never afforded a trial or a chance to defend himself against the charges. Even if Parmenio had no part in his son's plot, Alexander could not have allowed him to live. The risk that he would mobilize his army and move against Alexander was too great. Parmenio was sure to have sought revenge for his son's death.

The soldiers at Ecbatana were incensed when they learned that their commander had been assassinated. Cleander and the other generals managed to quell a mutiny only when they read Alexander's letter to the soldiers and revealed the plot of Parmenio and Philotas against the king. While the letters from Alexander quelled the threat of mutiny for the moment, the resentment of those soldiers toward Alexander for the death of their respected commander continued for years afterward.

Parmenio and his contemporary Antipater had been the senior advisors and commanders in Philip's regime. They had supported Alexander upon the death of Philip and helped him establish himself on the throne of Macedonia when they could have ended his career before it began. While Antipater kept Greece under control for Alexander, Parmenio had opened the way to Asia. Throughout the campaign from the western shores of Asia Minor to the gates of Persepolis, Parmenio steadfastly and wisely commanded the infantry in all the major battles while Alexander led the cavalry in the daring maneuvers that won him personal glory and made him famous. Parmenio was removed from the chain of command simply because he no longer fit in the new scheme of things. Parmenio's head was severed from his body and sent to Alexander as proof that his orders had been carried out.[48]

The confession extracted from Philotas was crucial for Alexander. It allowed him to execute all those who were named as conspirators as well as order the murder of Parmenio without running the risk of the army breaking into warring factions. Parmenio and Philotas had a strong following among the rank and file, both in the large army that Parmenio commanded in Ecbatana and in the cavalry commanded by Philotas. Parmenio and his sons were also the most conservative elements on Alexander's general staff. More than any of the others, they were the least likely to be cowed or intimidated into acknowledging Alexander as a god. They were the focal point for those in the army who were opposed to Alexander's rule. The Macedonians and the Greeks would acknowledge and obey Alexander as a king, subject to constitutional restraints, but they would never worship him as a god with unlimited powers. The next six years, until Alexander's death, would become the story of how he tried to force the idea of his divinity upon those around him and how in the end it cost him his life and his empire.

The purges did not stop with the deaths of Parmenio, Philotas, and the others accused of conspiracy. Another Macedonian nobleman, Alexander the Lyncestian, who had been charged with conspiring against the king three years earlier, was brought to trial and executed. He had been arrested and remained under guard, but his case had never been brought before the assembly of soldiers. This might have been because Alexander was reluctant to bring the matter to public light since the Lyncestian was related to Antipater through marriage. He belonged to a long-established royal family in Macedonia, and in the event of Alexander's death or incapacitation he would have been a strong contender to succeed him as king.

The Lyncestian's two brothers had been executed by Alexander several years earlier for their alleged complicity in the murder of Philip. Alexander the Lyncestian had been spared because he had promptly declared himself a supporter of the new king and pledged his loyalty. He had joined the expedition to Asia Minor but was arrested and placed under guard shortly thereafter. Now, with Parmenio dead, Alexander was confident and secure enough to bring the Lyncestian before the same assembly that had condemned Philotas. There, unable to find the words to defend himself, Alexander the Lyncestian was quickly condemned and executed.

Alexander continued to search for dissension or suspected cases of disloyalty. He encouraged his officers to urge their soldiers to write to their families in Greece and Macedonia. The pretext was that as Alexander was dispatching a special courier to take his correspondence to Antipater, the men could profit from the opportunity to send letters home to their families. On the surface it was a compassionate and magnanimous gesture on the part of the king that demonstrated his concern for his soldiers and acknowledged their homesickness. In fact, it was a deception. There was a courier dispatched to Antipater, but the invitation for the soldiers to write letters home was just a ruse for Alexander to determine if any dissension remained among the ranks.

The letters were carefully screened and censored by Alexander's agents. Those officers and soldiers who had written critical or unflattering remarks about the king, discussed the deaths of Philotas and Parmenio in critical terms, or complained about military service were placed in a special disciplinary unit.[49] There they could be isolated from the main body of the army and, when the time came, would be placed into the forefront of the combat where they would be given the chance to redeem themselves in the king's eyes or die. Alexander's special unit was a forerunner of the brutal political reeducation battalions that would characterize the military components of so many of the twentieth-century totalitarian regimes.

Alexander did not stop with merely rooting out dissension among the ranks. He reorganized the army and redefined the criteria by which officers were promoted. From now on, appointments and promotions were based on loyalty to the king and a man's actions in combat. Gone were the early days when officers were appointed or promoted based on their family ties in Greece and Macedonia. The only criteria now were loyalty to Alexander and bravery in battle. This allowed a whole new generation of soldiers, many from the ranks, to enter the officer corps. It also opened up the ranks of the officer corps to non-Greeks and non-Macedonians. Thus, Persians and other allies were able to rise to the highest positions in Alexander's new army.

With the reorganization of the army, the Companions, once commanded by Philotas, were now placed under a command arrangement shared by Hephaestion and Cleitus. After purging Parmenio and Philotas, Alexander did not want the command of any large and powerful body of cavalry in the hands of one man, not even if that commander happened to be his best friend and lover Hephaestion.

The purges also brought changes in the appointments of those entrusted with guarding the king. With the execution of Demetrius, Alexander appointed Ptolemy as his new bodyguard. Ptolemy, the boyhood friend of Alexander, would rise within the command structure to become one of the successors of Alexander and in a few short years the pharaoh of Egypt.

When news of the murders of Parmenio and Philotas reached Greece and Macedonia, it was not well received. The exploits of Alexander were becoming legend, and for what he was doing in the East against the barbarians he was a source of pride to both the Greeks and the Macedonians. But Alexander was also becoming an object of fear to many of his friends and particularly to his regent Antipater.[50] Many were apprehensive about their personal security and about the future of their countries that were firmly under the control of a man who had established himself as a tyrant and was rapidly beginning to demonstrate all the signs of a megalomaniac. Alexander was dangerous for Greece, and many feared his eventual return.

CHAPTER 4

OVER THE HINDU KUSH

FOLLOWING THE EXECUTIONS AND ASSASSINATIONS, ALEXander began to demand the strictest compliance with his orders. Eventually that came to mean limits on the exercise of free speech that many of the Greeks and Macedonians had known and valued. The stifling of free speech, coupled with Alexander's adoption of Persian manners and an increasingly luxurious and dissipating lifestyle, led to more dissension. To compensate, Alexander began to exercise a tight control over his officer corps. Loyalty to the king along with bravery in battle became the sole criteria for promotion. Promotion through the ranks was no longer a function of birth and family connections in Macedonia or Greece. That was how it had been when Alexander conquered Greece and in the first half of his campaign against the Persians. Now it was different. Promotions were made according to demonstrations of personal bravery in combat and loyalty to Alexander. Components of that loyalty included at least tacit acceptance of Alexander's claims to divinity and complete adherence to his philosophy of autocratic rule.

The execution of Philotas and the other conspirators as well as the murder of Parmenio had a chilling effect on the Greeks and Macedonians, but it had not suppressed all the pockets of discontent. The next phase of the campaign would see even more purges in the ranks to root out what Alexander termed disloyalty. While Alexander was able on the surface at least to bring about almost absolute compliance with his orders. he would never be able to eradicate completely the dissension within his army.

The farther east Alexander moved, the more he cultivated a cult of the personality around himself. He became the supreme authority in the army as well as the source of all law in the lands he had conquered. There could be no disagreement with him. Alexander set the direction, and the army followed; Alexander established the goals, and the army strove to meet them. Alexander rewarded, and Alexander punished. It was Alexander's vision that decided where they would go, and the farther east they moved the more he was able to convince the rank and file of the army that he alone was the only force that could take them home again. The common soldiers began calling Alexander "Father," and he encouraged their belief that without his leadership skills they would quickly succumb to the harsh environment and fall prey to the barbarians who surrounded them. Alexander skillfully constructed his image as the divine ruler and used it to manipulate the army. Compliance, loyalty, and performance were generously rewarded, while disloyalty, insubordination, and failure were punished severely, often by execution. This would apply not only to the army but to all those who served Alexander.

The resistance that Alexander and his army would encounter over the next few years would be different than what they had encountered in the West. In the eastern limits of the Persian Empire, they would be fighting a people they knew very little about in a land that few if any Greeks or Macedonians had ever heard of before, much less seen. The customs of the people were strange, and as Alexander and his army moved through the troubled lands that today comprise Afghanistan, Uzbekistan, Tajikistan, and Pakistan, they had to crush a national resistance movement led by men who even under the Persians had been fiercely independent and had maintained a great deal of their personal freedom. These were and still are a proud and autonomous people. They refused to accept being ruled by Alexander or anyone outside their own tribal world and still do so today, as successive generations of British, Soviet, and American invaders have continued to discover at considerable cost.

As the army moved farther and farther into the easternmost recesses of the Persian Empire, the soldiers had to deal with disease, hunger, thirst, heat, and cold in addition to the fighting that took place more frequently. While the common soldiers suffered the usual deprivations of men on the march, Alexander enjoyed a standard of living well beyond that of those he led. Although he had burned his personal treasure as a dramatic demonstration to the army of his resolve to move east, he still traveled with a royal entourage that rivaled anything seen in the ancient world. Alexander moved with his personal army of attendants, eunuchs, entertainers, concubines, slaves, and cooks who attended to his every need. The king had all the luxuries of a palace as he moved with his army over the mountains, plains, and deserts of Central Asia. Thousands made their living attending to the needs of the king.

Yet no matter how critical one might be about Alexander's comforts, no one could criticize him when it came to fighting. Over the next six years, he would place himself in the forefront of the combat, often unnecessarily. He would take needless risks during the fighting in Bactria, Sogdiana, and later in India, just as he had in the West. He would suffer a number of nearly fatal wounds over the next several years, and by the end of the campaign his body would be worn out from fighting and drinking.

Alexander's conquest of the East became a major logistical operation and an enormously profitable business enterprise. Not only did Alexander find silver mines in the Hindu Kush Mountains and gold in Sogdiana that would yield vast quantities of bullion for centuries to come, but the area became strategically important as a focus for controlling communications and trade between the East and the West. Central Asia became the converging point for several trade routes from China and the invasion route for hordes of Huns, Tartars, and Turks, who over the centuries to come would inflict on the West devastation in proportion to what Alexander brought to the East.

The first resistance Alexander encountered in Afghanistan came from Satibarzanes. Initially, he had fled from Alexander shortly after the murder of Darius but then returned to make his peace. Alexander had accepted his surrender and pledge of loyalty and then had restored Satibarzanes to his old position as satrap of Aria, the territory that today constitutes the area of southwestern Afghanistan along the border with Iran.

Initially, Satibarzanes proved very cooperative. But, as Alexander and the bulk of his army moved out of Aria and farther into

Afghanistan, he revolted against Alexander's rule. Satibarzanes massacred the Macedonian garrison Alexander had left behind to keep an eye on him, and when Alexander returned to Aria to confront him he fled to Bactria to join Bessus. After Alexander had left to resume his march deeper into Afghanistan, Satibarzanes returned to his province with a larger force of cavalry and incited the local people to revolt.[1] Alexander dispatched a portion of the army back to Aria under two trusted and experienced commanders, Erigyius and Stasanor.

Satibarzanes confronted Erigyius and Stasanor on the field of battle and, in a show of bravado, challenged Alexander's generals to come forward and engage him in individual combat. Erigyius, though advanced in years,[2] took up the challenge and in the ensuing fight killed Satibarzanes on the battlefield. The Bactrian army scattered, and the revolt was over. Erigyius and Stasanor rejoined Alexander in southern Afghanistan, bringing him the head of Satibarzanes as a trophy. His would be the first of many such human heads to be collected by Alexander in Central Asia.[3]

Alexander and his army continued to march through the south of Afghanistan without opposition and into the Persian satrapies of Drangiana and Arachosia. There Alexander founded two new towns, Alexandria in Arachosia and Alexandria Ghazni.[4] Then the army moved north into central Afghanistan and the area that today constitutes Kabul, where Alexander subdued the local people, known as the Parapamisadae. These tribes controlled the mountain passes of the Panjshir Valley, the valley at Kabul, and the Ghorband and Kabul Rivers. These were important areas for Alexander to control, as they were the crossroads of Central Asia. They were important links in the communications and trade routes between Iran and India. To secure them, Alexander founded Alexandria in Caucasus, near the site of what is now the American military base at Bagram.

By the beginning of December 330 B.C. there was little resistance from the local tribes. The army settled into winter quarters around Kabul and waited for the spring thaws, when the mountain passes would once more be accessible. When the first signs of spring came, Alexander was anxious to set out to find Bessus in Bactria. Alexander prepared to cross the Hindu Kush, a massive mountain range that ancient geographers often mistakenly referred to as the Caucasus.[5]

This high mountain range that stretches through northern Afghanistan divides the southern part of the country from the northernmost areas and the countries that today constitute Turkmenistan, Uzbekistan, and Tajikistan.

Since Alexander had pacified and settled the territory in Afghanistan south of the Hindu Kush Mountains, he had no worry that his lines of communication and supply might be disrupted. The pacification of southern Afghanistan had been the easiest part of the campaign; the hardest and costliest part still lay ahead. First, Alexander and his army would have to cross the mountains and descend into the vast and unknown territories beyond that constituted Bactria and Sogdiana.

Alexander and his army crossed the mountains but with considerable difficulty. Even though it was spring, the mountains were still covered with snow and the passes proved treacherous to cross. The soldiers were short on supplies and at one point were forced to butcher the pack animals for food. Many of the soldiers suffered frostbite and snow blindness. Yet in spite of the difficult conditions, Alexander led the army over the mountains and down into the satrapy of Bactria in only seventeen days.[6]

While the army was making its way over the mountain passes, some of Alexander's soldiers allegedly discovered a cave that they believed was where the legendary Prometheus had been imprisoned for offending the gods. Prometheus was one of the Titans. In Greek mythology they were a race of giants who had inhabited the earth and supposedly created man. Prometheus defied the gods when he stole the divine fire from heaven and gave it to men to make their lives easier. As punishment, he was chained to a rocky ledge on Mount Caucasus where a vulture fed on his liver in an eternal cycle of torment. Prometheus was thus important to the superstitious and religious soldiers, for to them he was the symbol of endurance and resistance to oppression. Since Alexander's men believed they were crossing the Caucasus and coming to the ends of the earth, it was only natural they would search for signs from the gods. When the army came down from the mountains and into Bactria, the soldiers rested at the ancient city of Drapsaka[7] and reprovisioned themselves for the next leg of their journey.

Bactria and Sogdiana became areas of widespread unrest for Alexander, and he would spend the next two years (329–327 B.C.) there suppressing resistance to his invasion and rule. The tribal men proved to be skilled horsemen and excellent warriors. The fighting would be much more difficult now, because Alexander was not liberating people from Persian rule but instead imposing his own form of tyranny on tribes who were used to being free. The resistance in Bactria and Sogdiana would grow into a national movement. Most of the casualties would be among the native people who were supporting their soldiers.

The resistance was first organized by Bessus in Bactria. When he was captured by Alexander the revolt was led by the Sogdian rebel Spitamenes. As Alexander and his army subdued one area, another would erupt in revolt. Even areas already pacified posed the danger of renewed insurgencies. The style and nature of the fighting changed as well. Bessus and Spitamenes tended to avoid set, placed battles with Alexander. Instead, they tried to wear down his army through guerilla tactics—irregular warfare by independent groups. They denied them supplies by burning their crops. They harassed the troops at every opportunity and let nature and the elements work in their favor. The conditions in this land were harsh; the summers were short and brutally hot, while the winters could be long and cold.

The terrain of Central Asia lends itself to rapid cavalry maneuvers and, in response, Alexander changed the nature of his tactics. He placed less reliance on his phalanx or infantry formation, the one he had used extensively against Darius in Persia. Instead Alexander divided his army into smaller, more mobile columns of infantry under his commanders Attalus, Gorgias, and Craterus. He relied more heavily on his cavalry, who could cover the vast distances of the steppes and deserts much faster than infantry.

Because the terrain was as harsh and unforgiving as the men who defended it, Alexander had to rely on speed and mobility to counteract the tactics of those who resisted him. The army had to adjust to fighting in terrain that could range from deep mud to scorching desert sand. Alexander sent out his columns to destroy the base of support that the rebels had among the people of the villages, towns, and cities. Thus, the warfare became particularly brutal, and Alexander directed most of it against the defenseless civilian population. Villages, towns, and cities were often burned and their people enslaved or massacred. There was nothing noble or heroic about Alexander's operations in Bactria and Sogdiana. Wherever his army moved, the countryside was devastated in order to deny the rebels any form of support. All males of military age whom Alexander's army encountered were routinely killed to decrease the pool of potential soldiers.

As Alexander moved throughout Bactria and Sogdiana, he had his engineers lay out a number of mud-brick enclaves, more so along the lines of military outposts and supply centers than towns. Each one was named Alexandria. While some of the settlements were incorporated into existing towns, others were built where no settlement had ever existed before. These towns and outposts allowed Alexander to establish a more secure line of supply and communication in the conquered districts. These Alexandrias were often involuntarily colonized by the king's more unfortunate soldiers—the lame, the wounded, the sick, and the malcontents. They were left behind to rule over the captured prisoners and the enslaved local population.

Bessus had proclaimed himself king of Asia, ostensibly in an effort to rally support among the tribes of Bactria. He started wearing the tiara and robes he had looted from the tent of Darius and established a court for himself at Balkh, the capital of Bactria.[8] During the course of a banquet at Balkh where there was much drinking, Bessus began bragging to the guests about how he would vanquish Alexander and his army. The new Artaxerxes boasted that he would bring together all the fierce tribes living beyond the Jaxartes River[9] in Scythia and assemble a force of cavalry such as the world had never seen before. Scythia was the ancient name for the unknown lands that lay on the vast steppes beyond Sogdiana and what the Greeks thought was the end of the world.[10] He bragged about how he would lead these fierce mounted warriors back into Bactria and crush Alexander and his army. One of the guests at the banquet was a partisan commander named Bagodaras.[11] Bagodaras had little confidence in the ability of Bessus to wage a successful war against Alexander, and he was not shy about making his feelings known.

Bagodaras remarked to the guests that Bessus was little more than a timid dog whose bark was worse than its bite. He then went on to suggest that given the limited skills of the new Bactrian king of Asia, Bessus would be better off simply surrendering to Alexander before the fighting began. In return, Alexander might take pity on him and allow him to retain the kingdom he had stolen from Darius. Bessus was drunk and quick to anger. He drew his scimitar but was restrained by his friends. Bagodaras left Balkh and made his way to the camp of Alexander, where he was welcomed as an ally.

When Alexander approached Balkh with his army a few days later, Bessus fled to the river Oxus,[12] which constituted the boundary between Bactria and Sogdiana. Once in Sogdiana, Bessus took refuge in one of its principal cities, Nautaca,[13] where he tried unsuccessfully to raise additional troops to fight Alexander.

Alexander left the aged Artabazus as satrap of Bactria and led his army toward the Oxus River. The army had to cross forty miles of blistering desert before it could reach the river, and in that desert summer temperatures routinely exceed 40 degrees centigrade. While crossing the desert, Alexander lost a number of men as the sun, intense heat, fatigue, and dehydration took their toll. There was such a critical shortage of water that some of the soldiers were driven by their thirst to drink wine. It proved to be a fatal error for many. The fortunate ones only made themselves sick, while the unlucky ones died.

When Alexander and his army arrived at the shores of the Oxus River, the few boats they found there had been destroyed by Bessus. The army was forced to improvise in order to cross the river, so the soldiers stuffed animal skins with straw and stitched them tightly closed. They used these stuffed skins as rafts to float across the river in a manner that was still reported to be in use by the locals as late as the twentieth century.[14]

Bagodaras entered Sogdiana in advance of Alexander's main force and infiltrated the entourage of Bessus. He was successful in organizing a cabal of discontented Bactrian and Sogdian nobles. Among these nobles were three prominent commanders of Bessus: Spitamenes, Dataphernes, and Catanes. Urged on by the promises and assurances of Bagodaras that they would be well rewarded, they seized Bessus, stripped him of his tiara and robes, and brought him into the camp of Alexander, where his ears and nose were cut off and he was bound to a cross. While accounts differ as to the exact manner of his death, they are consistent in recounting that Alexander turned Bessus over to Oxathres, the brother of Darius, for torture.[15] One account has Bessus dismembered when he was pulled apart by trees that had been bent together and then allowed to straighten when the restraining ropes were cut.[16] Another ancient source relates that Bessus was tortured for a long time and then cut up into little pieces, which were scattered over the land.[17] Yet another variation is that Bessus was tried and condemned by a Persian tribunal for the murder of Darius and then executed later in Ecbatana.[18] A final version recounts that Alexander had Bessus nailed to a cross, transported back to Iran, and executed in the same spot where he had killed Darius.[19] In any case, Bessus died after a prolonged period of torture. His mutilation and execution were barbaric by any standards and illustrate, like the torture and execution of Philotas, the orientalizing trend of Alexander's court. To inflict this type of sadistic torture and execution on those who opposed the king was regarded by the Greeks as a particularly Persian practice, and they noted how readily Alexander adopted it.

At the Oxus River, Alexander's army came upon a small town that was inhabited by a Greek-speaking people called the Branchidae.[20] These people were the descendants of Greeks who had been relocated to Bactria from the city of Miletus on the western coast of Asia Minor more than a century and a half earlier. Apparently, in 479 B.C. they had aided the Persians in looting the temple of Apollo just outside their city. Xerxes, the Persian king at the time, ordered them relocated to Bactria because he thought it was too dangerous for them to remain in the Greek world. The temple of Apollo near Miletus was as important a shrine to the Greeks as was Delphi, and what these people had participated in was regarded as the worst type of sacrilege. As a result of the violation, the oracle had remained silent for decades.

The Branchidae had settled in the border area between Bactria and Sogdiana, and their descendants, the current population of the town, still spoke Greek as well as the native dialect. These people had retained many of their old customs from Miletus, and they greeted Alexander and his soldiers as fellow Greeks. There was surprise on both parts when they discovered they spoke the same language, and initially there was considerable joy. The people graciously opened their town to Alexander and his soldiers.

After the army was encamped outside the town walls, Alexander learned the story of the desecration of the temple from his historians. Alexander's mood turned darker. He called all the officers from Miletus to his tent and recounted for them the story of the looting of their temple. He asked whether they bore any hatred for the people of this town for the sacrilege committed by their ancestors or whether they regarded the Branchidae as kinsmen because of their common language and customs. There was a general discussion, and opinions among the officers varied. When they could not, as a group, come to a consensus, Alexander made their decision for them. Once again, he took the role as the avenger of Persian sacrilege against the temples of the Greeks.

Early the following morning, Alexander assembled a lightly armed phalanx and entered the town. Once inside the gates, he gave the order to massacre the inhabitants. When the slaughter began, the Branchidae did not understand why. They were defenseless. The male inhabitants, all mostly unarmed, were killed where they stood or as they tried in vain to defend their families. The women were raped and then enslaved along with any children who survived the carnage. It was all over before lunch. Then Alexander ordered the town burned to the ground so that not a vestige of it would remain. This was another example of Alexander the Great at his worst.

When Alexander and his army were finished, what had once been a prosperous town was a wasteland. This was done to punish a people who had never even seen the Greek city of Miletus. Once again, Alexander imposed a collective guilt on the descendants of those who had taken the Persian side, and once again he extracted the maximum penalty.

After leaving the Oxus River, Alexander and his army marched nearly 300 kilometers northeast to the capital of Sogdiana, then called Marakanda.[21] As Alexander and his army were passing through the territory, a large force of local tribesmen kidnapped one of the foraging parties. Alexander led some of his army units out in search of their comrades. When they found the tribesmen and engaged them in combat, Alexander was wounded in the leg by an arrow. The head of the arrow remained deeply embedded in his leg even after the shaft was withdrawn. Alexander had to be carried from the field of battle back to the camp. When the tribesmen saw what had happened they feared retaliation if Alexander were to die. They sent envoys to the camp who expressed their remorse and asked for a peace treaty. Alexander agreed, his foraging party was returned, and the army moved on through the territory without further incident.

Four days later, Alexander's column reached the double-walled city of Marakanda. Alexander occupied the city, and the army ravaged and burned all the surrounding towns and villages. The men were massacred and the women and children enslaved. Then Alexander left a garrison at Marakanda and led the army 250 kilometers farther to the northeast, to the shores of the Jaxartes River and Cyropolis, a city founded centuries before by Cyrus the Great. For the geographers of the ancient world, the Jaxartes marked the end of Asia and the limit of the civilized world. Beyond this river, there was nothing but the endless steppes, the domains of the fierce nomadic tribes known as the Scythians. In August of 329 B.C., on the banks of the Jaxartes River, Alexander established Alexandria Ultima or Alexandria the Farthest,[22] a town to commemorate the farthest limits of his conquest. He had come to what the ancient Greeks believed was the edge of the inhabited world. Even Alexander was reluctant to venture beyond this point, for on the vast steppes was "the great hiving-ground of the world disturbers."[23]

Alexander's standard practice when it came to establishing his Alexandrias was to populate them with his sick and wounded as well as any malcontents—those who were of little use to him. He left behind as well a small garrison of healthy soldiers. When the sick and wounded recovered, they were expected to remain as permanent settlers. Some of the ancient sources imply that being ordered to remain as a colonist in one of Alexander's new cities was a punitive measure.[24] Two years later when rumors reached many of these settlements that Alexander had been killed in India, many of those who had been left behind as colonists deserted and set off for home. When Alexander discovered what they had done, many of them were severely punished, even executed, for their insubordination and defiance of his will.[25]

While Alexander was besieging one of the cities in the area around Cyropolis, he was struck in the neck by a rock with such force that it knocked him unconscious. When he regained consciousness, his voice was barely audible. The wound in his leg had not healed, and with the blow from the rock it took several weeks before he recovered enough to resume his command of the army and take to the field.

While Alexander was convalescing, Spitamenes, one of the Sogdian nobles who had surrendered Bessus and agreed to become an ally, started his own rebellion. Spitamenes declared that he could not endure the tyranny of Alexander toward his people; just as he did not endure the tyranny of Bessus, he would not endure the tyranny of the Macedonian invader. He declared himself in open rebellion and attacked Alexander's garrison at Marakanda. The relief column sent to rescue the garrison was ambushed by one of the nomadic tribes from the steppes of northwestern Sogdiana, and was nearly massacred to a man. The survivors who managed to escape and reach Alexander's camp were quickly isolated from the main army to keep them from telling the rest of the soldiers what had happened to the relief column.

The rebellion of Spitamenes grew over the last half of the year 329 B.C. and eventually spread from Sogdiana across the Oxus River and into Bactria. Support for the rebel leader grew among the local people. Towns and villages all over Sogdiana and Bactria provided supplies for his troops and information on the movements of Alexander's army. Spitamenes began to develop into the leader of a national resistance movement. He incited uprisings that spread to most parts of Sogdiana and attacked Alexander's outposts and garrisons with alarming frequency. Many of the tribes, especially the northern nomads who had massacred Alexander's relief column outside Marakanda, joined him.

Most of the uprisings and attacks on the garrisons occurred in the territory between the Oxus River to the south and the Jaxartes River to the northeast.[26] When Alexander had recovered from his wounds, at least to the point of riding a horse, he left Alexandria Ultima and led his troops back to Marakanda. They covered the distance in three to four days through a series of forced marches. Near Marakanda Alex-

Gate of All Nations: Also known as the Great Gate of Xerxes, this portal was the principal entryway into the city of Persepolis. It was through this gate that Alexander passed as the conqueror of Persia. The home of the Achaemenid kings and capital of the Persian Empire, Persepolis was reputed to have been the richest city in the ancient world largely because the royal treasury was housed there.

View of the ruins of Persepolis taken from the hills to the northeast of the ancient site. The city was practically defenseless except for its walls since its builders never envisioned that any conquering army could ever penetrate so far into the heart of the Persian Empire to threaten its capital.

Palace of Xerxes at Persepolis.

A bas-relief at Persepolis showing the Persian king fighting a demon from hell. Images such as this played into Alexander's perceptions of himself as a hero and eventually as a god.

Bodyguards of the king: known as the immortals.

Bas-relief at Persepolis: Lion devouring a deer.

Rock tomb of the Persian kings located at Naqsh-E Rostam about five miles northeast of Persepolis. There are four tombs hewn out of the cliff some fifty feet above the ground. The tombs are believed to have been those of Darius I, Artaxerxes I, Xerxes I, and Darius II. The Persian kings photograph show the tomb of Xerxes I, the most hated of all the Persian kings by Alexander and the Greeks.

Tomb of Cyrus the Great at Pasagardae: The modest tomb of the founder of the Persian Empire is located some eighty-five kilometers northeast of Persepolis in a small valley which was once the site of the ancient city of Pasagardae. Alexander came here to pay his respects to the Persian king. So impressed was Alexander by the simplicity and modesty of the tomb of this great king that he provided funds for its restoration and maintenance. The present effort at restoration is the courtesy of the government of the Islamic Republic of Iran.

Roxanne. The photo was taken in the grand bazaar at Samarkand, famous throughout history for its wide variety of spices and silks from the Orient. The beauty of the vendor is typical of the Eurasian women of Uzbekistan. Captivated by the beauty of the Sogdian women Alexander fell in love with Roxanne, the daughter of a Sogdian nobleman, and married her in 328 B.C. much to the displeasure of his Macedonian and Greek officers.

Greek ruins in the middle of modern-day Samarkand in the area known as the Afrasiab Hill. It was in this location, the highest point in the city, that the ancient city was located.

Mosque at Bukhara.

The archeological museum at Bukhara. The author posing in front of a collection of rare Sogdian artifacts dating from the time of Alexander which were made available to him courtesy of the museum director. From left to right are Dr. Golib Kurbanov, professor of oriental history at the Bukhara State University, the author, Dr. Makhsuma Niyazova, curator of the museum and Robert V. Almeev, director.

Syrdarija River outside of Bekobad on the border between Tajikistan and Uzbekistan. The river was known as the Jaxartes in ancient times and it marks the farthest point north that Alexander and his army pushed. Alexander founded a city nearby but its ruins have never been located. Although the Jaxartes is allegedly the farthest north Alexander ever went in Uzbekistan the author found a small city named Iskander (Persian for Alexander) located some thirty miles north of the modern-day capital of Tashkent.

Zeravsan River outside of Navoij in Uzbekistan. In Alexander's time the river was called the Polytimetus and it flows from the mountains of Tajikistan into Uzbekistan, through Samarkand, and west into the vast steppes of Central Asia. It was at approximately this location that some of Alexander's Macedonian commanders were defeated by the Messagatae tribes. The responsibility for their defeat became the cause of the argument between Alexander and his friend Cleitus at Marakanda (Samarkand).

The ruins of the ancient Greek city of Varkya. This largely unexcavated
site is located some thirty miles west of Bukhara.

View from the ramparts of Varkya looking south over the vast desert that
forms the border between Uzbekistan and Turkmenistan.

Walls of Paikend: a barely excavated Greek city lying some forty kilometers southwest of Bukhara in the deserts of Uzbekistan. The ancient Greek city, dating from the time of Alexander, was on the Great Silk Road linking China to the west.

Aerial views of the Hindu Kush Mountains in northern Afghanistan. Alexander and his army crossed this mountain range in the spring of 329 B.C. by way of the Kaiwak Pass in pursuit of the rebel Bessus who had murdered King Darius and proclaimed himself the new king of Persia. A tunnel, dug by the Soviets in the early 1980s, allows travelers foolish enough to trust it, a fast and convenient way of crossing under the range and avoiding the bandits as well as the treacherous passes. The tunnel is frequently shut down to allow debris to be cleared. The tunnel is dangerous because of its questionable engineering and its vulnerability to suicide bombers. Alexander and his army re-crossed the range again nearly two years later on their way to India.

The border crossing between Afghanistan and Pakistan at Torkham. Torkham is a border town and the entryway to the Khyber Pass from Afghanistan. Alexander's army crossed over the pass as they moved east into India. Today the pass is a virtual no-man's land in the tribal area of Pakistan and the main commercial and relief route between Pakistan and Afghanistan. Convoys travel the treacherous mountain road daily carrying everything from United Nations relief supplies for the Afghans to weapons and opium. Travel along the route at night is strictly prohibited and foreigners are not allowed into the tribal area without a permit.

Truck convoy on the Khyber Pass near the Afghan border.

The author at the narrowest point in the Khyber Pass. This is one of the most dangerous places in the long and winding thirty kilometer stretch because of the vulnerability to ambush.

The author standing on the site of ancient Bazira in the Swat Valley. The city was conquered by Alexander in 327 B.C. In the background is Mt. Elam, which some contemporary scholars believe is the ancient "Aornos" and the site of the Indian fortress of Pir Sar.

The Swat Valley looking north toward the foothills of the Himalaya Mountains. It was into this valley that Alexander came, conquered the cities, and drove the inhabitants into the adjacent Indus Valley.

The author pictured with Prince Miangul Aurangzeb, the Wali of Swat, on his estate in Saidu Sharif. The family of the prince was the hereditary ruling clan of the Swat Valley in the northwest territory of Pakistan.

Remains of a Greek column and Hindu/Greek figures at the ruins of the ancient city of Mingadra at Saidu Sharif in the Swat Valley.

The road leading over the Shangla Pass on the Swat Valley side. The single-lane road connects the Swat and Indus valleys. This road has carried traffic between the two valleys for millennia and might well have been the route followed by Alexander and his army as they pursued the fleeing inhabitants of the Swat Valley.

The Indus River at Mt. Aornos at dawn. In the summer temperatures in the narrow Indus Valley routinely reach to well over a hundred degrees with little relief at night.

Pir Sar: The mountain in the background was known in ancient times as "Aornos" from the ancient Greek word for sky. It was at the very top of this mountain that the inhabitants of the Swat Valley congregated in a natural fortress known as Pir Sar to resist Alexander. In the foreground is the Indus River.

Jandial temple: A unique example of the remains of a once magnificent ancient Greek temple constructed in the 2nd century B.C. facing the ancient city of Sirkap in Taxila. Around the interior of the temple once hung pictures on copper tablets which depicted the feats of Alexander and his victory over Porus the king of the Indians.

Taxila ruins: Preliminary excavations of an early Hindu-Greek city recently discovered buried under a farmer's orange grove a few kilometers outside of Taxila in the northwest territory of Pakistan.

The Gedrosian desert: Currently known as the Makran in the tribal area of Baluchistan, this area of southwestern Pakistan is perhaps among the most desolate and dangerous places on the face of the earth. Alexander led his army through this desert on his way back to Babylon from India. During the passage which took two months his army suffered more casualties at the hands of nature than in any battle they ever fought. When rumors spread that Alexander and his army had perished in Gedrosia revolts broke out all over his empire and spread to Greece and Macedonia.

Ruins of Babylon: all that remains of this once notorious ancient city, "the mother of all whores and earth's abominations," are a few crumbling walls and the modern palace which Saddam Hussein had constructed from the bricks of the ancient structures. The small museum on the site was looted during the recent war. It was into Babylon that Alexander entered in triumph following his victory over the Persian army at Gaugamela (331 B.C.) and it was at Babylon where Alexander died a few years later (323 B.C.). Alexander had intended that Babylon would become the capital of his new world empire.

ander attacked Spitamenes' base of operations—the villages and towns that supported him. The army units burned the fields and crops and destroyed the villages, leaving the survivors to starve and freeze that winter. All over Sogdiana men of military age were killed on the spot to deny Spitamenes necessary reinforcements.[27] It became a brutal campaign.

Spitamenes avoided a set battle with Alexander. He would attack garrisons and outposts, ambush columns, and retreat onto the steppes, but he would not stand and fight. Alexander would follow him only as far west as the Polytimetus,[28] a small river that flows midway between the larger Oxus and Jaxartes. This river begins in the mountains of Sogdiana and runs through Marakanda, then in a westerly direction out into the territories of the Dahae nomad tribe. Alexander would not venture onto the steppes much beyond what is today the Uzbek city of Bukhara. The area between Marakanda and Bukhara was probably the most fertile and flourishing in Sogdiana, so Alexander burned it and left the area a wasteland. He left Marakanda in the autumn of 329 B.C. and returned to Bactria, where he spent the harsh winter months in Balkh.

The following year, 328 B.C., saw even harder fighting as the insurrections continued. By the late spring of 328 B.C. Alexander was operating with his forces in eastern Sogdiana in the area that today constitutes Tajikistan. Then he moved his army west along the Polytimetus River back toward Marakanda. Alexander was determined to capture Spitamenes, who had been raiding with impunity from Marakanda all the way north to the villages along the Jaxartes River. In an attempt to limit the range of Spitamenes, Alexander established more small, fortified towns or outposts located close enough to each other so they could provide mutual support in case of attack.[29]

Part of Alexander's army, under the command of Craterus, remained in Bactria to deal with the insurrections there. All through the summer of 328 B.C., Spitamenes continued to raid at will throughout Bactria and Sogdiana, carrying off large quantities of spoils from many of Alexander's outposts. Alexander divided his army and spread his soldiers throughout Sogdiana. His columns of infantry and cavalry set out to hunt down the rebels, many of whom had now

taken refuge in the more mountainous sections east and south of
Marakanda.

When Spitamenes unexpectedly surfaced in Bactria, one of Alexander's garrison commanders made the mistake of setting out after
him. The Macedonian garrison left its fortified position and fell into
a carefully laid ambush, sustaining heavy casualties. On another
occasion, Craterus pursued Spitamenes and managed to inflict some
casualties on his forces before they could disappear into Sogdiana and
the safety of the steppes. Spitamenes eluded Craterus time and again
in Bactria. When pursued he would disappear onto the steppes or the
deserts or into the mountains and then surface in another part of
Sogdiana or Bactria. Each time Spitamenes managed to escape, but
his nomad allies began losing confidence in their leader. They could
see no conclusion to the war with Alexander—only continued devastation of their lands. So, in collusion with Spitamenes' disgruntled
wife, they cut off the rebel leader's head while he slept and sent it to
Alexander in Marakanda as a peace offering.[30] With Spitamenes dead
and his head in Alexander's collection, most of the resistance in
Sogdiana died out. There were only a few rebel strongholds left in the
mountain fortresses east of Marakanda, but those would have to wait
until the spring of the following year.

Because it was now late autumn, Alexander decided to remain at
Marakanda[31] for a few weeks before moving his army to more comfortable winter quarters farther south at Nautaca. There he planned
to await the spring and better weather before he resumed the campaign. It was already cold at Marakanda, and the nights were long.
There was little for the army to do, but Alexander filled his nights
with banquets where there was much drinking and feasting. The
boredom and the wine provided the catalysts for frequent flare-ups
of temper between men who lived daily with violence and habitually
drank too much. There was also the perennial generation problem
between a young king and his partying companions and the older,
more somber Macedonian and Greek officers.

Cleitus the Black was a senior Macedonian cavalry commander
whose family had a long and intimate connection to Alexander. He
was considerably older than Alexander, probably in his forties, with
a long and distinguished career of military service. He had served

first with Philip, and he had been with Alexander since the beginning of the campaign. At the battle of the Granicus, when Alexander first confronted the Persian army, Cleitus had saved his life.

Cleitus was also one of the most conservative of Alexander's commanders. He held to the old Macedonian traditions and was irascible either by nature or because of age.[32] As the years passed, he became one of the most outspoken critics of Alexander's claim to being the son of Zeus. He saw it as pretentious and disrespectful to the memory of Philip. For many Macedonians such as Cleitus, the king's demand that he be worshiped as a god meant that he had turned his back on a fundamental premise of Greek life, the equality of all male citizens. For Cleitus and many of the other senior officers, Alexander ruled as king by the consent and support of his nobles. They wanted a king who was a national figure, as Philip had been, and who ruled as the first among his peers—not a tyrant who thought he was a god. Alexander in the early years at least tolerated this criticism, especially from Cleitus who had saved his life in battle.

The king's increasing infatuation with all things Persian bothered Cleitus as well as his divine pretensions. Alexander had become addicted to Persian luxuries. Cleitus saw the king losing his self-restraint and degenerating into an arrogant tyrant.[33] As for the Persians, Cleitus saw them as barbarians, a vanquished enemy who should be treated as such.

By that autumn Cleitus had become tiresome, and Alexander had found a convenient way to be rid of him and his incessant criticism. Alexander appointed him satrap of Sogdiana and Bactria to replace Artabazus, who, if the manuscripts are to be believed, was approaching one hundred years old. The old Persian had begged the king to be relieved of his duty, as he considered himself too old to continue in the capacity of governor.[34]

The appointment as satrap meant that Cleitus would remain behind in Sogdiana and Bactria when Alexander and the rest of the army moved on to India the following summer. This was not an appealing prospect to the veteran Macedonian commander. He viewed being left behind with the other malcontents, the sick, and the lame to administer a network of military colonies supported by an enslaved native agrarian workforce as a demotion and punishment. Cleitus

knew that he might well remain in Sogdiana and Bactria, effectively
in exile by the king's order, until the end of his life.

Alexander had received a shipment of fruit as a gift from one of
the Greek cities in Asia Minor. Generous by nature, especially with
other people's wealth, he was anxious to share the fruit with his
friends, so he sent word to Cleitus, among others, that there would
be a banquet that night in the royal residence and his presence was
required.

Two nights prior to the banquet, Alexander had a dream that disturbed him to such a degree that he consulted his seers for their opinions. In his dream the king had seen Cleitus sitting with the sons of
Parmenio. They were all dressed in black robes and were evidently
dead. The seers could not offer a satisfactory explanation, so the
matter was dismissed.

The night of the banquet there was much feasting and the usual
amounts of heavy drinking that had come to characterize these events.
Alexander had by this point in his life "taken to new and more barbaric ways in drinking."[35] The Macedonians had always been heavy
drinkers and tended to drink their wine undiluted, a practice that the
Greeks regarded as barbaric. The drinking in Bactria and Sogdiana
had become particularly heavy and frequent. One possible explanation scholars have offered is that Alexander and his officers drank
wine so heavily because the water was so bad and the temperatures
in summer so hot. A general boredom that characterized those periods
when the army was not occupied fighting or foraging may also have
played a part that night in making tempers edgy and tongues dry.

After the banquet, in the traditional Greek manner, the symposium followed. This was the period after the meal when the drinking and the discussions became serious. Some of those present began
to compete with each other in flattering the king. They were "Alexander's Chorus," a mixture of Greeks, Macedonians, and Persians
who sought to ingratiate themselves to the king by appealing to his
vanity. Some did so by comparing Alexander's victories to the labors
of Heracles and others by maintaining that he had surpassed the
achievements of the illustrious twin gods Castor and Pollux. The
parallel with the divine twins pleased Alexander. They were important figures in Greek and later Roman mythology because they had

started life as mortals and, because of their achievements and bravery, had been elevated to the status of gods. Alexander identified with them, and along with Heracles and Dionysus they were his particular favorites within the Hellenic pantheon.

The sycophants continued to flatter Alexander, maintaining that it was only the envy of men that prevented him from receiving the divine acclamation he was due for his great accomplishments. Why, they asked rhetorically, should the world have to wait until Alexander's death to honor him as a god? Achievements such as his merited divinity during his lifetime. The flatterers competed with one another to the delight of the king, who was particularly susceptible to their words. They played on his vanity, and when the flattery finally subsided the entertainment began. This was much to the relief of a number of Alexander's senior Macedonian commanders who had remained silent during the flattery.

One form of entertainment for the guests that night was a recitation of verses set to music by a poet in the imperial court. Apparently, Alexander had commissioned the verses, which ridiculed some Macedonian commanders who had been recently defeated by the Sacae, a tribe of particularly fierce and skilled horsemen from the territories north of the Jaxartes River. These tribesmen had caught one of the Macedonian contingents at the Polytimetus River, and some of the commanders had been killed in the fighting. Alexander was apparently anxious to place the blame for the defeat on these dead commanders and avoid criticism that he had placed his men in a perilous position by underestimating the strength and skill of the Sacae.

The verses that the poet had composed were at best in bad taste and at worst intended to humiliate. They conveyed to all present Alexander's displeasure at the defeat of his Macedonian commanders by barbarians. A number of the Macedonian officers present were offended. They called out for a stop to the entertainment, while Alexander and those around him who were enjoying the recitation called out for the poet to continue. The mood was at first festive, and raucous. At first, the bantering between Alexander and his officers over the verses was loud but relatively harmless. Then the situation quickly deteriorated and became tense.

Cleitus by this time had already had a lot to drink. Even when sober he had a quick temper and a sharp tongue. He was typical of the breed of senior Macedonian officers who had been with Alexander since he first crossed over into Asia Minor. Encouraged by the support of those around him and heated by the wine, he cried out from his couch that it was wrong to insult the Macedonians. The men who fell in battle at the Polytimetus, he shouted, had been loyal and brave officers who had met with misfortune in combat. Those around Cleitus supported him with shouts of approbation. It was insulting, he admonished Alexander, to mock the memory of brave Macedonians in front of barbarians and former enemies, men who were markedly inferior to those who had died. Cleitus could not bear to see barbarians reclining at Alexander's table and laughing at the memory of Macedonians who had died fighting for their king.

Alexander retorted from the other side of the room that perhaps it was not misfortune at the Polytimetus but cowardice that Cleitus was excusing. Those around Alexander vigorously applauded his retort. Cleitus sprang to his feet in anger. The bantering had now turned to insult, and insult among Macedonians demanded satisfaction. Cleitus cried out that his so-called cowardice had saved the "god-born king" from death at the battle of the Granicus. During that battle, the Persian satrap Spithridates had gained the upper hand over Alexander in combat. With Alexander down, the Persian was preparing to strike the deathblow when Cleitus severed his arm and killed him. Cleitus had saved Alexander's life, and this act had earned him a privileged place in the royal entourage.

In his anger Cleitus had let slip a sarcastic reference to Alexander's claim to being the son of Zeus. Then Cleitus raised his right hand, the hand that had saved Alexander from death at the Granicus, and made an insolent gesture. Not content with that, Cleitus then hurled the worst insult yet. Alexander at the battle of the Granicus had "turned his back on the spear of Spithridates."[36] The implication to everyone at the banquet was clear. Alexander was running away when he fell, and Cleitus had intervened to save his cowardly life.

The battle of the Granicus River had always been a sore point for Alexander as well as a blemish on his war record. Although he had won the battle, his judgment in the opening engagement of the campaign in Asia Minor had been rash, impulsive, and costly. He had led a pointless and disastrous charge against skilled Greek mercenaries who held the high ground. As a result, the units Alexander led into combat suffered heavy casualties on the first day of battle and were forced to retreat. It was only the mature tactics of the stable and experienced Parmenio that had saved the army on the second day and given Alexander his first victory.

Alexander was in no mood to be reminded of his failure at the Granicus, but Cleitus had the floor and would not hold his tongue. He continued to berate Alexander, reminding the "god-born king" that it was spilled Macedonian blood that had made him great. Then Cleitus told the guests how Alexander was full of himself and had even disowned his true father Philip, the architect of his success. The representation of Alexander as the son of Zeus might impress Persians and other barbarians, Cleitus went on, but it earned nothing but mockery and contempt for the king from the Macedonians and Greeks. This was Philotas all over again. Alexander was on his feet in a fury. He accused Cleitus of treason and of attempting to cause dissention among the Macedonians. The charge of treason had become the preferred method of Alexander for quelling dissension in the ranks. Cleitus replied that he envied the Macedonians who had died in battle because those men had been spared the shame of seeing Alexander surrounded in his palaces by Persians.

The situation was completely out of hand. It had degenerated into a potentially violent confrontation in only seconds. Those physically closest to Alexander closed ranks around him, while several of the older Macedonian officers present tried to restore calm among the other guests. The Persians and the other barbarian guests present, while outwardly alarmed and careful to detach themselves from the events that were unfolding, watched with a sense of gleeful amusement. Macedonians at each other's throats was a prospect that secretly must have pleased them.

The situation improved, but only for an instant. Alexander, restrained by his friends, recovered from his outburst of temper. In a calmer voice, he commented to those around him that the Greeks among them that evening seemed like demigods when compared to the animal-like behavior of the Macedonians present. Cleitus heard

the remark and shouted back that perhaps Alexander should surround himself with more Persians and barbarians at his banquets,
those who willingly worshiped him as a god rather than free men
who spoke their minds.

Alexander became enraged, picked up an apple from a nearby bowl,
and hurled it at Cleitus. The apple reached its mark, striking Cleitus
squarely on the head. Then Alexander looked for his dagger, which
one of his bodyguards had wisely moved out of reach. Panic and confusion broke out everywhere in the banquet hall. The Macedonians
were on the verge of fighting among themselves, the guards were
confused, and the Persians were amused.

Alexander's bodyguards and closest friends Ptolemy, Perdiccas,
Lysimachus, and Leonnatus all tried to calm him. But Alexander was
in a fury and in his anger reverted to speaking in his native Macedonian tongue. When the king could not find his weapon, he became
alarmed and thought his friends and bodyguards, in collusion with
Cleitus, were attempting to assassinate him. Alexander ordered his
herald to sound an alarm that would alert the guards outside that
the king was in danger. The herald hesitated. If he had sounded the
alarm, the guards would have entered the banquet hall anticipating
a coup against the king and could have taken hostile action against
all those present. A bloodbath would have ensued, with many killed
over nothing more than what started as a simple argument between
the king and Cleitus.

Alexander struck the herald for failing to comply with his order
and cried out that he had come to the same end as Darius.[37] The
implication of these words was clear. Alexander continued to call for
his guards. By disobeying the order the herald, whether by intent or
not, probably prevented a massacre of Alexander's top officers.

All the while Cleitus continued to rail against the king. His
friends finally succeeded in pushing him out of the banquet hall, but
Cleitus broke free of their grip and reentered by another portal. Once
more in the banquet hall, he could not resist grandstanding by quoting a line by the Greek playwright Euripides on the evils of tyranny.

That was too much for Alexander, who seized a spear from a distracted guard and ran Cleitus through.[38] Cleitus fell on the floor and
lay groaning for several minutes before he expired. The instant Clei-

tus fell, Alexander's anger was spent and replaced by overwhelming remorse and grief. He withdrew the spear from the lifeless body of the man who had once been his friend and tried to impale himself upon its bloody point. His bodyguards and friends restrained him and prevented his suicide. They carried the king to his quarters on their shoulders and lay him, sobbing, on the royal couch.

Alexander was to blame for what happened. His outburst of temper and his drunkenness caused the death of Cleitus. Drunkenness was perhaps the more disgraceful of the two faults, for as a king and "divinity" he held an exemplary position among men. But drunkenness and kings are not incompatible. Alexander's father Philip was a notorious drunk who routinely made a spectacle of himself at court banquets and weddings. In the next few days, the court flatterers and the philosophers would move to excuse and justify the king's actions. After all, that was what they were paid for. At least Alexander, to his credit, was able to call what he had done by its proper name—murder.[39]

Some of the ancient sources blame Cleitus for what happened and call the murder a "tragedy that caused Alexander much suffering."[40] Never mind that it killed Cleitus. What is evident from the episode is that these were violent men with fragile egos. Killing, for Alexander and those around him, had been a part of their daily routine for many years. For men who are at war for long periods, resorting to weapons when angered is a natural but tragic reflex.

The confrontation between Alexander and Cleitus was more than an argument between two drunken friends that turned violent. Cleitus had as much of a temper as Alexander, and issues between them had obviously been unresolved and festering for some time. Events that night constituted a clash that was bound to have come sooner or later between the old conservative Macedonian guard and the "multicultural" order of Alexander's new world. Alexander was intent on becoming the master of a new world order, and he would crush, without hesitation, any resistance to his plans or criticism of his vision. Cleitus was confronting Alexander with the folly of his ways, and this drove him to violence.

Alexander was lost in grief. All that night and throughout the next day he lay on the royal couch and cried out for his murdered friend.

He also cried out the name of Lanice, the older sister of Cleitus,[41] who had nursed him when he was a child. She had helped to raise him, and her sons had died fighting for him. When Alexander no longer had a voice left to cry out with or tears left to shed, he lapsed into depression. He barely moved on the royal bed and refused all food or water for almost three days and three nights.

Alexander's closest companions remained by his side and became more concerned the deeper he lapsed into his depression. One by one they tried to console him with words, but he would not respond. The death of Cleitus was not his fault, they told him. It was due to the jealous wrath of the god Dionysus. They reminded Alexander that just before the banquet he had sacrificed to the Dioscuri, Castor and Pollux, and had neglected to sacrifice to Dionysus. Dionysus had become jealous, and his anger—not Alexander—was to blame for the death of Cleitus. Alexander countered that it was he who had killed Cleitus, not the gods.

On the second night Aristander, the king's seer, was admitted to the chambers and sat by the royal bed. In a calm, reasoning, even fatherly voice, he reminded Alexander of his dream of just a few nights before when he had seen Cleitus sitting with the dead sons of Parmenio. Aristander told the king that the dream was an omen— the gods had willed that Cleitus should die. The words of Aristander helped to soothe the suffering soul of the king.

Then Callisthenes, the court philosopher and official historian of the expedition, came to the king's chambers accompanied by Anaxarchus, another philosopher but of lesser standing. Callisthenes approached the king first and took up where Aristander had left off. By gentle persuasion, he tried to console the grieving king and alleviate his suffering. But the philosopher's words came to nothing. Alexander remained withdrawn.

Next, Anaxarchus approached the king. Where the seer and the philosopher had been gentle and respectful of the king's grief, Anaxarchus was direct and confrontational. "Is this Alexander, the son of Zeus, and the source of law on earth for all men? Is this the man who calls himself king, lying upon his couch and weeping like a frightened slave?"[42] Alexander was shocked. No man would dare speak to him in such a manner. He roused himself and turned to face

Anaxarchus. But Alexander was too weak and grief-stricken to become angry. He was emotionally vulnerable, and Anaxarchus knew it. He played the soul of Alexander like a skilled musician plays an instrument.

Now that Anaxarchus had the king's attention, he went on to explain that because he was a "god-born king" all his actions were the manifestation of the will of the gods. Alexander was the counterpart of Zeus on earth. Thus, his actions could not be questioned by mortals. Alexander could never make a mistake since his acts were by definition just. Remorse was inappropriate to Alexander's exalted position as a divinity, a god among men. Anaxarchus roused Alexander from his depression. He had taken a calculated risk, and it had paid off. Anaxarchus could well have found himself on the torturer's rack for the confrontational approach he had used to rouse the king.

Alexander responded favorably because Anaxarchus had played into his vanity. Anaxarchus had brought the king back, but into a new and more pernicious phase of megalomania. Anaxarchus had justified in Alexander's mind the idea of an unrestricted monarchy. It was tyranny in its worst form. For the Greeks and Macedonians, it was unacceptable. Callisthenes had watched the drama unfold, and he left the royal tent that night uneasy for the future.

The next day, Alexander appeared before a jury of the Macedonians to answer the charge of murder. Even though Alexander now considered himself to be the only source of law, when it suited him for political reasons he would adhere to the traditional practices of the Macedonians. This was one of those occasions. The soldiers welcomed the king into the assembly, and in a mock trial they heard the facts and exonerated him for the murder of Cleitus. Alexander asked for permission to give Cleitus a proper funeral. It was a staged production, and it did not sit well with many of the senior Macedonian officers who remained silent throughout.[43] The hearing before the assembly of soldiers was a politically expedient move and indicated that Alexander was careful as to how hard he was willing to push the idea of his divinity or divert from tradition.

Anaxarchus had always been one of the king's flatterers. He was among the first who encouraged Alexander to have his subjects worship him as a god, and he applauded Alexander when the king adopted Persian manners and dress. It was Anaxarchus who had suggested that since the Greeks had Dionysus and Heracles, it would only be fitting that the Macedonians have Alexander as their own special god to worship. Anaxarchus introduced the idea that it would be more fitting to honor Alexander now in his lifetime than to wait until after his death.

Following the murder of Cleitus, freedom of speech was gone for the Greeks and Macedonians. This would be difficult for many of them to accept. Gone as well was the amiable nature Alexander had exhibited at Persepolis when many of those around him could criticize him openly.[44] At Persepolis, he had accepted criticism with the good-natured quip that "it was the fate of kings to reward those around them, and in return have to endure ingratitude and criticism from the very ones they had rewarded."[45]

Anaxarchus had convinced Alexander that his word was law and that his father Zeus, the king of the gods, sanctioned all his actions. Alexander now considered himself the very embodiment of justice on earth and thus began the most repressive period of his reign.

Aristotle had taught Alexander that in every age a man comes forth who by virtue of his superiority is above the laws that govern mortals. While Aristotle had deplored monarchy, he made an exception for that rare occasion when a unique man came forward to become king. That man would rule as a part of natural right, a "god among men" by virtue of his "arête," or achievement.[46] Alexander believed he was that man for his age, and Anaxarchus, by justifying the murder of Cleitus in those terms, had unleashed the monster.

Callisthenes was an Athenian who had joined Alexander's expedition as the official court philosopher and historian when it left Macedonia. He was related to the great philosopher and Alexander's teacher Aristotle.[47] It had in fact been Aristotle who had recommended him to Alexander. Callisthenes commanded considerable admiration and respect among the Greeks and Macedonians in the army, both because of his connection to Aristotle and in his own right as a philosopher and teacher. He was an academic and, by nature, reclusive and pensive. Callisthenes has been characterized as "boorish in manner"[48] and a plain-speaking, detached, and emo-

tionally reserved man. Yet he was a man capable of incredible eloquence, especially when circumstances required it.

Because of their differences in personality, Alexander and Callisthenes never developed a close relationship. He was brought to Asia
to play the role of Homer while Alexander played Achilles. It was to
have been a mutually beneficial relationship whereby Alexander's
fame would live forever in the words of Callisthenes and the reputation of Callisthenes would be immortalized by his recounting of the
accomplishments of Alexander.

After the murder of Cleitus, Callisthenes became critical of Anaxarchus. He chastised his fellow philosopher for violating his trust as
one of Alexander's teachers.[49] Callisthenes admonished Anaxarchus
for neglecting to tutor the young king on his obligation to rule the
Macedonians and Greeks by respecting custom and law. The Greeks
were a people who valued freedom, and they would not be ruled by
a tyrant, even one who thought he was a god. Callisthenes argued
that Alexander should receive the honor due him for his accomplishments as a great military leader, but Greeks and Macedonians
should not be forced to worship him as a god. Let the barbarians
do that.

Yet Callisthenes was not without fault. He had been one of those
who years earlier had put the idea of divinity in Alexander's head.
Once when the army was moving along a particularly difficult stretch
of the coast of Pamphylia,[50] the sea normally came right to the
rocky mountainous coast and made passage by foot impossible along
that stretch of coastline. On the day when Alexander arrived, the sea
receded due to a combination of an unusually low tide and shifting
winds. A wide stretch of beach was exposed, which allowed Alexander to avoid the rocky coastline and reach his objective in a shorter
period of time. Callisthenes made capital of the matter by proclaim-
ing in extravagant and exaggerated terms that the sea had bowed to
its new master. Those words had now come back to haunt him.

One night Callisthenes was summoned by Alexander to attend a
banquet followed by the usual symposium. On this particular occasion, Alexander excused himself after the dinner and retired to his
quarters. When the king had left, some of the guests who remained

entered into a discussion of how appropriate it would be to honor him as a god during his lifetime rather than wait until after his death. The subject was introduced by one of the court poets, Cleo, who had come from Sicily to join the expedition. Cleo was one of a number of poets who had joined the royal entourage and "debased their art" by composing poems flattering Alexander.[51] While Callisthenes and other Greeks had been willing to support the idea of divine honors for Alexander, it was something to be bestowed posthumously, not during his lifetime.

Cleo began the discussion by enumerating all the great deeds of the king, and the other flatterers joined in. Alexander, they maintained, was a hero who was greater than the legendary Heracles. While it was true that Heracles had accomplished great deeds, Alexander's were even greater. And while Heracles had to wait until he went to heaven to receive his divine honors, Alexander merited having them bestowed on him now, while he lived. Cleo ended his monologue by proposing that all of the members of the court, as a sign of Alexander's divine status, should adopt the Persian custom of prostrating themselves before him when he entered their presence.

Callisthenes objected, arguing that divine honors were "inappropriate to the nature of man." A man, he maintained, could not cope with the emotional and psychological weight of becoming a living god. It would crush him. Worship of a man in such a manner was not only offensive but unnatural. It was hubris, overweening pride and arrogance, the ultimate sin for the Greeks, and it invited divine retribution. A free Greek might choose to prostrate himself before his gods, Callisthenes argued, but never before another man.[52] Had they come half a world away, conquering everything in their path, just to lose their freedom?

What Cleo was suggesting was the act of proskynesis, a practice that had been introduced into the Persian court by Cyrus the Great. Proskynesis was required to be performed by all—Persians and foreigners alike—who came before the great kings of Persia, and interpretations vary among scholars as to exactly what it entailed. The act had a social as well as a religious connotation. The lowest form was a simple ritual kiss, made with the right hand brought up to the mouth and then blown in the direction of the king. Proskynesis could be offered by a man to his superior as a gesture of respect. At the most extreme end, the subjects of the king were required to greet his royal person by literally throwing themselves on the ground before him, chin to the floor. The Greeks and the Macedonians regarded it as a uniquely oriental and contemptible practice. They considered proskynesis in this context as a ridiculous mode of reverence that reduced a free man to the level of a slave or, worse, to the level of the barbarians whom they despised.

In spite of their disdain for the practice, the ancient sources make no mention as to whether or not Greek ambassadors to the Persian court performed proskynesis in the presence of the king. Greek ambassadors had been accredited to the Persian court since the time of Darius I, two centuries before. While the sources are silent on this question, in all probability the Spartans and Athenians, the proudest of the Greeks, performed proskynesis in front of the Persian kings when they came to ask for money.

What Callisthenes and most of the others who were debating the matter did not know was that the entire discussion was contrived. Alexander had suggested the matter be brought up at the symposium and Cleo, along with several of the king's flatterers, staged the discussion. They raised the subject to the Macedonians and Greeks while Alexander listened, hidden behind some tapestries that had been hung behind the couches to conceal his presence.[53] The king noted who favored the practice and who did not. Callisthenes was first on the list of those who displeased the king by their attitudes.

While for the modern reader proskynesis seems a particularly debasing practice, scholars are divided on whether or not it indicated that the Persians regarded their kings as living gods in the manner of the Egyptians or whether it was nothing more than an exaggerated expression of reverence for the royal person. Trying to force this practice upon the Greeks and Macedonians was a risky undertaking. Alexander must have known that while the practice might be natural to the Persians it would be offensive, demeaning, and even heretical to his countrymen. However, since the murder of Cleitus, Alexander had become increasingly preoccupied with his divine status, and he was anxious to see it acknowledged by the Greeks and Macedonians.

Furthermore, Callisthenes had lately taken it upon himself to lecture Alexander on the dangers of tyranny. He warned him that those Persian kings who had been chosen to be worshiped as gods, men such as Darius, Xerxes, and Artaxerxes, had all been defeated by men who were free, that is, the Greeks.[54] Those words did not please Alexander, and Anaxarchus henceforth became the favorite philosopher in the royal entourage and Callisthenes was shunned.

The sentiments of Callisthenes, however, found favor with many Greeks and Macedonians who, because of their fear of the king, would never have dared to speak openly. Callisthenes did cause Alexander to back down, at least temporarily, on his demand for proskynesis. Meanwhile, the Persians in the king's entourage continued to treat him as a god and bow down to him. Emboldened by the criticisms of Callisthenes, some of the Macedonians now openly took to mocking the Persians when they performed proskynesis before the king.[55] As the weeks and months of the winter passed in Sogdiana, Callisthenes continued to express his objections to the worship of Alexander as a god. It was Callisthenes alone who was seen as standing firmly against Alexander and was credited with forcing the king to yield. Alexander came to hate Callisthenes because many of the Greeks and the Macedonians regarded him as the "defender of the public liberty."[56]

Callisthenes rejected invitations to dine with Alexander and his company, and this further alienated him from the king and his inner circle. On those rare occasions when Callisthenes did join them, his aloofness made the king and those around him uncomfortable. They perceived his silence as disapproval, and they resented Callisthenes for sitting in judgment on their drinking and whoring. On the rare occasions when Callisthenes did speak, his remarks could be scathing. On one such occasion, Callisthenes was commanded by the king to attend a symposium. After dinner, the philosopher was requested to demonstrate his eloquence by speaking extemporaneously in praise of the Macedonian people.

Callisthenes stood and delivered a speech that was so eloquent and moving that the guests rose from their couches in a spontaneous outpouring of praise. They applauded Callisthenes for his eloquence and threw garlands at his feet. It was not what Alexander had anticipated. Displeased, the king turned to one of his companions reclining on the couch next to him and, quoting from a play of Euripides, said, "I hate a wise man."[57]

When the applause and cheering had subsided, Alexander was obliged to rise and comment on the speech. He praised Callisthenes for his words and then commented to the guests that it was easy to find eloquent words when one was asked to speak on an easy subject. The king then challenged the philosopher to speak as eloquently on a difficult subject such as the shortcomings of the Macedonians. In this way, the king chided Callisthenes, the guests might not only be entertained by another demonstration of his eloquence and wit, but the Macedonians might profit as well by hearing a recitation of their faults.

Callisthenes took up the challenge and with equal skill proceeded to denounce the Macedonians. He spoke at length and concluded his speech with the summation that Philip of Macedonia had conquered the Greeks only because they, as a people, could not put aside their differences long enough to unite and stop him. This time there was no applause and no garlands were thrown. The room was silent. Alexander rose and commented that Callisthenes had demonstrated not only his eloquence but also his ill-will toward the Macedonians. Years later this episode was reported to Aristotle, who allegedly said that while Callisthenes was a man who had great ability as a speaker he had very little in the way of common sense.[58]

It was not long after that incident when Alexander attempted a second time to introduce the practice of proskynesis among the Greeks and Macedonians. This time, he used his close friend and lover Hephaestion to set the stage. At another symposium that Callisthenes was required to attend, each of Alexander's closest friends, men who were privy to the plot, planned to drink from a large gold cup of wine that Alexander would circulate among the assembled guests. After drinking, each guest would spontaneously fall down before Alexander and perform the act of proskynesis, then the guest would rise to receive a kiss of friendship from the king. There was no question that the Persians present would follow suit, and it was anticipated that the Greeks and Macedonians not privy to the plot would be intimidated into following the others. Toward the end of the evening, the great cup was circulated and each guest in turn took his drink, performed his act of obeisance, and came before Alexander to receive his royal kiss.

All was proceeding according to plan until the cup came to Callisthenes. The room fell silent, but Alexander pretended to be engaged in conversation and took no notice. Callisthenes took his drink and then proceeded to the royal couch to collect his kiss. Since he had failed to perform proskynesis, Alexander denied him his kiss. Callisthenes turned to the assembled guests and commented, "I go away then, the poorer by a kiss."[59] Many of those present that night could not help but be impressed by his fearless stand against the wishes of the king, yet in the process Callisthenes had signed his own death warrant. Because Callisthenes had refused to bow down to Alexander, the practice was expected only from the barbarians at court.

At a subsequent banquet, a Persian noble performed proskynesis before Alexander and one of the Macedonian officers present began to mock him when his chin touched the ground. Alexander became so angry that he dragged the young officer from his couch and pinned him to the ground.[60] The officer would not dare to resist or struggle against the king. Alexander turned him on his belly and made him perform obeisance. Alexander inflicted upon this young man a humiliation equal to the disrespect he had shown to the king's dignity before the court. The officer was taken to prison, where he remained "a long time" before Alexander pardoned and released him.[61] The effect of the incident was that Alexander never again demanded proskynesis from the Macedonians or the Greeks, although we know from the ancient sources that the practice was still in use up to the time Alexander died in 323 B.C. The mockery of the Persians did not end, for years later when Cassander, the son of Antipater, visited Alexander at Babylon and saw the Persians performing proskynesis, he allegedly burst into laughter and Alexander, in a rage, dashed his head against a wall.

Rumors began to circulate within the royal entourage that Callisthenes was disloyal and plotting to overthrow the king. Younger officers were flocking to take instruction from the one man in the army they regarded as being truly free. When one of them asked how to become famous, Callisthenes replied, "By killing a famous man."

It was said that Callisthenes had encouraged Philotas with similar words when it came to the question about the value of murdering a tyrant.[62]

Callisthenes' reputation was now a threat to the king, and his words classified as treasonous. His very presence, Alexander feared, served as encouragement to the younger officers to defy his will and attempt to assassinate him. But there was no proof that Callisthenes was involved in any kind of conspiracy. There were no grounds to arrest him and bring him to trial before the army. In addition, Callisthenes was an Athenian citizen and a civilian, and charging him presented a difficult question of jurisdiction. The assembly of the Macedonian army, Alexander's strongest venue for disposing of his political opponents, had no jurisdiction over a Greek civilian. Given that many Macedonians and Greeks admired Callisthenes, the assembly of soldiers might well be sympathetic toward him and give him a larger forum to criticize the king. Alexander would have to wait until he could find the right circumstances to charge the philosopher with treason. That occurred within a few short weeks when another plot against the king's life surfaced.

The king had about him a retinue of young male attendants who were the sons of Macedonian nobles. Some of these nobles were serving in the army as Alexander's officers. Since the time of Philip, it had been the practice for Macedonian nobles to place their adolescent sons in the service of the king. The practice served several purposes. First, the young boys acted as hostages to guarantee the loyal behavior of their fathers. Second, it was a training ground for the young men who would later become the officers in the king's army and enter his circle of nobles. Last, it provided the king an opportunity to indoctrinate these boys and inculcate in them a loyalty to his person.

There had been pages with Alexander from the time he had left Macedonia in 334 B.C. The pages had served throughout the campaign on a rotation basis as they attended the king. While some of the tasks they performed could be menial, such as escorting the concubines to the king's chambers through a special entrance or drawing his bath, their responsibilities could also be very important, such as standing guard over the king in his quarters while he slept.[63] There were privileges in being a page, among them dining with Alexander on those occasions when he remained alone in his quarters and receiving an education from Anaxarchus and Callisthenes. There were risks as well—accompanying the king into battle or incurring his displeasure for some trivial matter could result in being soundly beaten. The pages also accompanied Alexander when he hunted, one of his favorite pastimes.

Those pages who successfully finished their period of service to the king were often promoted to officers and had the potential to eventually pursue careers as governors and administrators of his provinces. As the older pages completed their internships and moved on in their careers, younger boys came from Macedonia to take their place. The boys in the first group who came with Alexander had finished their service and been promoted as junior officers in the Companion cavalry.

A new group of fifty young pages arrived from Macedonia and took up their duties with Alexander sometime in the winter of 329–328 B.C.[64] They came in the period following the execution of Philotas and the murders of Parmenio and Cleitus. The excesses of the court life, the heavy drinking, the presence of so many Persians around the king, the whoring, and the proskynesis all must have been disturbing to those who had come from a very conservative and rustic background in Macedonia. In the court of Alexander, they witnessed all the traditional values they had been brought up to respect abandoned in favor of the "orientalizing ways" of the Persians.[65] They saw the older and respected Macedonian officers who, while reluctant to speak out, nevertheless communicated their disapproval of Alexander's behaviors. The silence of these men, brought about by their fear of incurring Alexander's anger, must have caused some of the boys to take a jaundiced view of the king.

One of the pages who had been sent from Macedonia to join Alexander was a young man named Hermolaus. Little is known of his background except that his father, Sopolis, was an officer in Alexander's army. The page is described as having been zealous in his duties and eager to please. As a student of philosophy, he took his lessons with Callisthenes and listened attentively to all his teacher had to tell him. On one occasion, while accompanying Alexander on

a hunt, Hermolaus impulsively stepped outside the bounds of protocol. In the excitement of the hunt, the young page shot a wild boar
before the king could get off his own arrow. Alexander was furious at
the impertinence of the page and whipped him in front of the others.
Under Persian custom, the boy could have been put to death for his
infraction.[66] Hermolaus was humiliated by the whipping, and as the
days and weeks passed he grew to hate Alexander more and more.

His hatred of the king grew to become so strong that Hermolaus
decided to murder Alexander. He enlisted another page, Sostratus,
who was also his lover, to help him. The boys enlisted other pages to
join in the plot, and the group of young conspirators eventually grew
to nine.[67] That the other seven boys agreed to take part in the murder is an indication of how widespread had become the general discontent with Alexander among the Macedonians and Greeks. Some
scholars have speculated that this small cabal of nine boys might
have been sent from Macedonia specifically to assassinate the king.

The pages planned to murder Alexander while he slept, since that
was when he was most vulnerable and completely in their care. The
guard duty at the king's bedchamber was rotated among the pages, so
they decided to wait until a night when they all were on duty together
before striking. That night came nearly a month later.

That the pages' plot never came to light during that time demonstrated how strong their resolve had become and how tight the bond
of loyalty was that bound them. On the night they intended to murder Alexander, the king unexpectedly decided to attend a banquet. The
pages escorted him to the banquet hall and took their customary
positions outside. There they would wait until the king was ready to
return to his chambers. Throughout the night, the pages anxiously
waited for Alexander to leave. But as the hours wore on, it became
evident that the king was going to drink until dawn. This necessitated
a change of plans. Some of the boys wanted to wait until another
opportunity, but Hermolaus argued that it would be best to murder
the king on the way back to his quarters. Hermolaus feared that the
longer the delay, the greater the chance one of them would lose his
nerve and the plot would be revealed. As the king returned to his
chambers that morning, they knew he would be drunk and probably
sleepy. They would stab him with their daggers, and killing him in

such a state, they surmised, would be easy and quick. The problem was that according to the routine, the pages would be relieved at dawn by a new group that would assume watch over the king for the next shift. They had to get to the king before the change of shifts.

The pages remained by the banquet room awaiting Alexander even though their shift had ended. When Alexander exited the banquet shortly after dawn and saw the boys waiting for him, he was touched. The boys had remained faithfully by the door awaiting him, he thought, so he rewarded each one with a gold piece. In a jovial mood, he set off to his quarters escorted by the pages.

As the pages were escorting the king to his chambers, a deranged woman unexpectedly placed herself in his path. She was a Syrian, and Alexander allowed her to wander about the royal quarters since according to Persian tradition the gods often communicated with the kings through the medium of a mad woman.[68] She often gesticulated to the king using bizarre facial expressions. Because over the years some of her predictions had come true, the king put his faith in her along with his Babylonian priests. Alexander as a young boy had seen a similar emotional and physical possession of the body by the god Bacchus in his hysterical and overwrought mother Olympias. It was something that had left a strong impression on him. The Syrian prophetess indicated to Alexander in an agitated manner that he should return to the symposium at once. Alexander was surprised but, given his love of wine and his belief in her powers, he complied. The king returned to the banquet and ordered that the entertainment continue for another two hours. His life was saved by a mad woman's premonitions.

Hermolaus and the other pages were relieved by the next shift and ordered to return to their quarters. In the course of the next few hours, one of the boys lost his nerve. Now that the plot had failed, he had become fearful for his life and confessed to his brother, another page. That morning, the two brothers talked about the potential consequences of what the younger one had involved himself in. They recalled the torture and execution of Philotas for his involvement in the plot to assassinate the king and the murders of Parmenio, Alexander the Lyncestian, and Cleitus. The more they talked, the more fearful they became for their own well-being. Finally, they decided to save themselves at the expense of the others. So, "hand in hand,"[69] the boys went to Ptolemy and Leonnatus, the king's official bodyguards, and confessed. The bodyguards immediately entered the bedchambers and woke the king "whom wine had buried deep in sleep."[70] They were not about to delay in reporting the matter and risk suffering the same consequences as Philotas the year before.

When Alexander heard what the boys had to say about the plot and listened to the recitation of the names of those involved, he realized how close he had come to death at the hands of those he trusted. Alexander immediately inquired if Callisthenes had been part of the plot, and the boys explained that while he had never taken a direct role he had lent a sympathetic ear when they had complained to him about the king's excesses. They had recommended that when Hermolaus had shown Callisthenes the marks of the whip on his back, the philosopher had told him that he was becoming a man and should act accordingly. Whether this was said as consolation for the whipping and advice to Hermolaus to bear the punishment without complaint or to incite him to revenge himself upon the king was never clear.

But it did not matter. Alexander was convinced that Callisthenes had put the boys up to it and would find the evidence to support the charge later. The king rewarded the brother who had been part of the conspiracy by sparing his life and rewarded the second brother with a considerable amount of gold and the estate of a former Persian noble. Then Alexander issued an arrest order for all those pages named as conspirators by the two brothers as well as for Callisthenes. Alexander was worn out from too much drinking and a lack of sleep, so he went back to bed for the remainder of the day and slept through the next night. It had become the king's pattern—nights of heavy drinking and days of "sleeping it off."[71] Then on the following day, refreshed, he turned to the matter of the conspiracy.

Alexander called an assembly of the Macedonians as was traditional in a matter involving an attempt upon the king's life and as he had done with Philotas. The fathers and other relatives of the boys were placed under guard, since under Macedonian law all those related by blood to anyone who conspired to murder the king, whether guilty or not, were condemned to die as well. All the boys were brought before the assembly bound in chains. Alexander, acting as prosecutor as he had at the trial of Philotas, questioned the terrified boys as to their motives. What, he cried out to the assembly, had he done to deserve this from those he entrusted with his safety? All the boys had been tortured in the same manner to extract their confessions.[72] Although the boys readily confessed to the plot when they were arrested, they were probably tortured to extract information that Callisthenes had been involved. But according to the ancient sources, none of the boys implicated Callisthenes.

Alexander gave each page the opportunity to defend himself on the charges. Only Hermolaus, the page who had been tortured the most, had the courage to respond. The boy stood before the assembly, his body broken and bleeding, and struggled to find his voice. He began by thanking the king for his generosity in allowing "a boy with no experience in public speaking" to address the Macedonian assembly in his own defense. As he found his voice and confidence, the boy explained to the soldiers that he alone had formulated the plot to rid the Greeks and Macedonians of a tyrant who sought to make slaves of free men.[73] The boy's father broke free from his guards and, embracing his son, covered his mouth to prevent him from speaking further treasonous words. Perhaps his father hoped that by silencing him the king might spare the rest of his family and kinsmen. The father cried out that the boy was crazed and begged the king not to allow him to continue to speak. It was a useless and pathetic gesture. The boy's death was already a certainty. Alexander had the father restrained and continued to question Hermolaus.

Alexander demanded that the boy tell the assembly how Callisthenes had encouraged him in his plot. The boy responded that it was not Callisthenes who had encouraged him but the king himself by his actions. The boy spoke of how Parmenio was murdered and of how his noble son Philotas was tortured on the rack for the amusement of the Persians and then executed. He recounted the murders of Attalus, Alexander the Lyncestian, and Cleitus the Black. He spoke of how few Macedonians survived Alexander's displeasure. Any who defied the will of the "god-king" by intention or by accident rarely survived his displeasure. Alexander had become a tyrant of the worst kind. He used those around him to murder those who spoke out against his injustice. Then the tyrant turned upon those who had done his dirty work and had them butchered by others in turn. All the while the king surrounded himself in luxury and cavorted with those whom Macedonians had shed their blood to conquer.

The father of Hermolaus broke free of his guard once more and, grabbing a sword, lunged at his son to kill him. The father was again restrained, and Alexander encouraged the boy to continue with his treasonous words in order to further incriminate himself. In these, the last hours of his life, Hermolaus demonstrated every quality of a brave man. Reconciled to his death, the boy showed an inner bravery as he spoke openly about those things that he believed to be wrong. The page asked why Callisthenes, a man who was skilled in speaking, was not allowed by Alexander to address the assembly. Was it because Alexander feared to hear the words of an innocent man, a free Greek, who would speak out against injustice and tyranny?

Hermolaus told the assembly that Callisthenes had no part in planning the assassination of the tyrant. The pages, he said, undertook the plot on their own because they could no longer endure the arrogance of this tyrant who renounced his father Philip and demanded to be worshiped as a god. It was not a Macedonian king they had tried to assassinate but, rather, a Persian king. Hermolaus said he could not live under such a tyrant. Better that he die on his feet as a free man than live on his knees a slave to Alexander. In the end, all Alexander's campaign would amount to would be thirty thousand mules laden with captured gold for a tyrant who would return to Greece and Macedonia to enslave more free men. The Macedonians who survived long years of suffering in the service of this tyrant would return home with heavy hearts and only the scars of battle to show for their efforts. Alexander was a tyrant, and Hermolaus was seeking to free the Greeks and Macedonians from his yoke. All that the boy said was pure Callisthenes. Hermolaus concluded his words by saying that he was prepared to be led to his execution. But death would not be easy, quick, or merciful for the young page and his associates.

When Hermolaus had finished, Alexander rose to address the assembly. He reminded the Macedonians who sat in judgment and those who were watching the proceedings how generous he had been by

allowing the page to speak freely. Without censorship, he had allowed
the boy to speak all the evil he had been taught by his teacher Callisthenes. What had Alexander done to this boy? True, he had whipped
him for his impertinence on the hunt as any father had a right to
whip his son, his wife, or his slave under the most ancient practices
of the Macedonians.[74] The members of the assembly nodded in assent,
and Alexander continued.

What the boy should have borne as a simple, even fatherly lesson
on his way to manhood he instead transformed into a heinous plot
of revenge against a king whom the entire world knew to be natu-
rally disposed to kindness. Alexander was not to be outdone by a boy
when it came to eloquence and managing a stage production like this
one. If the boy were speaking the truth, it did not matter. He was an
amateur, and Alexander was a seasoned orator.

Furthermore, Alexander could not let this boy have the last word.
The king felt compelled to address and defend each issue the boy had
raised to the assembly. From the execution of Philotas to the thirty
thousand mules laden with gold to his claim to be a god, Alexander
refuted point by point each argument the boy had raised. Scars? The
Macedonians would only have scars to show for their service with
Alexander the Great? Let the boy look out at the army of Alexander.
Men who once slept on the cold ground in their native Macedonia
and Greece now took their leisure on couches of silver. Men who
once ate from simple tables now had their tables laden with gold.
Men who once had to tend to themselves now had slaves to wait on
them and concubines to fulfill their every wish. It would take more
mules than could be found in all of Asia to transport back to Greece
and Macedonia all the riches Alexander had won for his army.

To the charge that he favored the Persians, Alexander responded
that he treated all, including the vanquished, with mercy, generosity, and kindness. True, they had once been enemies, but why had he
come to Asia? It was not to conquer these vast and wealthy lands by
the sword but to hold Asia through clemency, kindness, and the everlasting gratitude of its people. It was his intent to incorporate the
vanquished into his new regime, to give them a share in a bright new
future, not to alienate them further and keep them forever hostile

and on the verge of rebellion. As to the charge that he was attempting to replace the old Macedonian ways and values with Persian ones, there was no merit to it. These empires had valuable contributions to make beyond merely their gold and silver. The Greeks and Macedonians would be foolish to ignore and fail to incorporate them. They should learn from those whom they had conquered.

Alexander then turned to address the charge that he claimed to be a god, the son of Zeus. It was the oracle of Zeus-Ammon in Egypt that had declared him the son of the god. It had not been Alexander's idea. Alexander maintained that he could not control the responses of the gods. If they wished to declare him the son of Zeus, who was he to dispute them? Alexander declared that he had accepted the designation because it would assist him as he conquered the peoples of Asia. These were highly religious and superstitious peoples, and it would make their acceptance of Macedonian rule that much easier if they looked upon Alexander as a god.

What was it that he sought to accomplish in his life? True, it was his goal to "subdue the whole world."[75] And it was this glory, which would be shared by every soldier who marched with him, that Hermolaus was seeking to deny them by killing their king. Even worse, had the pages succeeded, they would be leaderless and were sure to be defeated and destroyed by the barbarians. It was he who held the army together, and it was his vision that had brought them to Asia and would take them home safely.

As a display of the mercy and kindness for which he was known throughout the world, Alexander informed the assembly that he would suspend the traditional Macedonian practice of executing the innocent relatives and kinsmen of those who had been found guilty of plotting against the king. The fathers and kinsmen of the pages would be spared execution and would retain their positions in his army. As for Callisthenes, he knew why the boy wanted the philosopher present. It was so that Callisthenes could reiterate those same tired and worn criticisms they had all heard from him previously. Alexander contended that on legal grounds he could not bring Callisthenes before a council of Macedonians because as a Greek he had no right to be admitted.[76]

When Alexander finished, the pages were found guilty as charged and the king sentenced them to death by stoning. These sons of some of the most prominent Macedonian nobles were placed huddling and terrified in a circle, where they were pelted with rocks by the thousands of soldiers who surrounded them. They were executed in a most cruel and prolonged manner as their tormentors used the opportunity as a sadistic demonstration of their loyalty to the king.[77] Some modern scholars have been so disgusted by the barbaric execution of the young pages that they have termed it "repugnant" and an "atrocity that no reason of state can justify."[78] The vicious manner in which the pages were executed and the torture and crucifixion of Callisthenes that was to come showed how twisted and warped Alexander's mind was becoming.

The reality of life under Alexander was that anyone arrested by order of the king on suspicion of treason and prosecuted by the king in an assembly of soldiers convened by the king had no chance of acquittal. Being arrested on orders of Alexander was by this point in the story in and of itself a de facto death sentence. Any trial was a mere formality.

All the sources are in agreement that Callisthenes was tortured in an effort to force him to confess to his involvement in the plot to assassinate Alexander. He would not. This was the man who had prepared for Alexander his little book of the Trojan War that in more congenial times Alexander had said he treasured most of all his possessions, so much so that he reputedly slept with it under his pillow each night.[79]

The general consensus among historians and scholars is that Callisthenes was not guilty of having had any direct part in the plot. It was a convenient way for Alexander to be rid of a man he had come to dislike intensely since, like Cleitus, Callisthenes had become a constant source of criticism.[80] Callisthenes had been losing favor at court for some time due to his criticism of proskynesis and his resistance to the idea of divine honors for Alexander. His only crimes seem to have been believing that Greeks should be free and that Alexander's lifestyle was excessive. Some time later Alexander wrote to Antipater that he believed Callisthenes was part of a larger plot to murder him that had been hatched in Greece and Macedonia. He vowed to punish not only Callisthenes "but those who sent him to me and those who harbor in their cities men who plot against my life."[81]

Since Callisthenes was both a civilian and a Greek, he presented Alexander with a unique dilemma in regard to his trial. The army could not try him, as he was a civilian and not Macedonian. He could not simply be executed since as a Greek, by law, he was entitled to a trial by the Athenians. One option Alexander considered was to send him back to Greece to be tried at Corinth by the council of city-states called the synhedrion, perhaps with Aristotle in attendance.[82] But Alexander dropped that idea because the trial might easily become a general forum for the expression of the political discontent that was brewing in Greece.

There are conflicting accounts as to exactly how Callisthenes died. Some sources maintain that the philosopher was tortured on the rack and then hanged or crucified shortly after the execution of the pages.[83] Other sources believe that for months he was dragged behind the army as a prisoner in chains until he died of disease.[84] Others assert that he was bound hand and foot, kept in a prison, and allowed to die from disease, obesity, and lice.[85]

When news of the torture and later the death of the respected philosopher reached Greece, it engendered considerable animosity, even hatred, toward Alexander.[86] Many Greeks, especially the philosophers of Athens, were critical of Alexander, as they believed he had violated a fundamental tenet of Greek law; he had tortured and executed a citizen without giving him the benefit of a trial. The death of Callisthenes was viewed by many as murder and paralleled the fate of Socrates, the teacher who had been executed for allegedly corrupting the youth of Athens by encouraging them to question authority. Callisthenes had spoken to the pages on the virtue of killing a despot, and this had influenced the impressionable young boys to attempt the assassination of Alexander. In subsequent years the Peripatetic School of philosophy in Athens, established by Aristotle, condemned Alexander as a tyrant and as a man who wasted everything the gods and fortune had bestowed on him.

Alexander was characterized as a man intoxicated by his power and not mature enough to make the right use of what fortune had bestowed upon him.[87] He was seen as having failed to learn the most important lesson Aristotle had sought to teach him, that self-control was the key element in the character of any great man. Aristotle believed that a man who was able to conquer himself was to be admired more than a man who conquered others. Yet in spite of the execution of Callisthenes and the hostility of the Greek philosophers, Alexander and Aristotle continued their correspondence.

CHAPTER 5

DOWN THE
INDUS RIVER

IN THE SPRING OF 327 B.C., ALEXANDER ONCE MORE SET OUT to suppress any remaining resistance and pacify Bactria and Sogdiana. By the end of that summer, he had devastated the countryside and imposed his peace on its people. While he was campaigning, Alexander received considerable numbers of Greek reinforcements and news that Erigyius, one of his older and most competent and faithful generals, and the one who had defeated and killed Satibarzanes in combat in Aria, had died of natural causes.[1]

As Alexander had suppressed the last remaining pockets of resistance in the northern parts of Sogdiana and was returning to Bactria in the south, he came upon a number of fortified positions in the mountains that constituted the last of the resistance to his rule. The first was under the control of Sisimithres, the incestuous satrap of Nautaca. Nautaca was a city as well as the name of the mountainous area situated southeast of Marakanda. Sisimithres had married his mother and had two children by her, a common practice in that part of the ancient world according to the sources.[2] After some initial resistance, Oxartes, a Sogdian noble and ally of Alexander, was able to convince Sisimithres to surrender. Alexander kept his two sons as hostages to ensure their father's continued loyalty.[3]

In the same area another rebel leader, Ariamazes, had secured a much higher mountain fortress called the Sogdian Rock. Scholars contend that this mountain can be found about 170 kilometers due south of Samarkand in the small village of Derbent. On this rock, which according to the ancient sources was thirty stadia high,[4] Ariamazes

had massed nearly thirty thousand armed men and enough provisions
to hold out against Alexander for years. Among those sequestered
with the defenders on the mountain was a Bactrian noble named
Oxyartes and his family. The mountain seemed impregnable, and the
Sogdian defenders taunted Alexander and his men from the heights
above, telling them they would need to grow wings and fly up to do
battle with them. Alexander recruited a group of some three hundred
of his men who had experience in climbing mountains and sent them
during the night to scale the cliffs that loomed above the fortress.
In their ascent, more than thirty of these men fell to their deaths.
The next morning when Ariamazes and Oxyartes saw that Alexander's men were above them, they quickly negotiated a surrender.
What they did not know was how small a detachment of Alexander's
men actually held the heights above them and how weakened those
men were from their arduous climb the night before. Ariamazes and
his men could easily have overpowered them, but the psychological
effect of what they had done so unnerved Ariamazes that he surrendered without a fight. Alexander had Ariamazes crucified at the foot
of the rock for his taunts about growing wings but spared Oxyartes
and his family. The Sogdian Rock and the region around it were then
handed over to Artabazus to be administered within the confines of
his Bactrian satrapy.[5]

Oxyartes cooperated with Alexander, and over the following
months he became a strong ally of the king. The Bactrian nobleman
accompanied Alexander when the Macedonians and Greeks laid
siege to a third mountain fortress near the Varduj River, an area of
eastern Afghanistan where the mountains rise to heights of fifteen
thousand feet.

At this mountain stronghold, Alexander's army found the fortress
further protected by deep ravines on all sides. Like the Sogdian Rock,
it seemed impregnable until Alexander ordered his engineers to do
the impossible. They systematically started filling in the ravines with
felled trees and dirt. As the ravines were slowly filled, Alexander's
troops advanced toward the walls of the fortress. When it became
inevitable that Alexander's troops would reach the fortress walls,
Oxyartes convinced the Bactrian noble Chorienes, who was also his

friend, to surrender. To show his good faith, Chorienes provisioned Alexander's army and later hosted the wedding of Alexander to Roxanne in his fortress.[6]

Roxanne was a young girl who had been captured along with her father, the baron Oxyartes, at the Sogdian Rock.[7] Her name in Uzbek means "pretty face." Alexander allegedly first saw her at a banquet given by the baron Chorienes.[8] At this banquet, she performed a ritual dance for the guests during which Alexander allegedly fell passionately in love with her. She was reputed to have been the most beautiful woman in Asia, and her beauty rivaled that of Stateira, the deceased wife of King Darius who was described as the most beautiful woman in Persia. Alexander, according to the sources, could simply have taken Roxanne and added her to his collection of concubines, but instead he chose to marry her. Alexander was now twenty-nine years old, and while those around him had urged him to marry they had not anticipated that he would choose a barbarian bride. According to the sources, the marriage was motivated by love and was a true affair of the heart.[9] But more skeptical scholars view the marriage as another shrewd political move by Alexander. One scholar even maintains that the only woman Alexander ever cared about during his entire life was "his terrible mother," Olympias.[10] The political advantages of the marriage were obvious. It was a gesture of reconciliation between Alexander and his former enemies and an attempt to cement his recent alliances. That the lord of Asia, Alexander of Macedon, would take an Asian bride was a move intended to flatter the Persians and the local leaders and keep them loyal. It did not sit well with the Greeks and Macedonians.

This was not the first time Alexander had considered marriage to a barbarian princess. The Sacae, a tribal people who occupied the areas on the far eastern frontier of Sogdiana, several months earlier had sent ambassadors to Alexander with a proposal that he marry the daughter of one of their chiefs. Alexander declined the proposal but did think the political ramifications of the idea were so good that he persuaded several of his officers to marry daughters of the local nobility in Sogdiana. The officers were probably the ones who were being left behind to administer the provinces, and the marriages were arranged to strengthen Alexander's control of the area. The proposal of the Sacae that Alexander marry one of the daughters of a tribal chief probably influenced him to marry Roxanne some months later.

The marriage of Alexander and Roxanne was performed at the fortress of the Bactrian noble Chorienes and, according to at least one source, was carried out according to Persian rituals. Another source contends that the ceremony was carried out in the traditional Macedonian fashion by dividing a round of bread that both parties to the marriage tasted. Some modern scholars have seen in the marriage to Roxanne a reflection of Alexander's ideal of the equality of the Persians, Greeks, and Macedonians.[11] The marriage in this light is viewed as an example of how Alexander intended to fuse the Asian people with his Macedonians and Greeks. The mass marriages between Persians and Macedonians that would be carried out just a few years later near the end of Alexander's life were, for these scholars, the culmination of that idea.

The Macedonians and the Greeks did not care for the marriage of Alexander to Roxanne or his ideas on the fusion of Greek and barbarian civilizations. They had fought long and hard against these barbarians, and they did not embrace the prospect of the Orientals becoming their equals or their king's marrying a barbarian woman who would become the queen of his new empire. To them, Alexander was following his passions and not his intellect. It was one thing to lie with a barbarian woman; it was another thing to marry her. In their eyes, the king had contracted a marriage with a woman markedly his inferior in personal qualities and by birth.[12] For the Greeks and Macedonians, marriage was regarded as the patriotic duty of every male citizen to strengthen the state. Marriage needed to be to an appropriate partner. To be motivated, as Alexander allegedly was, by passion was for them a sign of weak and undesirable conduct. Roxanne became pregnant in short order, and Alexander eagerly attended the birth of his heir the following year.[13]

After the wedding ceremony, Alexander returned to Balkh. He sent Craterus east along the Oxus River to build two new Alexandrias. Craterus had the two mud-brick towns built near the river, one by the modern Uzbek city of Termez and the second one at Ay Khanom about 250 kilometers farther east along the river.[14] At each of these new towns Craterus forcibly settled more of the Greek and Mace-donian mercenaries.

Some of the colonists no doubt took advantage of the generous land grants that Alexander must have extended as an inducement for them to settle there. When both towns had been laid out and fortifi-cations were in place, Craterus left the colonists to begin their new lives while he returned to join Alexander.

As Alexander pacified Bactria and Sogdiana, he absorbed many of his former enemies into his own army as allies. This was a technique that had worked well for him with the Persians, and Alexander anticipated that his new allies would supplement his forces for the next stage of his campaign—the invasion of India. Some of the allies Alexander enlisted were fierce nomads from the steppes of Central Asia. Among them were the Dahae from western Bactria, the Sacae from eastern Sogdiana, and the Massagetae who had brought him the head of Spitamenes.

By the late summer of 327 B.C., Bactria and Sogdiana had been stabilized enough that Alexander was able to begin his preparations for the invasion of India. Large numbers of Greeks and Macedonians were left behind to populate the new cities and towns founded by Alexander. Alexander left Oxyartes, his father-in-law, as satrap of Bactria and Sogdiana to replace Artabazus.

As Alexander prepared to leave Bactria, he ordered the establish-ment of a special school to train thirty thousand native boys who had been orphaned in the fighting of the past few years. They were to be educated in Greek and taught a Macedonian style of warfare. The school was staffed with instructors who were ordered to complete the training over the next several years and then bring the boys to Alexander.

The provision to train these boys and form them into a significant paramilitary force is evidence that Alexander was establishing the core for a future army. It is doubtful that he established this school solely for altruistic and compassionate reasons. It was composed of young men who would be conditioned to Alexander's way of think-ing and would have no allegiance to any family or country. It was evident that Alexander was planning an empire where Greeks and Macedonians would not play a prominent military role. Many of the veteran soldiers were aging, and a significant number of them were reputed to have reached their sixties.

By the autumn of 327 B.C., Alexander's army had come to exceed 120,000 people. This figure seems high to most scholars, and a more probable estimate is 40,000–50,000 fighting men who were now a multinational force of Greeks, Macedonians, Persians, Bactrians, and Sogdians. Alexander's army for the invasion of India, trained by fighting in Bactria and Sogdiana, had become much more mobile than it had been in Persia.

In addition to the combat forces, there was a siege train comprised of a staff of engineers from Greece and Macedonia as well as formidable war engines. There were catapults to keep the defenders of besieged cities hunkered down behind their walls while Alexander's assault troops stormed them on the other side. There were wooden towers, some as high as fifty meters, mounted on wheels five meters in diameter. These towers were filled with Alexander's archers, who concentrated their fire on the upper walls of the cities, keeping the defenders pinned down, while the engineers worked to undermine the walls from below. There were assault ramps that were often constructed on the spot and then pushed up against the city walls and battering rams to smash through the gates. There were wooden shelters called tortoises that protected the soldiers from burning oil poured down on them as they stormed the city walls. The Macedonian siege warfare was an effective battle tactic because it combined a strong infantry attack on the walls with the well-engineered machines of destruction.

We know from the sources that there were many camp followers and noncombatants with the army. Among the noncombatants were engineers, surveyors, and architects who would lay out and build the king's new cities and towns. There was an extensive commissariat that was charged with collecting and distributing supplies from each district the army conquered as well as supervising and storing the treasures taken from those territories. The secretariat was responsible for keeping a daily journal, the official record of the expedition, that included not only the events of the expedition but such mundane factors as distances covered each day. Then there was a host of resident philosophers, historians, scientists, artists, poets, and other entertainers who followed the expedition to either chronicle and immortalize the king's conquests or keep him amused. The geographers and cartographers plotted the new terrain and collected other relevant information on the route, while the botanists collected specimens of new plants and cataloged the varieties of new animals they discovered. A staff of Greek doctors tended to the sick and wounded. Among the camp followers who traveled behind the army were the usual assortment of merchants and prostitutes as well as cooks, tradesmen, craftsmen, artisans, scribes, common laborers, the wives and captive women of the soldiers, their children, large numbers of slaves, and the native guides. In all, the combined numbers could well have reached the level of 120,000 people mentioned in the sources.

In the autumn of 327 B.C. Alexander crossed back over the Hindu Kush Mountains before the winter snows blocked the passes. Once more, in a dramatic gesture to prepare the army for the new phase of the campaign, he ordered all the carts loaded with treasure and burned before they crossed over the mountains. Just as he had done in Iran, Alexander started with his own possessions and promised his men that there would be more treasure for them when they reached India.[15] While it is fairly certain that Alexander entered the Panjshir Valley and took the Khawak Pass (4,431 meters) over the mountains when he entered Bactria, his return was over much lower passes and easier valleys. The army marched over the far easier Ak-Robat (3,125 meters) pass that today leads from Mazar-I-Sharif over the mountains and into the Bamyan Valley. From there the army would have moved east to Kabul. Today in that same valley are the remains of the once magnificent Buddha statutes recently destroyed by the Taliban. These two statues, which each rose to a height of more than 50 meters, were estimated to have been nearly two thousand years old. They had been carved into the side of the rock cliffs in a style known as Gandhara or Indo-Greek and were probably the work of descendants of the Greek artists who came with Alexander and remained behind. Traveling along the Bamyan Valley, Alexander took either the Shibar Pass near the village of Sar-e-Kotal (2,987 meters), or he could have come directly from Mazar-I-Sharif over the Salang Pass (3,172 meters), which today leads directly to Kabul through a long tunnel. Either of these routes would have been much easier to follow than the hellacious inward march over the Khawak had been nearly two years before.

After arriving at Alexandria Caucasus (Kabul), the army gathered provisions and then followed a route east along the Cophen (Kabul) River until it reached what is today Jalalabad in Afghanistan. There Alexander founded another new city that he named Nikea, which means "victory" in ancient Greek. Traces of this city are still visible near the village of Mandrawar on the lower Alingar River, northwest of modern-day Jalalabad. Perdiccas and Hephaestion, two of Alexander's principal commanders, led the larger part of the army east along both the north and the south banks of the Cophen River toward India.[16]

The army was met at the Khyber Pass by emissaries from Alexander's first Indian ally, Taxiles. Taxiles was the ruler of the kingdom of Taxila in what is today Pakistan. He sent his son Omphis to Alexander with a gift of twenty-five war elephants. Taxiles died shortly thereafter, and Omphis took the name of his deceased father. Taxila was the first principality in India that received Alexander as an ally.

During the spring of 326 B.C. Alexander carried out a series of devastating campaigns, first against the inhabitants of the Cophen Valley along the Kabul River and then against the towns and cities of the Swat Valley in what today is the northwest territory of Pakistan. He justified his actions by maintaining that he was not going to allow the same thing to happen to him in India that had happened in Bactria and Sogdiana. His armies would no longer march through the countryside unopposed by the local population only to have pockets of resistance spring up behind them. The campaign into the Swat Valley was particularly brutal. It was a campaign of calculated terror and slaughter intended to cow the local populations and spread word of Alexander's might to the other kingdoms of India. That did not happen. Resistance to Alexander's invasion continued throughout his campaign in India.

At Jalalabad, Alexander took a mobile force of infantry and his cavalry and branched off from the slower moving main column. Following the Choaspes River north into the Chitral Valley of Afghanistan, he crossed over the Nana Pass and moved his forces east into the

Swat Valley near Mingadra (the ancient capital of Swat). Alexander had undertaken a flanking movement, probably suggested by Taxiles and intended to cover the main army from any possible attack by hostile forces from the Swat Valley. The first city Alexander attacked was called Massaga, located in the lower Swat Valley.[17] This city was the capital of an Indian people known as the Assaceni who were ruled by a queen, Cleophis.

The city was defended by a large number of experienced Indian mercenaries who had been brought from the eastern parts of the country to reinforce the native defenders. The mercenaries numbered close to ten thousand men, and they resisted Alexander's assault for nine days.[18] Alexander was injured in the fighting and is reported to have been surprised that blood flowed from his wound instead of the ichor that flows in the veins of gods. The court philosopher Dioxippus was right by the king's side to assure him that even gods felt pain and not to be distressed.

After several days, Alexander negotiated a settlement with the queen. He offered her mercenaries and their families safe conduct out of the city in return for the surrender of the city. The Indian mercenaries agreed, and when the last elements of their column had cleared the city gates Alexander had them ambushed. The mercenaries formed a circle to protect their women and children against the attack of Alexander's infantry. It was a futile defense by men who had been caught unprepared. The mercenaries and their families were all massacred. When asked why he had failed to honor his word, Alexander replied that while he had given the mercenaries his assurances of safe conduct out of the city he had said not one word about what would happened to them once they left.[19] In the course of occupying the city Alexander had an assignation with the queen,[20] thus putting to rest any misconceptions of his romantic infatuation with Roxanne, who was about to give birth to his son.

From Massaga, Alexander moved north into the upper reaches of the Swat Valley. As his army advanced, the local people fled and took refuge in the next valley to the east. There they congregated on the top of a massive natural fortification called Aornos.[21] Aornos is still today an imposing mountain that according to legend even Heracles, the son of Zeus, could not conquer.[22]

That was all that Alexander had to hear. He had to capture the rock and best Heracles. Heracles was a special figure for Alexander. The legendary son of Zeus had performed so many heroic deeds during his lifetime that the gods had granted him immortality for his service to humanity.

The storming of the great rock, however, was not just motivated by Alexander's ego. It was also consistent with his strategy not to leave an enemy force behind him. Those who resisted Alexander when he conquered their lands either ended by joining him as allies or were buried in the ground he left behind. With the lower Indus and Peshawar Valleys secured by the larger army of Hephaestion and Perdiccas and no threat from the upper valleys, Alexander was able to concentrate on taking Aornos.

The mountain rises nearly seven thousand feet above the Indus River and covers a circumference of some twelve miles. The river wraps around three sides of its sheer cliffs, and the only ascent to the plateau at the top was via a single path surrounded by deep ravines and inaccessible cliffs.

Aornos is composed of two high ridges known as the Pir-sar and the Una-sar. These ridges are part of a number of spurs that the Himalaya Mountain Range throws out to the south. Pir-sar, the higher of the two, is level at the top and offers ample space for raising crops and grazing animals. The winter snows melt rapidly in the full sun of springtime, so there is abundant water for the inhabitants to drink as well as to irrigate their fields. The nearly level portion of its top extends for more than a mile and a half and offers dramatic views of the plain of the Peshawar Valley to the south. A conical hill called the Bar-sar (meaning "high end") is located at the northern end of Pir-sar and rises to a height of nearly a thousand feet above the plateau. It was on this hill, archeologists and historians have speculated, that the defenders fortified themselves against Alexander's attack.

Aornos was first located and identified in the Indus Valley by the noted British explorer and archeologist Sir Aurel Stein in 1904 and then extensively surveyed by him in 1926. The Swat and Indus Valleys only became accessible to Europeans after the warring tribes who inhabit them were pacified by the British in a series of campaigns in 1880 and 1892 known as the Black Mountain Campaigns. The area today is one of the most dangerous in Pakistan and is still largely under tribal rule. The current ruler of Swat is Prince Miangul Aurangzeb. Swat is home to a thriving father-and-son arms industry that dates back at least a century. Small storefront shops manufacture, trade, and sell a variety of weapons to buyers from all over the world, especially Africa and Asia. Portraits of Osama bin Laden are everywhere.

Alexander determined that the main assault against Aornos would have to be against the fortress on the Bar-sar.[23] The position, in addition to its strategic location and height, is further protected by a deep ravine. This ravine, two hundred meters deep and nearly five hundred meters across, separated Alexander's army camp from the fortress. Alexander ordered his men to fill in the ravine with tree trunks and earth just as they had done at the fortress of Chorienes in Bactria. It took several days to complete the task, and when it was done Alexander ordered an assault up the steep slopes.

Alexander's general Ptolemy was sent ahead with a lightly armed force to occupy a smaller but higher plateau above the level of the fortress. It was the side of Bar-sar where Alexander had determined that an attack would have the best chance of success. Ptolemy's forces were able to guard the route leading up from the river and were in position to support the main force as it made its assault.

When the main elements of the army had reached the plateau and were in position, Alexander selected thirty young boys from among his pages to lead the assault. No doubt he had selected them so that they might demonstrate their loyalty and remove the stain on their reputation from the assassination conspiracy of the year before. Without the option of refusal, the pages took up their weapons. They were inexperienced boys and perished in the very first attempt to storm the fortress. The Indians rolled large rocks down on the pages as they were climbing up the cliffs. Those who were struck by the rocks lost their grip on the steep crags and fell to their deaths several thousand feet below. Two of the pages managed by some miracle to get high enough to engage the Indian defenders in hand-to-hand combat. Their efforts came to nothing, as both boys were quickly overpowered by the defenders and hurled to their deaths.

Casualties among the Macedonians and Greeks were high as they persevered in their assault on the rock fortress. Then the Indians sent heralds to Alexander and offered to discuss terms of surrender. They had no intent to negotiate a surrender but only to stop the assault in order to allow their main force to abandon the fortress and disperse into the surrounding countryside. Alexander realized their plan and even while negotiating with the Indian ambassadors elements of his army laid an ambush for the Indian soldiers and their families as they were leaving the fortress. The Macedonians slew many and drove countless others to their deaths off the steep precipices. At a high price in casualties, Alexander finally took the rock that legend said even Heracles could not conquer.

After his victory at Aornos, Alexander had a fortified post built on the mountaintop and erected altars to the god of victory, Nikea. Alexander then descended the Indus Valley and entered Taxila, a city even greater in size and splendor than Massaga. It was now the early summer of 326 B.C. Taxila was a thriving commercial center with a university and a community of artists, writers, poets, and philosophers. It was reputed to be the most magnificent of the Indian cities between the Indus and the Jhelum Rivers and controlled a kingdom as big as Egypt and equally as rich.

When Alexander entered the city, King Taxiles greeted him warmly and proposed that there was wealth enough for them both to share and no need for war between them. The Indian king asked only that Alexander and his army not deprive his people of water and food. All the rest was of little value and could well be shared. Alexander conferred gifts on Taxiles, who responded to this generosity by conferring even more gifts on Alexander. Back and forth it went, each man trying to outdo the other in his generosity. In the end, in spite of their amicability toward each other and pledges of friendship, Taxiles like so many other kings before him became a vassal to Alexander.[24] No king no matter how kind, wise, or generous, as Taxiles was reputed to be, would ever be allowed to rule his kingdom as the equal of Alexander.

The area around Taxila and most of the adjoining territory along the Indus River, especially the area of modern-day Pakistan known as the Northwest Frontier, eventually became the favored location for the majority of the colonists in India. It was the only place in this country where the Greeks and Macedonians could tolerate the extremes of temperatures[25] and endure the array and number of dangerous animals and vipers that existed there. Taxila became the seat of government for a long succession of Greco-Bactrian rulers.[26]

As Alexander and his army continued to move east, the minor principalities and the cities of India fell to him one by one. Many capitulated without a fight, but many more resisted. The principal opponent of Alexander in India became Porus. Of all the kings in India, this giant of a man alone refused to surrender. He assembled his army and prepared to do battle with Alexander on the shores of the Hydaspes River (modern-day Jhelum) sometime between May and July 326 B.C. The battle with Porus is among the most dramatic and well documented of all Alexander's military encounters.[27] Alexander's planning and battle tactics were developed and executed without flaw. He has traditionally been portrayed, in this battle, as the commander who foresaw every possible move by his adversary and planned for every contingency. Scholars have speculated that the battle might have taken place around Jalalpur, a small town just southeast of the modern city of Jhelum. Porus was himself a clever tactician. His army of infantry, cavalry, chariots, and war elephants held the eastern bank of the Hydaspes River and waited for Alexander and his army to come across the river to them.

Porus was reputed to have been nearly seven feet tall—a giant among the men of his time. In his golden armor and seated astride the biggest elephant the Greeks and Macedonians had ever seen, he was an intimidating sight. The Indian king drew up his forces on the banks of the river and waited. Alexander made a show of preparing to cross the river on several occasions. Each time, there was an immediate counterresponse from Porus. At the same time that Alexander was pretending to cross, he sent scouts farther upriver to find an easier crossing and one that was not defended. The scouts found a place some twenty-five to thirty kilometers above where Porus was camped. To keep Porus from discovering what he was planning, Alexander continued to make his feints at crossing the Hydaspes in front of the Indian camp. This kept Porus and his army continually on the alert both day and night. When no threat ever materialized and after several stressful days and sleepless nights, the Indians grew weary of mobilizing every time Alexander made a move. Finally, they stopped reacting to his feints. Then the one time they let their guard down, Alexander moved against them.

On a stormy night, Alexander led a portion of his army out of camp and up the river to the crossing point his scouts had marked out. The larger part of his army remained in camp in full view of the Indians. As Alexander and his soldiers marched upriver, the rains increased. There was considerable lightning and thunder, which served to cover his army's movements. The lightning strikes became so frequent and the bolts so intense that a number of Alexander's men were struck and killed as they crossed the river. Most of Alexander's force made it across the river, which though running swiftly and in spite of the heavy rain was only chest-deep and fordable.

When Alexander's soldiers had regrouped on the far bank, the king, as was his nature, immediately set off with the faster-moving cavalry units and headed downstream toward the Indian camp. The slower-moving infantry followed behind in formation for battle. At a prearranged signal, the main force, which had been left behind in camp, entered the river and made a frontal assault against the Indian camp. By the time Porus and his army realized what was happening, it was too late—Alexander was on them, and the battle ensued. As Porus turned his forces north to meet the threat, Alexander and his horsemen assaulted the left flank of the Indian army while Coenus and his cavalry detachments attacked the right. This left the middle of Porus's army, where the massive war elephants and heavily armored infantry were concentrated, with no enemy in front of them to fight. There was confusion in the ranks of the Indians as both wings of their army collapsed under the Macedonian envelopments. The battle lasted all through the night in the thunder and lightning until, at daybreak, the Indians gave up.

During the course of the fighting, Porus was wounded by a number of spears. His elephant, sensing its master had been hurt, allegedly knelt on the ground and with its trunk gently pulled the spears from the king's armor. It was a sight that moved not only the Macedonians who saw it but Alexander himself. When Porus was captured, his wounds were treated; when he was well enough, he was brought before Alexander. The two proud kings faced each other. Alexander spoke first and asked Porus how he wished to be treated now that he had been defeated. The giant Indian looked down on the diminutive Macedonian who had dealt him such a resounding defeat and replied "like a king."[28] The answer so impressed Alexander that he not only accepted Porus as a vassal but increased the size of his kingdom by adding to it some of the areas that had already been conquered by the Macedonians and the Greeks in the area of the Indus.

While Alexander had defeated Porus at the Hydaspes River, it was clearly a Pyrrhic victory for the Macedonian king. The battle with Porus had drained the last of the strength and morale from the army. Yet Alexander continued to drive his men farther east. He would not quit. Alexander had visions of conquering everything to the known limits of the ancient world. He would continue to fight as long as there was someone left to fight with. For him, death in the pursuit of glory was a guarantee of immortality. He would live on forever in history. It was an attractive prospect by which to end his life, and it had been the choice his hero Achilles had made. The Macedonians and Greeks shared none of his vision. For most of them, all they could see before them was an unmarked grave in some barbarian land far from their homes and families.

Finally, after more than two months of slow and relentless marching under the worst of conditions, Alexander and his army reached the Hyphasis River.[29] They had only traveled 170 kilometers since they had left the shores of the Hydaspes. Nature finally forced Alexander to give up. His men had endured all they could over the last two months of endless marching and incessant fighting in bad weather. The monsoon season had begun, and conditions for the army had become miserable. The rains were unending and often violent. Beginning during the battle with Porus was a period of seventy straight days of the worst weather they had ever encountered.[30] In addition to the continual rain, there were often heavy thunder and deadly lightning strikes.[31] Everything was always wet, and the equipment rotted. There was disease everywhere in the camp now along with a plague of rats, mosquitoes, and poisonous snakes, which made conditions miserable during the day and deprived the soldiers of sleep at night. Malaria came into the camp daily to take away more of them. On the banks of the Hyphasis, Nature dealt Alexander the first major defeat of his charmed career, and she was preparing to deal him yet another equally severe blow in the months to come in the deserts of southern Pakistan.

It was now September, and on the western shores of the Hyphasis River Alexander gave orders that the army was to prepare to march east to the Ganges River.[32] The Ganges, Alexander's geographers and native scouts told him, could only be reached after a twelve-day march through a vast desert. Beyond the Ganges they would find the land of the Praesii and the Ganderites. Rumors began to circulate among the troops that even if they got through the desert and reached the Ganges they would never be able to cross it. The river was more than two kilometers wide and was hundreds of meters deep and filled with man-eating reptiles.[33] On the far side waited the combined armies of two kings reputed to number more than eighty thousand cavalry, two hundred thousand infantry, eight thousand war chariots, and six thousand elephants.[34] Porus confirmed Alexander's worst fears about the size and composition of the Indian army they would be facing. Alexander's men were tired and despondent, and they were frightened of what lay ahead. The Macedonians and Greeks had subdued the Punjab for Alexander, and they vowed that they had done enough.[35] They wanted to go home, and there were doubts about whether or not they would fight.

What really lay beyond the Hyphasis? There was no desert between the two rivers. The Thar Desert does separate the lower reaches of the Indus basin from the Ganges and extends to a width of some 360 kilometers, but not at the latitude where Alexander and his army were crossing. The desert is much farther south. The ancient geographers often were wrong in their calculations.

Alexander believed that beyond the Ganges River there was a rich and populous land with an aristocratic constitution and elephants bigger than anything they had seen in all their travels. The irony, according to at least one credible source, is that Alexander might have conquered all of India if he had pressed on. Xandrames, the stronger of the two kings opposing him on the Ganges, was allegedly disliked by his people. If Alexander had invaded, speculation is that the local people as well as units of the king's army might have revolted. Alexander would have been welcomed as a liberator, conquered the lands east of the Ganges, perhaps reached China, and fulfilled his dream.[36]

However, the Hyphasis River was the limit of Alexander's eastern conquest. He was forced to stop there for three reasons: his troops were fed up with his wars; they feared what the future held for them; and the incessant rains had sapped their will to go on. Alexander sensed that his men had reached their limit, so he tried to improve their mood by allowing them to sack the rich territory between the rivers. While his soldiers plundered, murdered, and raped, Alexander remained in camp making generous dispensations to their wives and children in terms of gifts, bonuses, and retirements. But these were only temporary measures that bought a little time and some compliance with his wishes. In the end, nothing he did was able to stifle the discontent that eventually came to mutiny.[37]

It fell upon Coenus to confront Alexander with the arguments for returning home. Coenus had been among the most loyal and obedient of Alexander's commanders. He had tortured Philotas to prove his loyalty to Alexander. He had commanded cavalry, infantry, siege troops, and naval squadrons for Alexander throughout Asia Minor, Egypt, Persia, Bactria, Sogdiana, and India. Of all Alexander's officers, except perhaps Craterus and Hephaestion, Coenus had taken the most responsibility for the campaigns in India. He had conveyed Alexander's fleet to the Hydaspes River and had played a key role in the recent battle against Porus. Coenus had supervised the crossing of the dangerous Acesines River and directed the siege of the Indian city Sangala, the last military action before the mutiny. His credentials as a commander and his loyalty to Alexander were above question.

Coenus was also well regarded among his soldiers. He had shared the hardships of his men both on the march and led them in battle. He knew how they felt and probably sympathized with them. He was caught in a dilemma every officer dreads—feeling sympathy for the plight of those serving under him and having to obey the demands of his commanding officer. Yet Coenus knew the dangers incurred in speaking up for the army against the wishes of the king. He knew the sentiments of the army had become dangerous for the king—the soldiers were on the verge of mutiny, and Coenus believed that Alexander had to be made fully aware of just how serious this crisis was.[38]

Coenus went to see Alexander, and the king listened quietly and calmly as his commander explained to him the sentiments of the army. Coenus was careful and tactful in explaining to the man who considered himself to be a god and destined to rule the world that the army was refusing to follow his orders. This was a dangerous position to be in. If Alexander lost his temper, as he often did, Coenus could forfeit his life in an instant as many others had before him. Alexander could be impetuous and violent or restrained and moderate depending on his mood and the circumstances.

On this occasion the king listened to Coenus. When Coenus had finished, Alexander replied to him in a calm voice. Because the common soldiers could see no end in sight to his wars was no reason for him, Alexander the Great, lord of Asia, to end the pursuit of his dreams and turn around. Alexander lectured Coenus that he set no limits for a man of noble spirit. Like Achilles, his personal hero, Alexander had vowed to fulfill the Homeric ideal of never giving up and always striving to be the very best. And like Achilles, Alexander would chose a glorious death in place of a long and mundane existence. The fear of the soldiers was that they would die with him.

Now Coenus had to respond to the king's argument that men, real men, would never give up until they had achieved their goals. It was clear to Coenus that Alexander intended to push on to the ends of the earth no matter what the cost in human suffering. Then Coenus suggested to the king that he end the campaign in India because a great man knows when to stop. Coenus told Alexander that there had to be an end to their labors and something for them other than death. Many of the Macedonians and Greeks had grown old. Some were in their sixties now, and they wanted an end to the incessant marching, misery, and fighting that had come to define their lives. This was the most dangerous point of the exchange. Coenus was in effect lecturing the king on the characteristics of a great man, and given the volatile nature of Alexander's personality that was a very risky thing to do. Coenus had tried as tactfully and subtly as he could to convince the king that the very magnitude of his achievements in conquering so much of the world required that some limit be set. Coenus would be dead three days later, killed in combat.

Alexander would promise anything to get his way. Six years before at the battle of Issus, he had told the army that victory on the field of battle that day would mean an end of labor and the enjoyment of empire for all of them.[39] At Hecatompylus nearly four years later, he promised only a few more days of marching before the campaign would end. Now, as the soldiers looked east over the Hyphasis River, all they could see before them was an abyss filled with more suffering and death.

Alexander, refusing to accept the argument of Coenus, called an assembly and addressed the army. He began by stating his intention to advance east, even if he went alone. He attempted to shame his men into following him by telling them that they would have to return to Macedonia and Greece to explain why they had left their king alone in India. Then, once again, he resorted to the themes that had worked for him before. He reiterated his belief that acquisition of an empire such as his, one that encompassed the entire ancient world, was only possible through a combination of his iron will, the support of the army, and triumph over the obstacles that nature placed in their path. Alexander recounted, as he had when he spoke to the soldiers in the past, how they had marched eastward and overcome all the natural obstacles in their path. They had passed through the Caspian Gates then crossed over the Caucasus Mountains (the Hindu Kush) and finally the Jaxartes River, which was the boundary between Europe and Asia. Now they had come to India and defeated the armies of its kings. They were on the verge of reaching the great eastern Ocean and the limits of the earth. He begged them not to stop now that they were so close to realizing their goal. Alexander acknowledged the hardships they had all endured, but he emphasized that without hardship there could be no achievement in life. He promised that those who remained with him would become the envy of those who returned home.

At the end of Alexander's speech, there was silence.[40] There were no cheers or shouts of support for the king like there had been years before. There was just a deafening silence from men who had enough and wanted to go home. Alexander asked the soldiers why there were no shouts of approval, and there was no reply. He asked again and again. Each time there was only silence. Alexander, like his hero Achilles in the Trojan War, retired to his tent to sulk for three days and three nights. He was incapable of taking satisfaction in what he had already accomplished and contenting himself with returning home to bask in his glory. For him, retreat from the shores of the Hyphasis was nothing less than an admission of defeat.

Alexander sequestered himself in his tent, refusing to see anyone, sulking and self-indulgent in his anger. He had used the same tactic following the murder of Cleitus. Alexander remembered that the ploy had worked then, and he hoped for another display of hysterical devotion by the army. This time it was different. The Macedonians and Greeks would not give in. They proved as stubborn as their leader. What had worked before for Alexander failed this time. The soldiers allowed the king to sulk for three days, then they surrounded his tent and by their presence convinced him to give in. The army had won. Alexander the Great had been defeated.

Alexander emerged from his seclusion and ordered that sacrifices be held to determine if the army should continue forward. On the banks of the Hyphasis, the sacrifices were held and the omens read as the entire army watched. The priests declared on the first reading that the omens were unfavorable for a crossing of the river. Alexander had his excuse for turning back, and he did not ask for a second reading. In this way, he was able to save face by pretending to capitulate to the will of the gods, not to the demands of his men.

In reality, the sacrifices were a sham. Ptolemy, as expected of a loyal officer and friend, reported in his memoirs that Alexander's intentions in sacrificing were genuine and that it was the unfavorable omens, not the refusal of the army to advance, that deterred him from crossing the river. What is interesting to note is that there were techniques among the Greeks and Macedonians for circumventing unfavorable omens,[41] and there were occasions during the campaign when Alexander chose to ignore unfavorable omens. Yet Alexander conducted only one sacrifice that day and then capitulated to the demands of the army. While it is true that in general the Greeks and Macedonians took their sacrifices seriously, Alexander had been cavalier in the past about altering unfavorable omens. His ready compliance indicates that he had already decided to withdraw and arranged the charade of the sacrifice to save his pride and make it seem that he was yielding to the will of the gods.

It was the custom of the Greeks to set up pillars, or altars, to mark the farthest point reached on a military expedition.[42] Alexander had set up altars on the shores of the Jaxartes River at Alexandria Eschate to mark his farthest point of conquest in the north, and now on the Hyphasis he set out to mark his farthest point of conquest in the east. The god Dionysus, the hero Heracles, and the legendary Queen Semiramis who had founded Babylon had all supposedly set up altars in India. Alexander followed suit but ordered that his altars would be three times larger than normal. Twelve oversized altars were erected on the shores of the Hyphasis River, one for each of the Olympian gods. But the altars were not enough. Alexander ordered his engineers to build a camp that would be left behind as an additional memorial. Everything in this camp, from the armor of the soldiers to their beds in the barracks and the stables for their horses, would be oversized. Alexander wanted the Indians and their kings who lived beyond the river to believe that the Macedonians and Greeks in his army were giants among men.[43]

The statues of the twelve Olympian gods erected on the banks of the river rose to a height of nearly twenty meters each.[44] In Alexander's mind, he had to exceed anything that a god such as Dionysus or legendary heroes such as Heracles and Semiramis could accomplish so that he too could join them and become a god in his lifetime.

The army got its way, and the soldiers began the long journey home. They would travel south by way of the Indus River then west over the Gedrosian Desert and finally through southwestern Iran to Persepolis, Susa, and Babylon. But along the way they paid a heavy price. Instead of an easy retreat home, along the more northern route they had used to invade Afghanistan and India, Alexander led them into unknown territory and against new enemies. South along the Indus River, the army engaged in some of the bloodiest fighting of the entire campaign, and Alexander nearly died.

The retreat started at the Hyphasis River (modern-day Beas River). Then the army fell back to the Hydroates River (modern-day Ravi) and then to the Acesines River (modern-day Chenab). Finally they retreated to the Hydaspes River (modern-day Jhelum) where the fleet that would transport them south to the Arabian Sea was under construction. When the fleet was completed, the army was transported along the Hydaspes to the Indus. From the completion of the fleet until the army reached the sea, the journey took nearly a year.[45] They would not reach the Arabian Sea until July of 325 B.C.

When the flotilla was completed, it numbered nearly a thousand ships of all types, from warships and troop transports to supply barges. Nearchus, the boyhood friend of Alexander, had been recalled from his satrapy in Persia to rejoin the army in India. Initially, Alexander had planned for Nearchus to command a fleet, which would set out to explore the great Ocean that Aristotle told them lay at the ends of the earth, but now he would command the fleet that was taking the army home. Onesicritus, another of Alexander's close companions, was appointed helmsman of the lead ship.

When the fleet was ready to depart, Alexander sacrificed to the gods of the river and to Poseidon, the Greek god of the sea. The omens were favorable, so the fleet set off down the Hydaspes River, whose currents quickly brought them to a point where they reached the Indus. Because of its size, part of the army was forced to remain ashore where it was divided into two columns, which marched along the banks of the rivers. Craterus took command of the column on the right bank, while Hephaestion commanded the column that followed along the left bank. On both sides of the river, the army was accompanied by a huge contingent of Indian nobles, merchants, women, children, and slaves—people who followed the army simply because they had nowhere else to go.

As Alexander and his flotilla sailed along the Hydaspes River toward the Indus, they assaulted nearly every city on its banks and subdued the surrounding countryside for several miles inland. Even scholars who have portrayed Alexander as a heroic and noble figure admit that this aspect of the campaign is as disturbing in its record of slaughter and massacre as were the campaigns in Bactria, Sogdiana, and the Swat Valley.[46] Tribes known as the Malli and the Sudracae dwelled along the banks of the Indus, and with the approach of Alexander they thought it prudent to make an accommodation with him rather than resist. They hoped he was only passing through, so they sent one hundred envoys to pay him homage. These envoys had been selected from among their foremost citizens, and their robes were of linen embroidered with gold and purple. They arrived at Alexander's camp in magnificent chariots that were bedecked with gold and other precious metals and were pulled by matched pairs of horses. The ambassadors had come to surrender themselves and their cities to Alexander, relinquishing their freedom that they told Alexander they had guarded and defended for generations. There was little doubt that these people had decided it would be easier to pay homage to Alexander and let him pass on than to resist him and suffer the destruction that was bound to occur. What they did not know was that even though Alexander had accepted their submission, he would turn on them with a vengeance.

Alexander imposed upon these tribes a tribute of gold and conscripts. Then the king ordered a feast to be prepared in their honor on the shores of the river. Magnificent tents were erected, and golden couches equal to the number of guests were arranged within. Hung from the walls of the tents and draped upon the couches were purple tapestries gleaming with gold. Alexander intended to impress the Malli and the Sudracae with his wealth, so he ordered that the banquet display all the luxury and fashions he had accumulated from his newly conquered empire. The Macedonian and Greek guests were ordered to attend in Persian dress.

Invited to the feast that evening was a Greek mercenary, Dioxippus by name. An Athenian, he had once won a crown in the Olympic Games for boxing and was known in Alexander's army for his skill and strength. Also present was a Macedonian companion of Alexander's named Corratas. Corratas was also renowned for his strength and bravery in battle. As the night wore on and the drinking intensified, bantering between the Macedonians and the Greeks began. At first it was good-natured and harmless. Then as egos flared, fired by the wine, and as men vied to impress the king, it turned more serious in nature. The jests that in the beginning had about them a lightheartedness now became more perilous. Corratas, overcome with wine, challenged Dioxippus to prove his courage in single combat.[47] The Macedonians around Corratas urged him on, and the Greeks encouraged Dioxippus to accept the challenge. Alexander was amused,[48] and the Indian guests were impressed. A contest between the two men was set for the following day.

A large number of spectators gathered to watch, and among them were the Indian envoys who, curious about the spectacle, had decided to delay their departure. An arena had been hastily constructed for the contest, and when all was ready the two warriors entered from different sides. The crowd roared its approval. Corratas, clad in expensive heavy armor, came to the contest prepared to fight in the traditional Macedonian style of a soldier in war. He carried a bronze shield and a long uniquely Macedonian spear known as the sarisa. In his right hand he had a much shorter spear, and about his waist hung a short sword. Corratas had come prepared to fight an army, not one man.

The Greek Dioxippus, on the other hand, came to the contest naked. His body was oiled, and he wore on his head the garland he had won at the Olympic Games. He carried a purple cloth in his left hand and in his right a knotted and well-balanced club. His muscles were toned, and all the spectators remarked on his physical condition. Yet at the same time the spectators commented to each other that Dioxippus was mad to have entered the arena so lightly armed to fight against a man in full armor.

Alexander and his entourage sat on a platform that had been constructed to give the king the best view of the combat. As the Macedonian and the Athenian stood to face each other, the crowd was filled with excitement and anticipation. The spectators were about to witness a battle between gods. Corratas opened the combat by hurling his short lance in an attempt to kill Dioxippus from long range. It was a mistake. He was encumbered by his equipment, and the spear missed its mark when the Athenian moved quickly to the side. In an instant, Dioxippus countered by closing in on the Macedonian as he moved to transfer the long sarisa from his left hand to his right. Dioxippus struck the sarisa with a massive blow from his club and broke the long spear in half. Corratas fumbled again when he attempted to draw his sword, the last weapon left to him. Dioxippus struck Corratas with a vicious head-butt. The Macedonian fell backwards and lay on the ground stunned.

Dioxippus was on him in an instant. Kicking the sword away from the Macedonian, the Greek placed his foot on the fallen man's neck and immobilized him. Then he raised his club overhead and prepared to inflict the deathblow. Alexander leapt to his feet in anger and shouted for Dioxippus to lower his club. The Athenian complied with the angry king's order and lowered his club, but he kept his foot firmly planted on the neck of his opponent. This forced Alexander to ask the Greek to spare the fallen Macedonian. It was a humiliating moment for the king. The Greeks were cheering wildly for Dioxippus, and the Macedonians were sullen. Alexander ordered the gathering broken up and left the arena in anger and embarrassment.

The Indian envoys and the other barbarians had witnessed the defeat of a Macedonian champion and the humiliation of the king. There was no award of a prize to the victor by the king, yet a few nights later Dioxippus was invited to a feast in Alexander's quarters. In the course of the banquet, the Greek was accused by the Macedonians of stealing a golden cup from his host. When Dioxippus protested his innocence, a servant retrieved a cup from under one of several pillows placed about the couch upon which Dioxippus had been reclining.

Dioxippus knew that the Macedonians had set him up, and he left the banquet in embarrassment. He returned to his own quarters and wrote Alexander a letter maintaining his innocence in the theft of the cup. Dioxippus was a proud man, and the humiliation of being called a thief by those about the king compelled him to take his own life with his sword. When word was brought to Alexander that Dioxippus had died, the king was still drinking with his friends. The Macedonians received the news with pleasure, and someone commented aloud to the company that the problem with Dioxippus had been that he had a great body but little in the way of brains. They all laughed at the quip and then resumed their drinking.

Initially Alexander was angry that Dioxippus had taken his own life, not because he saw that the Macedonians had wronged an innocent man, but because Dioxippus had been indignant enough to take his own life rather than to repent. Sometime after Dioxippus died, however, Alexander came to regret that he had wronged an honest man. The entire incident is noteworthy not only because it illustrates the tension that must have existed between Alexander and his Greek officers but also because it shows the ego-driven and violent world these men lived in. Shortly thereafter, Alexander gave orders for the army to resume its march along the river.

A few days later Alexander attacked the town of the Malli, located along the Indus River near the modern-day Pakistani city of Multan. The territory of the Malli was called Aspasia, and it is reputed to have been a fertile and wealthy area. While the Malli, according to the ancient sources, had a reputation as a warlike people among the Indians, the destruction of their town and the slaughter of its people by Alexander have been condemned by scholars as nothing more than a premeditated act of terror. The ambassadors of the Malli had already surrendered to Alexander, yet he ordered the town attacked without warning or quarter for its people. The army attacked the town as well as the surrounding villages with particular fury, showing no quarter to anyone and taking no prisoners; this included murdering the women and children.

In spite of Alexander's sudden attack on the city, resistance proved tougher than he expected. The defenders were able to close the city gates before Alexander's soldiers entered and thus forced the army to assault the walls. When the defenders put up considerable resistance and casualties in Alexander's army began to mount, his soldiers began to hesitate when given the order to resume their attack on the walls. The reluctance of large numbers of Alexander's soldiers to storm the city walls again is significant. It indicated that many in Alexander's army had had enough of the fighting and the dying. Alexander had to lead the second assault on the walls himself in an effort to motivate his soldiers. On two occasions he scaled the walls, and the second occasion nearly cost him his life.

Alexander led one of the assault parties attempting to scale a wall that was heavily defended. Prior attempts had failed, and casualties among the Macedonians and Greeks were mounting. Alexander was the first to reach the top, but the ladder he was using broke and the men following him fell to the ground. The king found himself alone on the ramparts without support and surrounded by the Malli. He was struck in the chest by an arrow and badly wounded. So hard was the force of the arrow when it struck his breastplate that Alexander fell to his knees and nearly lost consciousness. Peucestas and Leonnatus, two of Alexander's close companions and bodyguards, mounted the wall by another ladder and managed to reach the king. They protected Alexander from the arrows with their shields and kept the

Malli at bay. The three men were badly outnumbered, and as a result Peucestas was wounded and Leonnatus was killed before the Macedonians were able to take the ramparts and rescue them.

Alexander had lost consciousness. Before the soldiers could carry him down an assault ladder and to the royal tent for treatment, the shaft of the arrow had to be cut off. Peucestas, even though he was wounded, removed the shaft from the chest of the king but was forced to leave the arrowhead buried in one of Alexander's ribs. When Alexander was brought back to his tent for treatment, word spread throughout the army that he had been killed. The surgeons removed the arrowhead from his ribs, and Alexander nearly died from the loss of blood.[49] Alexander eventually recovered, but it took a long time for him to regain his strength and he remained under his physicians' care for several weeks.

The incident among the Malli showed once again the darkest side of Alexander. Angry that his men had forced him to turn back at the Hyphasis River and angry at their reluctance to fight, he vowed to extract the maximum suffering not only from the local people he encountered along the route home but by inflicting the greatest number of casualties on his men as well. As the flotilla moved downriver the atrocities against the local inhabitants continued. He had the Agalasseis burned alive in their town and massacred eighty thousand of the Sambastae on the lower Indus. Then he ravaged the lands of the Oreitae just before he entered the Gedrosian Desert for no other reason than that they happened to be unlucky enough to be in his path. The slaughter that Alexander inflicted on the Punjab and the Sind caused outrage among the Indian philosophers, the Brahmins, who urged the local people to take up arms against Alexander. The resistance to Alexander eventually resulted in the placement of a native king on the throne of a partially united India. While this new king, Chandragupta, came to power after Alexander left India, he enlisted the people in wiping out nearly every trace of the invaders and their influence east of the Indus River, probably including Alexander's great altars to the gods.

As Alexander advanced along the Indus River, he came into contact with a number of the Indian philosophers who lived in many of the cities along the river. Many of these philosophers were called the

Gymnosophists, and along with the Brahmins they encouraged their people to resist Alexander and not relinquish their freedom. These philosophers had a reputation for being particularly clever men, so Alexander had ten of them captured and brought to him for questioning. He decided to test just how clever they were by posing a question to each and judging his reply. Alexander appointed as the judge of their answers the most senior philosopher among them and declared that each philosopher who gave an incorrect answer would die.

The contest was held before an assembly of the soldiers. Alexander posed the first question: Who are more numerous on the face of the earth, the living or the dead? The first Indian philosopher replied that of course the living were, for the dead no longer exist. Alexander was delighted by his wit and went on to pose a question to the next philosopher: Which contains the largest animals, the earth or the sea? The earth, the second philosopher replied, for the sea is but a part of the earth. Then Alexander asked posed a question to the third philosopher: What animal is the cleverest of all? The philosopher replied that it was the one that had not yet been discovered by man. The questions went on in that manner until all ten philosophers had answered and Alexander was delighted with their responses. Then the king asked the most senior among them, the one he had appointed as judge, to render his verdict. The old man replied that each philosopher had answered worse than the one before. Alexander ordered the old man to be executed first for rendering such a verdict. The old philosopher replied that he could not be put to death unless the king were a liar. Alexander had declared before the entire assembly that he would put to death the philosopher who had answered his question incorrectly. Alexander was pleased by the old philosopher's response and released all the Gymnosophists, sending them home with gifts. Then, still curious, Alexander sent Onesicritus, one of his Greek historians, to visit the two most noted and revered of all of the Indian philosophers, Calanus and Dandamis. These men lived in self-imposed isolation. Onesicritus first went to visit Calanus, who demanded that they sit naked together while they conversed. Onesicritus was so impressed that he convinced Calanus to accompany him back to the camp and visit with Alexander. When

Onesicritus met with the second philosopher, Dandamis, the Indian had only one question for Alexander: Why had he made such a long journey from Macedonia to India? Was it only for the purpose of conquering other people? Then Dandamis asked if the king understood how insignificant he was. Like any mortal man, all he owned was the small square of earth he stood on for the brief period while he lived.

When Calanus and the king came face to face, Alexander asked the philosopher for advice on how he might best govern his empire.[50] Calanus threw a dry and stiff animal hide upon the ground. He placed his foot on one edge and pressed it down into the ground. The other edges came up. As he went around the edges of the hide, no matter where he stepped and no matter how hard, another edge would pop up. Finally, Calanus stepped into the middle of the hide and while the edges rose up, the main portion of the hide remained firmly planted on the ground beneath the philosopher's foot. The lesson was not lost on Alexander. If he were to rule his empire effectively, it would have to be done from the center and with some latitude to allow for minor rebellions and limited degrees of autonomy on the outer edges. Alexander was so impressed with the simplicity and wisdom of Calanus that he asked the Indian philosopher to accompany him to Persepolis and Babylon. The Indian, curious about the world of the Greeks and Macedonians, agreed.

As Alexander and his army made their way down the Indus River, they continued to destroy city after city. Ptolemy was wounded by a poisoned arrow and nearly died. Alexander was distressed because they were close friends, and it was said that Ptolemy was the son of Philip by another woman and thus the king's half-brother.[51]

By the summer of 325 B.C. Alexander and the army had reached a place where the Indus River bifurcated. Craterus, with the baggage, the siege train, the elephants, the sick, the wounded, and three battalions of the phalanx as escort, left the main column to head due west toward Persepolis. He followed a route that today leads from Pakistan and the tribal areas of Waziristan over the Mullah Pass into southern Afghanistan. This area has been the scene of recent fighting between the Pakistani army, tribal factions, and al Qaeda guerillas. Once into southern Afghanistan, Craterus would follow a route that would lead him through Arachosia and Drangiana and into southern Iran directly toward Persepolis.

Nearchus and the fleet continued on their way down the Indus to the Arabian Sea. The fleet was down to between 100 and 150 ships. The supply ships had been emptied of their contents and abandoned along the upper reaches of the Indus while many of the troopships, especially those carrying the sick and wounded, were abandoned when Craterus left the column. The fleet had supplies remaining for ten days and water enough to last for five. Nearchus was given a mission by Alexander to find a sea route between the Indus and Euphrates Rivers. He was ordered to survey for harbors, islands, and possible sources of supplies along the shoreline of what today constitutes the Makran tribal area of Pakistan and the coastal section of Iran on the Persian Gulf. In September of 325 B.C., Nearchus left Patala but was delayed for twenty-four days at "Alexander's Harbor" (modern-day Karachi) until the fleet was able to pick up favorable winds and finally set sail into the Arabian Sea.

CHAPTER 6

RETURN TO BABYLON

ALEXANDER TOOK THE REMAINING COLUMN,[1] WHICH
numbered about fifty thousand to sixty thousand fighting men and
an equal number of camp followers, and started what was to become
his deadliest march of the campaign. The route Alexander selected
led the Greeks and Macedonians through the Gedrosian Desert,[2]
the desolate area of southernmost Pakistan along the coast of the
Arabian Sea that is known as the Makran or Balochistan Province.
Exactly why Alexander chose this route has been the subject of considerable speculation among scholars over the centuries. There was
no reason to cross this desert, which even today has seen limited
development and resembles the moonscape in its barren and desolate nature. The best route was the one followed by Craterus and the
remainder of the column through southern Afghanistan and into
Iran. But reason had long since been replaced in Alexander's mind by
fantasy and legend. He was intent on emulating or surpassing the
efforts of Queen Semiramis, a legendary figure who was supposed to
have invaded India centuries before Alexander and to have returned
to her native Babylon by way of the desert.

When Alexander and his army first entered the barren wasteland,
they encountered a primitive people known as the Oreitae. These
people were similar to the Indians in all their customs except in how
they treated their dead.[3] Their practices in this regard offended the
Macedonians and Greeks, who took particular care in the proper burial of their dead. The Oreitae stripped their dead of any clothing and
left their bodies in thickets to be eaten by the wild animals. This was

not the first time the Macedonians and Greeks had encountered such primitive practices when it came to the ritual treatment of the dead. In Bactria and Sogdiana, they found that the sick, the elderly, and the dead were routinely left in the countryside to be eaten by wild dogs, while the Scythian tribes further out in the steppes of Central Asia ate their own dead.[4] Alexander divided the army into three groups, and they set about burning the land of the Oreitae, pillaging and destroying their villages. When the army had finished subduing the local people, Alexander founded a city in Makran, which he colonized with men from Arachosia and named Rambacia.[5]

The desert was a place of terrible searing heat, poisonous plants, and no food. In more than sixty days of relentless marching in Gedrosia, Alexander lost thousands of people, many of them in the lethal flash floods that still extract a heavy toll of human life in that region. The rain in Makran falls often in torrents in the mountains, which are north of the desert. In the desert, the storms raging in the mountains are neither heard nor seen by the local people or travelers until a sudden wall of raging water and mud, racing along the gullies and ravines of the parched land, destroys the unwary and everything else in its path. Alexander and his column had camped one night, probably somewhere near the modern town of Turbat, when a column of water and mud struck them without warning.[6] The effect was catastrophic. Casualties were high, especially among the women and children who followed the army.

The conclusion seems to be that Alexander led his army through Gedrosia to continue to punish them for their defiance at the Hyphasis River. There certainly was no strategic or tactical reason to enter Gedrosia. Some of the sources maintain that Alexander did so to try to find water for his fleet as they made their way along the coastline of Makran. There was little if any water in the desert, and the only people Alexander and his men encountered as they pushed deeper into Gedrosia were the Ichthyophagi, or fish-eaters in ancient Greek. They were an unfriendly and brutish Stone Age people whose skins were blackened by constant exposure to the harsh sun and whose fingernails and toenails grew, untrimmed, to extraordinary lengths. With their matted and filthy hair, these people were a terrible sight. They lived along the coastal areas of the desert and subsisted on fish, which they cured in the sun, and the flesh of whales that became stranded on the beaches. The fish-eaters lived in huts whose walls and roofs were supported by the ribs of whales and then covered by their skins. The stench of fly-covered fish curing in the sun sickened the Greeks and Macedonians as they passed through, as even today it sickens the traveler to this remote area where practices have remained unchanged for centuries.

It was late in November when Alexander and those who had survived the march cleared the Gedrosian Desert and entered into the province of Carmania in southeastern Iran. After two months in Gedrosia, those who remained with Alexander had almost given up hope of surviving the ordeal. Conditions in Gedrosia had been the worst Alexander and his army had ever endured. The sun beat down on them relentlessly, hour after hour. There was little water or food, and the countryside was infested with a variety of insects that made life miserable. In the course of the march, the soldiers became so desperate for food that they slaughtered all the animals, including the horses, and then when there were no more animals to slaughter they dug into the ground with their hands searching for roots. Gedrosia was and remains the most desolate place imaginable.

Even with all the modern advances in technology, travel into Balochistan is a risky undertaking. It is part of what is known in Pakistan as the tribal region, an area beyond the control of the regular government and off-limits to foreigners. Permission to enter this tribal area must be secured in the form of a highly restrictive permit issued by the regional administration of Balochistan at the provincial capital of Quetta. Once secured, the permit must be further reviewed and approved by the central government in Islamabad. Even after receiving verbal assurance that the permit has been approved, it can be retracted at a moment's notice. Entry by foreigners without the permit can result in imprisonment and stiff fines, as it did recently for two French journalists.[7]

The tribes in Balochistan are self-governing through councils of tribal elders known as jirgas. The jirgas make the decisions for their members, and then those decisions are enforced by the tribal armies and militias known as lashkars. Punishments for the breaching of ancient tribal codes remain harsh. Sex outside of marriage may be punishable by stoning, and families may be required to sell virgin daughters as compensation in the settlement of feuds. This lawless tribal preserve is a place where feuds and vendettas flourish. Foreigners who enter the area run the risk of being kidnapped for ransom or beheaded by radical Muslim groups anxious to make a media statement.

There is only one two-lane road that passes through the nearly four hundred miles of desert that constitute the Kolwa and Kech Valleys in the central Makran mountain range. The condition of that route, which is the one most likely used by Alexander and his army, is never certain even today. The route is passable only by camel or in an air-conditioned four-by-four vehicle carrying adequate provisions of water, food, and ammunition. The journey begins in Karachi, where the route turns north to Bela and due west directly across the desert to the border between Pakistan and Iran. The barren mountains of the Makran range flank the northern side of the desert, and because it is such an isolated and lawless place security is always the primary consideration for the traveler.

The area is considered a wilderness and a haven for outlaws and terrorists. It is the preferred route for drug smugglers carrying opium out of Afghanistan bound for Western markets and the slave traders with their caravans of human cargo bound for the Arab world. Today much of the illicit caravan traffic moves at night because of the heat and to avoid detection. The preferred mode of transportation is, as it was in Alexander's day, by camel. The desert is almost impassible from early March until the end of November, and the skin of the local people is blackened from the sun just as described in Alexander's day. The food is terrible, and black flies, which made life miserable for Alexander and his army, still make life miserable for the modern visitor.

Conditions became so bad for Alexander's army that soldiers as well as hundreds of noncombatants fell out of the column and were left to die each day. The weaker ones—mostly women, children, and soldiers who were sick and wounded—fell by the wayside. Those who could walk were forced to ignore the pleas and cries of the sick and weak as the column moved slowly to the west.

It came to a point when Alexander ordered the pace of the column increased. On the surface, it was a cruel order because it increased the numbers who were left behind to die. But in reality, Alexander hoped that he could save at least the fittest of his men by completing the march and reaching the satrapy of Carmania as quickly as possible. Alexander had sent messengers to the satrapy, which bordered Gedrosia on the northwest, with instructions to send supplies to a point where the army would exit the desert. Conditions worsened each day. Disease brought about by the poor food and unsanitary conditions was rampant in the long column and took a toll as heavy as that taken by famine, exhaustion, and dehydration. As Alexander led the army, he tried to mask the depression and insecurity that each day increased and threatened to incapacitate him. The "god-king" had erred in trying to satisfy his own ego. He had led his army into the desert, and now he feared they would all perish in this desolate land.[8] Still, the column kept moving west, pushed on largely by its fear of stopping. At first the soldiers tried to move by day; then, forced to avoid the relentless sun, they took to marching at night. The scouts often lost their way on the track because of the shifting sands. All the column could do was move due west, navigating by the sun and the stars.

Then, as if they were not suffering enough, the Oreitae attacked one of Alexander's divisions under the command of Leonnatus and inflicted heavy casualties before being driven off. Alexander's losses in Gedrosia have been estimated as high as three-quarters of his fighting troops and nearly all the noncombatants.[9]

When Alexander and the army finally left the desert, they arrived at a city called Pura,[10] where a great store of provisions had been laid for them. The provisions had been sent by the satraps of the surrounding provinces in anticipation of Alexander's arrival and in compliance with his orders. The land around Pura was fertile, and there was an abundance of fruit and vegetables. Sacrifices were offered by the soldiers in gratitude to the gods for having spared at least some of them from death. Alexander ordered a great festival replete with "all the sports of Bacchanalian license."[11] During the period of the festivities, Bagoas, the king's young eunuch who had survived the march through the desert, won a competition for song and dance. This so delighted Alexander that when the eunuch, with his garland on his head, came and reclined on the couch next to him following his victory, the king, "well heated with wine" and overcome by passion, "threw his arms about him and kissed him tenderly."[12]

At Pura Alexander received couriers with news that Craterus and his column were moving to meet him. Craterus had successfully completed the trip from India, and most of his column was intact. The journey had been considerably easier than Alexander's, but it had not been without its perils. As Alexander read the correspondence that had been sent to him at Pura, he began to realize the extent of the corruption that had developed in the western parts of his empire during his absence. There had been considerable treachery and corruption among many of those whom Alexander had appointed as satraps in the Persian provinces.[13] In his absence, word had spread throughout the western parts of his empire and even reached as far as Greece and Macedonia that he had been killed in India. Then reports followed that most of his army had been lost in the desert of Gedrosia. As a result, there had been revolts as "restlessness and desire for change spread everywhere throughout his empire."[14] Many of the satraps he had left in Persia were now corrupt tyrants, and they had enriched themselves at the king's expense. Even Antipater, Alexander's regent, along with the king's mother Olympias and his sister Cleopatra, thinking Alexander dead had divided parts of Macedonia and northern Greece among them.[15] Harpalus, the treasurer at Babylon and trusted boyhood friend of Alexander, had squandered huge sums on whores and luxuries and then absconded to Greece.[16]

Alexander's empire needed attention, and it took only seven days for him to reach Persepolis from Pura. The satrap of Carmania was executed along the way because he was suspected of having contemplated revolt while Alexander had been in India.[17] Even though Alexander was anxious to reach Persepolis, the march through Carmania slowed and became a drunken rout.[18] As Alexander and the remnants of his army marched west, the king had ordered that the inhabitants of Carmania line the route with flowers and attend the soldiers with accolades, music, and great barrels and flasks of wine as they passed. Alexander reclined on a magnificent wagon pulled by eight horses while he feasted and drank with his companions all day long and into each night.

Behind Alexander came even larger wagons, many with embroidered canopies and freshly planted trees to provide shade for those who rode on them. These elaborate wagons conveyed the rest of Alexander's friends and commanders. While some soldiers followed on foot, most rode crowded on wagons. They were so festive and glad to be out of the desert that they marched unarmed through the countryside of what is today southeastern Iran. Not a shield, helmet, or spear could be seen among them. The soldiers drank and sang, dipping their cups into the large vats of wine that were transported on carts beside them or provided by the local people who lined the route. They saluted Alexander and congratulated each other on their success in having survived the desert. Musicians accompanied the soldiers, and the "reveling cries of women filled every place with music."[19] It was a Bacchanalian procession such as the ancient world had never seen before.[20] It was, as one source has commented, "a riotous procession" that would have been "easy prey" if the conquered peoples along the route had only risen up. Just "a thousand real men," the sources tell us, could have easily fallen upon the column and murdered a drunken Alexander and his companions.[21]

Along the route through Carmania, Alexander was reunited with Nearchus and his officers whom the king feared had been lost at sea. They had beached their ships on the shores of ancient Harmozica at the entrance to the Persian Gulf[22] and worked their way overland through Carmania to find Alexander. Alexander listened intently as Nearchus recounted the details of his voyage by ship along the Makran coast and into the Persian Gulf. It had not been an easy voyage, and they had suffered from a lack of food and water. They had encountered a large school of whales, which terrified the sailors. Yet what Nearchus had seen filled Alexander with a desire to circumnavigate Africa and enter the western Mediterranean through the Pillars of Heracles (Straits of Gibraltar).[23] Nearchus eventually left Alexander and returned to his ships with orders to sail from Harmozica along the shores of the Persian Gulf until the fleet reached the entrance to the Euphrates River.

In the early spring of 324 B.C., Alexander reached Persepolis and set about cleaning out his imperial household. The king instituted a new round of purges in which he called to account all his administrators and governors who had sought to enrich themselves during his absence and those who were accused of treason. In the course of the next several months, the innocent along with the guilty would suffer. The purge included many of Alexander's closest officers as well as Persians suspected or accused of corruption or disloyalty. Among those arrested and charged with corruption were the three generals from Ecbatana who, along with Polydamus, had murdered Parmenio for Alexander. They were brought to the king at Persepolis and, although spared execution, were imprisoned. Six hundred of their soldiers were executed on a variety of charges from theft to rape. Craterus brought in a number of officials and officers from the eastern provinces who were charged with treason and executed along with the condemned from Ecbatana.

Of the twenty-two satraps known to have been in office in 325 B.C., only four were untouched by the purges. Six were executed for treason, and most of the others were left to die in prisons. Alexander personally executed one Persian noble, Oxathres, on unspecified charges. Oxathres was the son of Abuletes, Alexander's Persian satrap at Susa. The father was imprisoned shortly after the execution of his son on the charge of having failed to furnish provisions for Alexander as ordered. Abuletes had made the mistake of sending gold coins to Carmania when Alexander had ordered food for his troops. When the coins arrived, Alexander commented that neither his men nor his horses could eat them, and Abuletes was condemned for insubordination.

The satrap of Persepolis was hung for corruption, and Peucestas, who had saved Alexander's life at the city of the Malli, was appointed the new satrap of the area.[24] Peucestas had become a particular favorite of Alexander's because, with perhaps the exception of Hephaestion, he was the most willing of Alexander's senior officers to adopt Persian dress and manners. He embraced the Persian lifestyle, and as satrap he learned the language and followed the customs of the people he ruled. Peucestas was one of only a few Macedonians who converted so enthusiastically to the Persian style of living.[25]

Executions became almost a daily occurrence at Pesepolis as men were brought in from all parts of the empire to answer to charges of treason and corruption. The fields around the city were soaked in blood. Alexander had become quick to believe accusations of treason, corruption, and disloyalty, no matter how baseless, and even quicker to order men executed.[26] Success and power had changed him over the years. They had turned his mind, and now at the whim of even his eunuch he took men's lives. It was a dark and murderous time in a dark and violent career.

When Alexander discovered that the tomb of Cyrus had been looted, he became enraged. He ordered the Macedonian officer he had left behind to guard the tomb executed and the guards tortured. The officer came from a prominent family, and when word reached them in Macedonia of his execution it further inflamed the hatred that was building toward Alexander.

The satrap of Pasagardae, Orsines, a competent and honest man, was executed as well but for other reasons. The crime of Orsines was that he had failed to honor the "whore" of Alexander, the eunuch Bagoas, with gifts.[27] Bagoas was close to the king and in moments of passion would fill Alexander's ears with lies about those who served him. Orsines, a descendant of Cyrus, had come from a noble Persian family and was regarded as a kind and good governor. Bagoas even participated in his execution.

As word of Alexander's purges spread, many of the satraps and generals in the provinces feared that they might be called to account. Some did not wait to be summoned to Persepolis but took as much treasure as they could carry and fled. Others attempted to resist the king's troops who had been sent to arrest them. When that began to happen, Alexander issued an order to all his satraps throughout Central Asia that they were to disband and dismiss their mercenary armies immediately. One result of that order was a flood of unemployed soldiers throughout Asia who became bandits and lived by plundering the countryside. Some of these dismissed mercenaries and their commanders made their way to Greece, where they joined forces with those seeking to free Greece from the yoke of Alexander.[28]

Among the satraps and commanders who looted the treasury deposits and fled was Harpalus. He had been Alexander's boyhood friend and was placed in charge of the vast treasuries at Babylon, Susa, and Ecbatana just before Alexander headed into the east several years before. While Alexander had been campaigning in Bactria, Sogdiana, and India, Harpalus had been living a life of debauchery. Thinking that Alexander would die in the East, the royal treasurer spent the king's money on everything from building palaces and private gardens to importing fish from the Mediterranean and harlots from Athens. When word reached Harpalus that Alexander was calling his satraps to account and that many were losing their lives, he looted five thousand talents from the royal treasury and, with a bodyguard of six thousand mercenaries, fled to Athens. Alexander considered crossing over to Greece to pursue Harpalus, but when he received word that Harpalus had been murdered he abandoned the idea.

As a result of the purges, power in Alexander's empire had shrunk to the close entourage around the king: Hephaestion, who had the title of chiliarch, the Achaemenid title of first after the king; Eumenes, who was Alexander's chancellor; and Craterus. There were a number of senior commanders who formed the king's bodyguard and shared power with Hephaestion, Craterus, and Eumenes. Among the most notable were Perdiccas, Ptolemy, and Lysimachus, men who would later compete among themselves as Alexander's successors.

When the Olympic Games were held in Greece the summer of 324 B.C., Alexander sent messengers with an order that all the Greek city-states must readmit those they had exiled for political reasons, with the exception of any who had been convicted of murder. Why Alexander issued such an order has never been satisfactorily explained by scholars; speculation is that his order, coupled with his dismissal of all mercenaries in Asia, was intended to create an enormous social and military problem in Greece and break the power of those who opposed him. Many of the Greek city-states were ruled by men who had been appointed by Antipater, and Alexander had come to distrust his regent and those loyal to him. These rulers had used the time-honored method of exile to rid themselves of many of their political opponents, and now Alexander was requiring them to readmit those opponents. The Greeks were unhappy with the situation Alexander had created but in the end reluctantly complied with the king's order. The Athenians alone among the city-states resisted Alexander's order and refused to pollute their city with a cesspool of men they had exiled.

At Persepolis, Calanus, the Indian philosopher who had accompanied Alexander, had fallen ill. He was in his seventies and had never experienced a day of sickness in all the years he lived in India. Now he was sick almost daily from intestinal disorders. Rather than attempt a cure prescribed by Alexander's Greek doctors, Calanus chose to end his life on the traditional Indian funeral pyre.[29] A pyre was built, and the philosopher bid farewell to all those who came to see his end. He told Alexander he would see him soon in Babylon— a prophetic remark—and climbed to the top of his pyre. There Calanus covered his head with the folds of his robe and lay back quietly upon his bed. Silently and without any movement, he allowed the flames that worked their way up the sides of the pyre to consume his body and release his spirit. The Macedonians and Greeks who witnessed his death that day were impressed with the contempt that the Indian had showed for death.

Following the immolation of Calanus, Alexander invited the mourners to a banquet to raise their spirits. After the meal the king proposed a drinking contest and offered a golden crown to the officer or noble who could drink the most at one sitting. Promachus, a Macedonian officer, won the prize after he consumed three gallons of wine. He was dead three days later along with forty-one others who were among the finalists.[30]

From Persepolis Alexander moved to his palace at Susa where he married Stateira, the eldest daughter of Darius, in a glorious ceremony. That marriage was followed shortly thereafter by a marriage to Parysatis, another princess of the Persian royalty. Parysatis was the youngest daughter of Artaxerxes III, who had been king of Persia before Darius. Roxanne was now confronted with Alexander's two new wives as well as his mistress Barsine, his lovers Hephaestion and Bagoas, and his more than three hundred concubines.

At Susa Alexander arranged marriages between his officers and the noblest of the Persian women. Hephaestion was married to Drypetis, the younger daughter of Darius, because the idea that the children of both royal marriages would be cousins pleased Alexander.[31] Craterus was married to the daughter of Oxathres, the brother of Darius, while Perdiccas was married to Atroptes, the daughter of the satrap of Media. Ptolemy and Eumenes were married to the daughters of Artabazus, the father of Alexander's mistress Barsine. Nearchus was married to the daughter of Barsine by a prior husband, and Mentor was married to the daughter of Spitamenes, the beheaded leader of the Sogdian revolt. In all, about eighty of Alexander's highest-ranking officers were married to the daughters of the noblest Persian and Bactrian families. Indications are that the Macedonians participated reluctantly to please their king. There were no marriages recorded to the daughters of any of the Indian kings.

The marriage ceremonies were performed, en masse, and in the Persian fashion.[32] Chairs were arranged for the grooms, and after each had been seated the brides were brought in and presented to their new husbands. Each groom then took his new bride by the hand and led her to their wedding bed. Alexander gave each bride a generous dowry to bring to her new husband. Compliance with Alexander's wishes always resulted in generous dispensations of other people's money.

From a reading of the ancient sources, it becomes evident that through these marriages Alexander intended that an alliance be formed among Greeks, Macedonians, and barbarians. With the birth of successive generations of children from these marriages, "all distinction between vanquished and victor" would, he hoped, disappear. All would be subjects of one king with equal rights under one empire. "Asia and Europe would belong to one and the same kingdom."[33]

Following the marriages, Alexander announced that his Macedonian bodyguard would be replaced by Persians and that all his attendants and servants from then on would be uniquely Persian.[34] Even more alarming for the Macedonians and Greeks was Alexander's order that Bactrian, Sogdian, Arachosian, and other barbarian cavalry units would henceforth be incorporated into the Companion cavalry.[35] Alexander formed a number of other mixed units— Macedonians, Greeks, and Persians blended to his own particular mixture.

Alexander encouraged even his common soldiers to marry Asian wives. He hosted a wedding feast for nine thousand newly married soldiers who each reclined at supper on a silver couch and received a golden cup as a memento of the occasion. As his personal wedding gift to each of the couples, Alexander paid off the debts of the husbands.

At Susa, the thirty thousand orphaned boys Alexander had left behind to be trained in Bactria several years before arrived. The boys were now young men, and while not experienced in war they had been well trained by their instructors in the use of Macedonian weapons and tactics. The king had spent a lot of money to ensure that they were well equipped. Alexander and the army assembled to watch the young Persians drill, and the king was impressed and pleased by what he saw. He named them the Epigoni,[36] or his successors, and this concerned the Macedonians, who became uneasy and fearful of what this new corps of Persians portended for the future.

With the arrival of the Epigoni and their warm reception by Alexander, many of the Macedonians and Greeks, both common soldiers as well as officers, believed that they were about to be replaced. Their discontent manifested itself in assembly. They had become unruly and frequently ridiculed Alexander, especially his pretense that he was the son of Ammon.[37] They would interrupt him with shouts and taunts when he addressed them. At one assembly, the soldiers were particularly disruptive and disrespectful when Alexander tried to speak to them. He lost his temper and in a rage leaped down from the platform and drove headlong into the crowd of soldiers. He seized the ringleaders, those men he deemed to have spoken out most disrespectfully toward him, and handed thirteen of them over to his guards. Not a man in the army that day resisted the king even though all of them were armed. The thirteen were led off to be executed by Alexander's Persian guards,[38] and the army stood there dumbfounded. The men were drowned in the nearby river as the army watched—executed at the whim of Alexander as an example to all that he would not tolerate insubordination or disrespect. There was no trial prior to their execution, and that angered the Greek and Macedonian soldiers who watched as much as the executions themselves. But no one spoke out. Such could be the force of the lord of Asia.[39] After the executions, the Macedonian and Greek soldiers became even more hostile toward Alexander, and as a result he increased the number of Persians who were appointed as generals in the army.[40]

By the late summer of 324 B.C., Alexander had become so distrustful of the Macedonians and Greeks that he routinely filled vacancies in the army with Persians and assigned a thousand Persians as his bodyguards.[41] When Alexander ordered Craterus back to Macedonia to replace Antipater and commanded him to take with him all the veterans who were weak, wounded, old, or lame, the Macedonians mutinied first and then the Greeks followed. The entire army demanded to go home. Alexander addressed the soldiers in assembly and tried to inspire them with new visions of glory and conquest. When he told them they would shortly set out to conquer new lands and share once again the same dangers and hardships, they shouted back at him that he should take his young Persian boys and go conquer the world with his father Zeus.

There were shouts and cries that the Macedonians and Greeks had been "used up" by the "god-king," and now when they were old and lame they were being replaced by young Persians. It was painfully evident that what they feared was true.[42]

Alexander lost his temper before the assembly and dismissed the army. The Macedonians and Greeks surrounded the palace of Alexander and begged him to forgive them and take them back into his favor. Alexander refused to see them for two days and nights. They kept their vigil day and night, crying out to the king. On the third day, Alexander emerged from his palace and embraced many of the old veterans. The king and his soldiers were reconciled and together cried tears of joy.

The army was once more united with Alexander, but the reconciliation would last only a short time. What this incident showed, as did the mutiny on the Hyphasis, was that while Alexander could still elicit the affection of the Macedonians and Greeks on occasion, he could not depend on it. Alexander had become more irascible and impulsive. The years of subservience and obsequiousness by the Persians and other barbarians around him had alienated him from the Macedonians and Greeks. Alexander was always suspicious of them and had become quick to accept accusations of disloyalty. He was inexorably cruel in dispensing the harshest of punishments. He had reached a point in his career where he inspired terror not only among those he conquered but also those who came into contact with him on a daily basis as his officers, administrators, attendants, or soldiers.

Those veterans who because of their age and attendant maladies wanted to return to Greece and Macedonia were discharged with generous bonuses. They left with Craterus. Alexander ordered that when they returned to Macedonia and Greece they would be honored for the remainder of their lives as heroes by having the best seats reserved for them at all athletic contests and theater productions. Then he ordered that the orphaned children of those Macedonians who had died in his service would receive the pay and bonuses due their fathers.[43] The Macedonian and Greek soldiers who returned home had left behind more than ten thousand young boys who were born of their captive women. There is no mention made of female children, and one can only assume they were either killed or sold into slavery. These men had no intent to return home dragging behind them sons born of barbarian women. Alexander adopted the boys and provided funds for their education and training, once again supplying for himself future generations of loyal soldiers.

Alexander ordered Craterus back to Macedonia to replace Antipater as regent. Craterus would take direct control over Macedonia, Thrace, and Thessaly and function as the protector of the freedom of the Greeks, a euphemism for their ruler. Antipater in turn was ordered to report to Alexander at Babylon along with a contingent of replacements for the troops who were being sent home. Antipater never left Macedonia to go to Babylon. There can be little doubt the aging regent feared that compliance with Alexander's order would only result in his own murder or execution. Antipater was not about to meet the same fate as Parmenio, and he began to set into place his own contingencies.

Alexander's mother Olympias had been feuding with Antipater for years. When word reached Macedonia sometime in 324 B.C. that Alexander had been killed in India, Olympias and Alexander's sister Cleopatra mobilized their forces to challenge Antipater's rule. Both women tried to establish their own independent kingdoms—

Olympias in Epirus, her father's old kingdom, and Cleopatra in Macedonia. It was only when word was received that Alexander was alive and returning to Persia that the feuding parties stopped short of all-out civil war.

At first Olympias wrote to Alexander complaining that Antipater had forgotten who had made him regent and that he ruled not in the name of Alexander but in his own right. She accused the elder general of coming to think of himself as king over the Macedonians and plotting with those in Greece who wished to free themselves from Alexander. This latter charge was bound to cause Alexander to take notice, especially given that he had just finished purging those men in his army and administration who had been charged with corruption and disloyalty.

On the other hand, Alexander's order to Antipater may not have been motivated from suspicion of any disloyalty. Perhaps Alexander intended through a change of command to prevent the conflict between his mother and his surrogate from weakening his political hold on mainland Greece and Macedonia. In any case, Antipater did not come to Babylon but instead sent his son Cassander, probably as a hostage. Alexander now had all of Antipater's three sons in Babylon.

The relationship between Alexander and Antipater and Craterus during this period has never been clear to scholars, and the paucity of sources has left much to speculation. What is known is that nearly a year after Alexander had issued the order for Craterus to leave Persia and take the reins of government in Macedonia, Craterus had only gotten as far as Cilicia in southeastern Turkey. Craterus did not leave Cilicia for Macedonia until the spring of 322 B.C., nearly a year after the death of Alexander. Antipater never went to Babylon.

From Susa, Alexander moved to the imperial residence at Ecbatana. There he ordered festivals and games to enjoy the talents of more than three thousand artists and entertainers who had come to him from Greece eager to perform for his pleasure. During the festival, there were the usual amounts of copious eating and drinking that had come to characterize so much of Alexander's life. His closest friend and lover Hephaestion fell ill with a fever during the festivities, and Alexander ordered his personal physician, a Greek named Glaucus,

to treat him.[44] Glaucus placed Hephaestion under rigid dietary guide-
lines and for seven days attempted to treat the fever. But Hephaestion was young, younger than Alexander, and difficult to control,
especially when it came to his appetites. He refused to follow his
physician's advice, and one morning while Glaucus was attending a
performance at the festival Hephaestion ate an entire boiled chicken
and drank a large container of wine. An hour later he was dead.

Alexander was summoned from the festival and told that Hephaestion had died. For the better part of that day, he lay weeping on
the body of his dead friend. Then Alexander cut off his hair over the
body of his friend as Achilles had done when his friend Patroklos
had died at Troy. Alexander's grief lasted but a short time before it
was transformed into rage.[45] The physician was blamed for the death
and crucified. All events at the festival were canceled, and the entire
empire was ordered into mourning. The temple of Asclepius, the god
of healing, was destroyed at Ecbatana.

Alexander ordered the body of Hephaestion sent to Babylon for
the funeral and burial. The king lavished huge sums of money on the
construction of a tomb and preparations for the most elaborate and
magnificent funeral the ancient world had ever seen. Alexander proclaimed that Hephaestion would be worshiped as a god throughout
the empire.

After a few days of seclusion, Alexander tried to find solace for his
loss by hunting. When killing animals no longer sufficed to keep
away the grief, he turned to making war on the Cossaeans, a tribe
living in the mountains between Susa and Ecbatana. The Cossaeans
had done nothing to warrant such a "slaughter." Ptolemy accompanied Alexander along with the cavalry and the infantry into the
mountains, where they systematically exterminated the Cossaeans
"from the youngest to the oldest"—all this slaughter simply to
assuage the king's anger over the death of his friend.[46] When the
campaign was finished, Alexander and the army set out for Babylon,
the city he had designated as the capital of his new empire. It was
now the late spring of 323 B.C.

As Alexander crossed the Tigris River he was met by Nearchus
and a number of Chaldaean priests of the god Baal. The priests had
come to warn Alexander not to enter the city facing in the direction

of the setting sun and at the head of his army because of omens that portended evil for him.[47] Alexander heeded the warning and established his camp some thirty kilometers away from the city. But after a few days, he was advised by Anaxarchus, his philosopher in residence, to ignore the warning and proceed to Babylon. Alexander was still apprehensive, so he attempted to enter the city with the sun behind him. The approach to Babylon by this direction was difficult for the army and its baggage train because of marshes.[48] As a result, Alexander was forced to change his line of march and enter the city with the sun in his face.

As Alexander neared the city walls, he saw ravens fighting with each other in the sky overhead. Several of the birds, exhausted by the ferocity of their struggle, fell to the ground dead. The Greeks believed in augury, the interpretation of omens derived from the flight and actions of birds. When Alexander entered the city, the garrison commander, Apollodorus, had sacrifices performed to learn the significance of the behavior of these birds. He called upon his brother, Pythagoras, who was a seer and expert in the interpretation of omens to read the entrails of the sacrificed animals. The seer was disturbed because the liver of the animal that had been sacrificed was found to have no lobe, something that he had seen weeks earlier when he sacrificed regarding the fate of Hephaestion. The liver of that sacrificial victim had no lobe,[49] and Hephaestion had died shortly thereafter. The results of the sacrifice were hidden from the king.

In preparation for the magnificent funeral of Hephaestion, Alexander had a long section of the city walls demolished. The bricks from the wall were used to build the foundation for a massive funeral pyre in the center of the city. The pyre was constructed on a leveled square with each side nearly half a kilometer in length. The pyre rose to a height of more than seventy meters in a series of elaborate levels. Each level contained intricate figures, from the prows of ships to armed men nearly five meters high. At the top were images of sirens carved of wood and then hollowed out. Within each siren was concealed a woman who sang a lament to the dead.[50] The world had never before seen such a magnificent edifice, much less one to be burned in honor of a man who had never even been a king. There were games and festivities for days, and during that period Alexander received ambassadors from all over the Mediterranean world. Envoys came from as far away as Rome, Gaul, and Carthage to pay their respects to the greatest monarch in history and acknowledge the conqueror of the ancient world.[51] The Romans and the Carthaginians were anxious to learn where Alexander intended to move next.

Cassander, the elder son of Antipater, arrived at Babylon. Nicanor and Iolas, Antipater's two younger sons, had been at Babylon for some time. Nicanor served as an officer, and Iolas brought the king his wine each day.

When Cassander arrived in Babylon and attended court, he saw the Persians perform proskynesis before Alexander for the first time. Cassander could not restrain himself at the spectacle and laughed openly before the king and the rest of the court. Alexander, in a rage, jumped down from his throne, grabbed Cassander, and dashed his head against the wall. Cassander survived Alexander's displeasure but was so shaken by the rage of the king that he never fully recovered psychologically. Years later, following the deaths of Alexander and then Antipater, Cassander became king of Macedonia and master of Greece. Even as king Cassander was unable to overcome the fearful memory of Alexander's rage, and once when Cassander was visiting Delphi and unexpectedly came upon a statue of Alexander, he is reported to have shuddered at the sight.

In the weeks following the funeral of Hephaestion, Alexander's superstition and paranoia became worse as he became "prey to his fears." Alexander had always been a superstitious man, as were the Greeks and Macedonians in general. Now, he began to see evil omens all around him. His pet lion was kicked to death in its compound by an angry jackass—a lion, the king of beasts, killed by the lowest and most stupid of animals. Then a few days later an idiot was discovered sitting on Alexander's throne wearing his royal crown and robes. The deranged man was removed from the throne, tortured, and then executed. The king spent most of his time sequestered in the palace sacrificing and drinking, often all through the night and into the next day.[52] He surrounded himself with seers, priests, mystics, purifiers, and diviners—all experts in the occult. The king became deranged from his excessive drinking. Everywhere he looked in the palace at Babylon, he saw treason and disloyalty among his soldiers, slaves, and family. He saw omens and manifestations of the divine will in everything around him, and this caused him to become more agitated. The more agitated Alexander became, the more he drank.

One evening Alexander attended a "comus"[53] (drinking bout) at the invitation of a friend named Medius. The comus had been arranged to commemorate the anniversary of the death of the king's hero Heracles. Medius came from a noble family of Larissa in Thessaly[54] and had accompanied Alexander on at least part of the expedition, although not in a military capacity. Medius was also alleged to have been the lover of Iolas, Antipater's youngest son and Alexander's wine-pourer. That night Alexander consumed large quantities of un-mixed wine provided by Medius and served by Antipater's son Iolas. Toward the end of the evening, the king drained a large beaker of wine in one gulp and then cried out in acute abdominal pain.[55] He was carried back to his chambers by his attendants and put to bed.

The pain intensified throughout the night, and the Greek physicians were unable to relieve the king's suffering. Then Alexander developed a fever. The symptoms were disturbingly similar to those that attended the fatal illness of Hephaestion. As Alexander's body dehydrated because of the fever, he continued to drink prodigious quantities of wine to quench his thirst. Soon the king became delirious. Contemporary scholars enamored of Alexander and defensive of allegations that he had become an alcoholic by this stage in his life[56] have insisted that he "began to drink wine as hard as he could to try and check the onset of the malaria that would kill him."[57]

The case for any cause of Alexander's death is ultimately forced to rest on his symptoms as they were recorded in the daily journals of the court at Babylon, known as the Ephemeredes.[58] Alexander's symptoms were acute abdominal pain, escalating fever, and great thirst. For ten days after the onset of the pain and fever, he suffered from delirium, loss of voice, and increased weakness that gradually progressed to paralysis and death.

Malaria could well have been the cause of Alexander's death, but then so could acute alcohol poisoning or a body simply worn out from too much abuse. Alexander's patient history as taken by a modern physician would have shown a young man who was widely traveled and thus had been exposed to a range of viruses and bacteria. He was sexually active with a number of wives, concubines, and male sex partners. He had a history of excessive alcohol consumption and a body that in spite of his youth must have been rundown from years of marching, riding, and fighting. Alexander had suffered a prior fever as well as a number of wounds, the most serious in the two years prior to his death.

In addition, Alexander had spent some time just before his death in the marshes and swamps that existed south of Babylon directing a project to divert the waters of the Euphrates River to irrigate some of the surrounding lands. Malaria, which is carried by mosquitoes, was a problem throughout the ancient Mediterranean world and remains a serious health risk in many parts of the Middle East today.

The question of what killed Alexander has always interested scholars and forensics experts, even today. Current speculation is that an infectious disease—not malaria, alcoholism, or poison—was the probable cause of death. Typhoid fever or a brain inflammation caused by a variation of the modern West Nile virus are two relatively recent possibilities. Because Alexander's corpse was eventually lost to history, scientists have no tissues from which to extract DNA samples for any conclusive testing. Rather, they have to rely on the methods of traditional medicine, analysis of patient history, and symptoms as recounted in the ancient sources to diagnose the cause of his death.

His symptoms have caused some contemporary forensics experts to speculate that typhoid fever was the likely cause of death.[59] Typhoid is a bacterial disease transmitted by contaminated food and water that can cause among other symptoms high fever, stomach pains, and paralysis. Contaminated food and water were a problem in the ancient world as they continue to be today in the Middle East.

Another possible cause of Alexander's death was a variation of the West Nile virus known as West Nile encephalitis. It is an unusual complication of the virus infection that can cause a syndrome termed flaccid paralysis in the victim. Birds, especially crows and ravens, are particularly susceptible to this variation of the infection. It is known from the manuscripts that ravens flew over Alexander's column as he entered Babylon and that several fell dead at his feet. This has caused some experts to conclude that these dead birds might have indicated the presence of the disease in the ancient world.[60] The disease is transmitted from birds to humans by mosquitoes, and it is known that Alexander passed swamps on his approach to Babylon.

The most compelling speculation on the death of Alexander points to poison. There was motive on the part of Antipater as well as a number of the officers around the king. The murders of Parmenio and Philotas as well as reports of the widespread purges at Persepolis, the excesses of the king at Babylon, and the discontent in the army had made Antipater anxious. One source says that the purges "struck terror into Antipater as into all of Alexander's friends."[61] So rather than wait to be summoned by the king and executed, Antipater probably took the initiative and "by the hand of his own son, who was the royal wine-pourer, he administered the poison to the king."[62]

The poison had been gathered up "like a delicate dew" from the cliffs of Nonacris, a mountain in Macedonia whose waters were considered fatal. The water was so caustic that it had to be stored and transported to Babylon in an ass's hoof, for no other material could contain it without being eaten through.[63] It was alleged that Aristotle himself had "counseled" Antipater to "do the deed"[64] and had even provided the poison.[65] Cassander carried the poison to Babylon, and Iolas administered it in the last cup of wine Alexander drank at the end of the evening.[66]

Alexander apparently suspected Antipater of conspiring against him. The king had often commented of late that Antipater had taken too much power upon himself and now thought of himself as a king,[67] especially after his victory over the Spartans at Megalopolis in 330 B.C. Olympias had complained to Alexander about Antipater for years. At first Alexander had dismissed her complaints against him and tried to keep peace between the two, but then he began to heed them. The stories of Alexander being poisoned on order of Antipater and the deed having been carried out by his sons probably did not appear in the manuscripts until long after Alexander's death for fear of offending the new rulers of Macedonia. Five years later, however, Olympias, the queen mother, took her revenge. She had a number of men murdered, among them Iolas. Olympias had no doubt that Antipater and his sons had poisoned her son.[68]

The daily journals of the court at Babylon inform us of the sequence of events that led to Alexander's death. The first night—June 2, 323 B.C.—the king was in considerable pain, so he slept in the bathing room. The next day, he had to be carried out of the palace on a stretcher when it came time for him to perform his usual sacrifices. Following the ceremonies, he lay in the soldiers' barracks for a long time until he felt well enough to be moved back to the palace. The second night, Alexander stayed in his bedchambers and felt well enough by the next morning to spend the following day playing at dice with some of his friends. The third night, Alexander bathed and performed his sacrifices. He spent the remainder of the evening talking to Nearchus about his sea voyages. The fourth night, the king's fever increased. The fever increased even more on the fifth night, and on the sixth night Alexander moved once more to the bathing room, which seemed cooler to him. There he conversed with some of his officers and staff about filling vacancies in the army.

On the seventh night, Alexander's fever worsened and he became violent. On the eighth night, he was carried to a palace on the other side of the Euphrates. There is a story that he rose from his bed and tried to make his way to the riverbank where he intended to drown himself. He intended that the river current would carry his body away from Babylon and his disappearance would cause his subjects to think he had been transported to heaven by the gods. Roxanne supposedly stopped him, and Alexander chastised her for begrudging him "the everlasting fame accorded to one who has been born a god."[69]

On the ninth night, the king lost his speech and some of the Macedonians around him thought he was dead because of his paralysis. Groups of soldiers began to congregate outside the palace gates, and as the day progressed their numbers grew by the hour. As night began to fall, they demanded to see their king and commander. They were allowed to enter Alexander's chambers in small groups, and thousands of men, silently and without weapons or armor, filed passed his canopied bed[70] to say goodbye to the man they had followed for so many years—a man they had come to fear, hate, and love. While Alexander was too weak to speak, he acknowledged their presence with his eyes or a feeble gesture as they filed past his bed. After the last of the soldiers had paid their respects and left his chambers,

Alexander was surrounded by his closest officers. Sensing that he was dying, Alexander was barely able to remove his signet ring from his finger and give it to Perdiccas. Perdiccas accepted the ring and asked to whom he left his empire. Alexander, in a barely audible voice, replied, "My kingdom goes to the strongest."[71]

On the tenth night, there was no entry recorded in the journals. Then, on the eleventh night—June 11, 323 B.C.—as dusk descended on Babylon, Alexander of Macedonia died. He had not reached his thirty-third birthday.

EPILOGUE

ALEXANDER'S ILLNESS AT BABYLON TOOK HIM AND THOSE around him by surprise—it was so sudden that it gives credibility to the suspicion that he had been poisoned. By the time he died, Alexander had become eccentric and bizarre, if not outright mad, running about his palace on the shores of the Euphrates with a gaggle of priests and seers following him, seeing evil omens everywhere, suspicious of his friends and family.

His dying words indicate that his concern was not for his empire or for the success of those who would rule after him, or even for the fate of his unborn son. Alexander had ruled his empire personally, demanding loyalty from his administrators and using the fear of severe punishment to ensure obedience. He had done nothing to impose a uniform structure of government that would survive him. Instead, he had used the existing bureaucratic structure of the defeated Persians and had made sure that all the conquered wealth came to him. The force of his personality and reputation had enabled him to hold parts of his empire together. Alexander was a great conqueror, but what he was not, as the Roman emperor Augustus so astutely commented, was a ruler. Once Alexander lay dying, his empire began to disintegrate.

Alexander had left his empire "to the strongest," and, with him gone, those words were all it took to plunge the eastern half of the ancient world—from Greece to the borders of India—into decades of turmoil and civil war. It would be more than a hundred years before the Romans would impose a unified system of government and administration over much of the western part of Alexander's old empire and the Parthians would unify and rule over the eastern reaches.

Perhaps Alexander made no provisions for his empire to continue in an orderly fashion after his death because it was inconceivable to him that anyone could carry on after him or for that matter that he could ever die. He had cheated death in innumerable contests, and in his mind he was immortal.

The ancients believed that when the gods wished to take vengeance on a man for his crimes they would grant him a lengthy period of impunity, and even considerable success, so that when the time came to destroy him he would feel it that much more painfully. Alexander's crime was that he envied the gods and was presumptuous enough to think that by his accomplishments he could join their company in his lifetime. He was guilty of what the ancient's called hubris—an immoderate level of pride, excessive self-confidence, and, most damning of all, arrogance.

Alexander was driven by the power of personal motivation and, later, by his own demons to accomplish what he did. For the lord of Asia, conquest was not a means to building an empire; it became an end in itself. His all-absorbing obsession through his short but crowded life was to become a god. War and conquest were the methods he believed would enable him to realize his goal. What resulted was his megalomania, his obsessions, and his extravagant, paranoid, and murderous behavior. In the end, even though other hands may have administered the poison, Alexander destroyed himself because he came to believe his own propaganda.

Alexander's psychiatric metamorphosis from a mortal to a god began in his youth with fantasies of Homeric heroes such as Achilles. As he matured and became successful, he claimed to be a descendant of Heracles, a man who became a god. Then, in Egypt, one of the conquered lands, Alexander found an oracle who confirmed his mother's contention that his true father was Zeus. Finally, by the end of his career, at the age of thirty-two, he had convinced himself that he was a living god. And conquest had brought Alexander the power and the resources to demand that the world worship him as a god.

Unquestionably, Alexander of Macedonia was one of if not the greatest conqueror the world, ancient or modern, has ever seen. In the short span of just thirteen years, he conquered more territory and amassed a fortune greater than anyone had ever done before. Seven years before he died, the young conqueror had stood on the palace terrace of Persepolis and looked out over the empire that was now his. It was his moment of greatest glory, and there would never be another like it in his life. He had come to Persepolis after four years of conquest, bringing to its knees in that short period a great empire, and he was now the richest and most powerful man in the ancient world. Alexander had reached the pinnacle of power by the age of twenty-five.

Yet in the next seven years all that Alexander accomplished would be lost. In the East, beyond the Persian borders of Iran in the mysterious lands of Afghanistan, Uzbekistan, Tajikistan, and Pakistan, lay a people and terrain that in the end would consume the soul of the man who subjugated them. Alexander's conquest of the East was ephemeral—he conquered only what he passed through—but the conquest of the East over him was permanent. The East changed his psyche and altered his soul, affecting what was weakest and most vulnerable in his character—his ego. As he traveled into the farthest reaches of the Orient, Alexander began a slow and steady demise. These would be years of slaughter and a chronicle of how senselessly cruel a conqueror can be to those he has subjugated. Alexander would lash out not only at the enemies before him but at those closest to him as well. He would drive his armies farther and farther into the East for no other reason than to gratify his ego. He would establish towns and cities, which he named after himself, in the most remote locations and populate them with his unwilling soldiers. He would lead his army into deserts, where they suffered unacceptable levels of casualties, for no other reason than to emulate the deeds of gods and legendary heroes.

In the end, what did Alexander achieve in his short lifetime? Perhaps he achieved that which he wanted most—immortality. He has taken his place among the giants of history, and he will live on in its pages as one of the greatest, if not *the* greatest, conqueror of all time. The world's great generals—men such as Hannibal, Caesar, and Napoleon—used Alexander as the standard by which they measured their own success, and there is little doubt that future generals will do so as well. Nearly everyone knows the name of Alexander the Great and has used him as a projection for dreams and aspirations. Each country, each generation, has looked at Alexander and seen reflected in his story the issues of their own times. Biographers and now filmmakers put as much of themselves into that great historical figure as they can. Legions of petty and some not-so-petty politicians, movie stars, and sports figures often succumb to the same seductions of power and believe that truth is a commodity to be bent to their own purposes and ends. The power and fascination of Alexander's character and accomplishments retain their attraction today, in our own generation, as much as they did two thousand years ago. In that regard, Alexander got his wish—he will live forever.

Yet Alexander's story is testimony to the darker side of the human condition. It validates the axiom that power is a dangerous commodity that must be handled carefully by those who possess it. Power corrupts quickly if not used judiciously and cautiously. It destroys those who seek it as an end rather than as the means to accomplish something of lasting and humanitarian value. The fear, however, is that little if anything will be learned from Alexander's experience and that the world will be forced to repeat his mistakes in an endless and increasingly more dangerous cycle of war and conquest.

WHO WAS WHO
IN THE
WORLD OF ALEXANDER

Alexander III, the Great—Son of Philip, Macedonian king who conquered the Persian Empire and all the lands east to the Indus River. Died 323 B.C.

Alexander IV—Infant son of Alexander the Great by Roxanne and designated heir to the throne. Murdered along with his mother during the years of turmoil that followed the death of his father.

Alexander the Lyncestian—Member of the Macedonian royal family, officer, and the most likely candidate for the throne of Macedonia should Alexander have been killed. Executed on the order of Alexander on charges of conspiracy in 330 B.C.

Anaxarchus—One of the Greek philosophers in the entourage who pandered and encouraged Alexander to think of himself as a god among men.

Antipater—Alexander's regent in Macedonia and Greece and one of his principal successors. Antipater had served as a senior commander and advisor to Philip and along with Parmenio had helped Alexander stabilize his rule in the early years. Died 319 B.C.

Ariamazes—Noble who defied Alexander at the Sogdian Rock. Crucified in 328 B.C.

Ariobarzanes—Persian satrap and commander in the army of Darius III. He defended Persepolis and trapped Alexander's army at the Persian Gates. Died in combat in 330 B.C.

Aristotle—One of the greatest of the Greek philosophers and the teacher of the young Alexander. Aristotle planted in Alexander's mind the idea that in every age a man came forth to lead who was above the laws.

Artabazus—Persian satrap, close friend of Darius III, and the father of Alexander's mistress Barsine. He later became a close ally of Alexander and satrap of Bactria (northern Afghanistan) and Sogdiana (Uzbekistan and Tajikistan).

Artaxerxes IV (Bessus)—The satrap of Bactria and one of the Persian king's principal commanders. He became the leader of the conspirators who murdered Darius and proclaimed himself Artaxerxes IV. Betrayed by his own men, he was tortured and executed by Alexander in 329 B.C.

Bagoas—Persian eunuch loved first by King Darius and then by Alexander.

Bagodaras—Bactrian commander who defected to Alexander and organized the coup against Bessus.

Barsaentes—Satrap of Arachosia and Drangiana in western Afghanistan. One of the co-conspirators in the murder of Darius. Captured and executed by Alexander in 329 B.C.

Barsine—Persian noblewoman who became the mistress of Alexander after her capture at Damascus. Reputed to have been a woman of great beauty and intelligence, she was considerably older than Alexander and allegedly first introduced him to the pleasures of heterosexual love. Murdered.

Calanus—Indian philosopher who accompanied Alexander on his return to Persia and committed suicide when he fell ill at Persepolis in 324 B.C.

Callisthenes—The most senior and respected of the Greek philosophers in Alexander's entourage. Callisthenes was related to Aristotle and implicated in the pages' conspiracy. Executed in 328 B.C.

Cassander—Son of Antipater and later king of Macedonia.

Cebalinus and Nicomachus—Fraternal catamites in the court of Alexander who revealed the plot to assassinate the king in what is now western Afghanistan.

Chorienes—Bactrian noble who surrendered his fortress to Alexander and became an ally. Hosted the wedding of Alexander to Roxanne.

Cleitus the Black—Senior Macedonian commander whose family had a long and intimate connection to Alexander dating back to the king's childhood. Murdered by Alexander during an argument in Sogdiana in 328 B.C.

Cleopatra—Younger sister of Alexander.

Coenus—Senior Macedonian commander and son-in law of Parmenio. Took the lead in the prosecution and torture of Philotas and later in India was instrumental in convincing Alexander to turn back. Died in combat in 326 B.C.

Craterus—Macedonian commander who became Alexander's most senior general and filled the advisory role that Parmenio had once held. Killed in battle in 321 B.C.

Darius I—One of the first and greatest of the Persian kings. He began the construction of Persepolis and invaded Greece in 490 B.C.

Darius III—The last and perhaps most tragic of the Persian kings. Murdered in the deserts of eastern Iran by his officers in 330 B.C.

Drypetis—The youngest daughter of Darius III, captured after the battle of Issus and later given in marriage to Hephaestion. Murdered 323 B.C.

Erigyius—Senior Macedonian commander who defeated and slew Satibarzanes of Aria in single combat. Died of disease 329 B.C.

Eumenes—Secretary to Alexander and royal chancellor. Executed in 316 B.C. during the struggle for the succession to Alexander's throne.

Harpalus—Boyhood friend of Alexander who became the royal treasurer but proved corrupt. He fled to Greece with a considerable portion of Alexander's treasure. Murdered in 325 B.C.

Hephaestion—Alexander's close friend and lover. Died of gluttony and alcoholism 324 B.C.

Heracles—Son of Alexander the Great by his Persian mistress Barsine. Murdered along with his mother after Alexander's death.

Hermolaus—Son of a Macedonian noble in the army of Alexander. Served as a page in Alexander's entourage and was the principal conspirator in the plot to assassinate the king in Sogdiana. Executed 328 B.C.

Iolas—Youngest son of Antipater and cupbearer to Alexander. It is Iolas who is suspected of having administered the poison to Alexander on order of Antipater. Murdered.

Leonnatus—Macedonian bodyguard to Alexander who along with Peucestas helped save the king's life in India.

Meleager—Macedonian officer and one of the principal players in the struggle for the succession after Alexander's death in Babylon. Murdered 323 B.C.

Nabarzanes—Commander of the Persian royal cavalry and the palace guard in the army of Darius III. He was probably the most powerful figure in the king's entourage. A co-conspirator with Bessus in the murder of Darius.

Nearchus—Boyhood friend of Alexander. Commanded the fleet that sailed down the Indus and into the Arabian Sea.

Nicanor—Macedonian commander and younger son of Parmenio. Died of disease in Afghanistan 330 B.C.

Olympias—The "terrible mother of Alexander the Great" and clearly the most dominant force in his life. Alexander allied himself with her emotionally and politically in the early years of his rule, and she continued to advise him on all matters until his death. Murdered 316 B.C.

Onesicritus—Greek historian in Alexander's entourage who studied the Indian philosophers.

Orsines—Satrap of Pasagardae. Executed in 323 B.C. for failing to honor Alexander's eunuch.

Oxartes—Sogdian noble from Nautaca and ally of Alexander.

Oxathres—Brother of Darius III. Joined Alexander after the death of his brother rather than be executed. His principal value to Alexander was symbolic. His presence on Alexander's staff, even though he seems to have had no rank of importance, symbolized the acceptance of Alexander's rule by the Persian nobility.

Oxathres—Son of Abuletes, the satrap of Susa. Personally executed by Alexander for corruption in 324 B.C.

Oxyartes—Bactrian noble, father of Roxanne, and ally of Alexander.

Parmenio—The most senior of the Macedonian commanders. Advisor first to Philip then to Alexander. Along with Antipater, responsible for stabilizing the early years of Alexander's rule. Often credited with being the principal force behind Alexander's early military successes in Asia. Assassinated by order of Alexander in 330 B.C.

Parysatis—Youngest daughter of the Persian king Artaxerxes III. Alexander took her as his third wife at Susa. Murdered 323 B.C.

Patron—Greek commander of the mercenaries who fought against Alexander in the army of Darius III.

Perdiccas—Macedonian commander and one of the entourage of Alexander. Perdiccas was one of the principals in the struggle for power after Alexander died. Executed 321 B.C.

Peucestas—Macedonian bodyguard who saved Alexander's life and later was rewarded with the satrapy of Persepolis.

Philip II of Macedonia—King of Macedonia and the father of Alexander. Murdered 336 B.C.

Philip III Arrhidaeus—Half-witted older brother of Alexander who was put on the throne following the king's death at Babylon. Murdered 316 B.C.

Philotas—Senior Macedonian commander and elder son of Parmenio. Tortured and executed by Alexander in 330 B.C. on a charge of plotting to assassinate the king.

Polydamas—Close friend of Parmenio and one of his assassins.

Porus—One of Alexander's principal adversaries when he invaded India. Porus later became an ally of Alexander following his defeat at the battle of the Hydaspes River.

Ptolemy—Senior Macedonian commander and close boyhood friend of Alexander. Following the king's death at Babylon, Ptolemy became one of his successors and then pharaoh of Egypt. Died in 285 B.C.

Roxanne—Young Sogdian noblewoman and the principal wife of Alexander. Murdered 310 B.C.

Satibarzanes—Persian satrap of Aria in western Afghanistan. He was one of the co-conspirators in the murder of Darius III and later went on to lead the resistance against Alexander. Beheaded 329 B.C.

Seleucus—One of the successors of Alexander. Allotted Babylon after Alexander's death. Assassinated 281 B.C.

Sisigambis—Mother of Darius III. Captured following the battle of Issus and held prisoner by Alexander. She developed a close relationship with Alexander and according to some sources became a surrogate mother to him. Unable to go on living when she learned of Alexander's death at Babylon, she starved herself to death.

Sisimithres—Incestuous Sogdian satrap of Nautaca (Uzbekistan).

Spitamenes—Leader of the Sogdian revolt against Alexander and the man who caused Alexander more problems in Central Asia than any other. Spitamenes is considered to be the first national hero of modern-day Uzbekistan. Beheaded by his wife 328 B.C.

Stasanor—Senior Macedonian commander who along with Erigyius defeated Satibarzanes in Aria.

Stateira—Wife of Darius III and reputed to have been the most beautiful woman in the Persian Empire. She was captured by Alexander following the battle of Issus when she was deserted by her husband. Stateira lived only two years as a captive before she died in childbirth, allegedly bearing the child of Alexander.

Stateira—Elder daughter of Darius III. Second wife of Alexander. Murdered by Roxanne shortly after Alexander's death in 323 B.C.

Taxiles—Indian king of Taxila who became a close ally of Alexander.

Thais—Athenian courtesan and later mistress of Ptolemy. Instrumental in the burning of Persepolis.

Thalestris—One-breasted queen of the Amazons who came to Alexander on the shores of the Caspian Sea in the hopes of conceiving a child with him.

Tiridates—Royal treasurer of Darius III at Persepolis who turned the city over to Alexander in return for personal gain.

Xerxes I—One of the most famous and powerful of the Persian kings and the son of Darius I. He invaded Greece in 480 B.C., defeated the Spartans at Thermopylae, and burned Athens. Xerxes was the most hated of all the Persian kings and the pretext for the Greek invasion under Alexander.

NOTES

Chapter One

1. 522–485 B.C.

2. 485–464 B.C.

3. Peter Green, *Alexander of Macedon* (Berkeley, 1992), p. 314.

4. The Persians sacrificed horses to their god, while the Greeks sacrificed bulls to theirs.

5. Those same bulls now stand guard half a world away at the Oriental Institute of the University of Chicago.

6. A. T. Olmstead, *History of the Persian Empire* (London, 1992), p. 162.

7. Xenophon *Cyropaedia* 8.3.10.

8. Herodotus *Histories* 7.16; Curtius *History of Alexander* 8.4.17.

9. Plutarch *Parallel Lives* 37.5.

10. Curtius *History of Alexander* 4.10.19–21.

11. The term "hegemon" referred to the position of Alexander as "boss" of the Greeks, not their king. It was a title for life conferred upon him by the Corinthian League, a feudal council of the Greek city-states established by his father Philip and to which each city-state sent deputies proportionate to its military strength. The term "strategos" refers to Alexander's title as commanding general of the Greek expeditionary force sent to Asia for the "war of vengeance" against Persia. This title was also conferred upon Alexander by the Corinthian League but only for the duration of the war against Persia. According to some scholars, the Greeks did not look upon the Macedonians as equals but as their less sophisticated barbarian cousins. Ulrich Wilcken, *Alexander the Great* (New York, 1967), pp. 23 and 45.

12. Estimated at twenty-five thousand infantry and some three thousand cavalry.

13. Siculus *Library of History* 17.68.4.

14. Curtius *History of Alexander* 5.5.2–3.

15. Curtius *History of Alexander* 5.4.34.

16. Alexander scholars such as Bosworth agree that Persepolis was surrendered to Alexander from within. A. B. Bosworth, *Commentary on Arrian's History*, Vol. 1 (Oxford, 1980), pp. 329–33.

17. A talent was an ancient measure of weight in gold or silver, and no really reliable estimate exists of its modern equivalent in dollars. The most conservative estimate is that Alexander found close to a billion dollars. Plutarch *Alexander* 7:35, Curtius *History of Alexander* 5.6.9.

18. Wilcken, *Alexander the Great*, pp. 142–43.

19. Curtius *History of Alexander* 5.6.9.

20. Plutarch *Alexander* 7.37 wrote that it took five thousand camels, while Siculus *Library of History* 17.71 wrote that it took three thousand. In either case, it took a lot of animals to haul away the treasure from Persepolis. Siculus in the same passage mentions Susa as a repository, while other sources mention Ecbatana.

21. Curtius *History of Alexander* 5.6.9, Siculus *Library of History* 17.71, and Justini *Epitoma Historiarum Philippicarum* 12.1.3 all agree that the totals varied between 176,000 and 190,000 talents. Plutarch and Arrian do not mention how much money was taken, only that it was a lot.

22. Cyrus, 560–534 B.C.

23. *Cyropaedia* and the *Anabasis*.

24. Alexander's soldiers discovered Greek ambassadors in the camp of Darius after the Persian defeat at Issus. Then just before the battle of Gaugamela, letters allegedly from Darius were discovered in the Greek camp that offered sizable rewards to any Greek who would assassinate Alexander. Curtius *History of Alexander* 4.11.18.

25. Curtius *History of Alexander* 5.6.11.

26. Siculus *Library of History* 17.71.3.

27. New Testament, Revelation 17:5.

28. Curtius *History of Alexander* 5.1.38–40.

29. Wilcken, *Alexander the Great*, p. 130. The Greeks considered the Macedonians as their barbarian cousins even though Alexander spoke Greek and had been educated by Aristotle.

30. Plutarch *Alexander* 7.2

31. A. B. Bosworth and E. J. Baynham, eds., *Cambridge Ancient History* (Cambridge, 1994), chap. 17.

32. Green, *Alexander of Macedon*, p. 315.

33. Curtius *History of Alexander* 5,6.1.

34. Olmstead, *History of the Persian Empire*, p. 162.

35. 405–359 B.C., the longest reign of the Persian kings.

36. Olmstead, *History of the Persian Empire*, p. 520.

37. Estimates on the number of these maimed Greeks vary from eight hundred (Siculus *Library of History* 17.69) to four thousand (Curtius *History*

of Alexander 5.5.6). Maiming as a form of punishment is still prevalent throughout the Middle East and Central Asia today.

38. Siculus *Library of History* 17.70.2.

39. Olmstead, *History of the Persian Empire*, p. 520.

40. Siculus *Library of History* 17.70.

41. Bosworth, Fox, Green, Olmstead, Tarn, and Wilcken are examples.

42. Green, *Alexander of Macedon*, p. 314.

43. Arrian *Anabasis of Alexander* 2.15, 3–5, and Curtius *History of Alexander* 3.13.15.

44. Siculus *Library of History* 17.70, Justini *Epitoma Historiarum Philippicarum* 11.14.10, Plutarch *Parallel Lives* 37.2; and Curtius *History of Alexander* 5.6. Arrian ignores the episode.

45. Demaratus of Corinth, who in earlier years had reconciled Alexander with his father. Plutarch *Alexander* 9.12.

46. Curtius *History of Alexander* 5.2.13. In this version a Persian slave wept tears of shame to see a Macedonian upon the throne.

47. A cluster of six visible stars in the constellation Taurus by which the ancients determined the onset and end of winter.

48. Plutarch *Alexander* 41.

49. Bosworth, *Commentary on Arrian's History of Alexander*, 1:332.

50. Siculus *Library of History* 71.2, Curtius *History of Alexander* 5.6.9, and Plutarch *Parallel Lives* 37.4.

51. Arrian *Anabasis of Alexander* 3.18.11, Siculus *Library of History* 72, and Curtius *History of Alexander* 5.7.

52. Arrian *Anabasis of Alexander* 3.18, 11–12.

53. Robin Lane Fox, *Alexander the Great* (London, 1973), p. 263.

54. Curtius *History of Alexander* 5.7.2 and Plutarch *Alexander* 23.

55. Curtius *History of Alexander* 5.7.

56. Arrian *Anabasis of Alexander* 3.18.

57. Livy *Roman History* 30.14.6–7.

58. Curtius *History of Alexander* 5.6.2.

59. Herodotus *Histories* 1.53.

60. Plutarch *Alexander* 23.

61. Plutarch *Alexander* 4, 21, and 38 for Alexander on wine, women, and song.

62. Curtius *History of Alexander* 5.7: "non quidem quas violari nefas esset, ebrium scortum."

63. Plutarch *Alexander* 38.

64. Curtius *History of Alexander* 5.7 and Siculus *Library of History* 17.72.

65. Curtius *History of Alexander* 5.

66. Plutarch *Alexander* 38.7.

67. Plutarch *Alexander* 38.11.

68. Curtius *History of Alexander* 5.7.11.

69. Arrian *Indica* 6.30.1.

70. Siculus *Library of History* 19.21.

71. Olmstead, *History of the Persian Empire*, p. 522.

Chapter Two

1. Ecbatana was the summer palace of the Persian kings and corresponds to the modern Iranian city of Hamadan.

2. Curtius *History of Alexander* 5.9 and Arrian *Anabasis of Alexander* 3.21.

3. Arrian *Anabasis of Alexander* 3.22.

4. Siculus *Library of History* 18.6.1, Justini *Epitoma Historiarum Philippicarum* 10.3.3–5. "How was it that the man selected for the Persian throne on his record of personal bravery underwent such a metamorphosis after his accession and became such a chronic coward?"

5. Curtius *History of Alexander* 4.12.

6. Curtius *History of Alexander* 4.10.

7. Curtius *History of Alexander* 4.12–13 and Plutarch *Alexander* 31.

8. Curtius *History of Alexander* 4.13.

9. Thomas Harbottle, *Harbottle's Dictionary of Battles* (New York, 1981), p. 121.

10. Arrian *Anabasis of Alexander* 2.11.4 and 3.14.3.

11. Curtius *History of Alexander* 4.11.

12. Arrian *Anabasis of Alexander* 3.19.

13. Curtius *History of Alexander* 5.11.4 says four thousand mercenaries, while Arrian *Anabasis of Alexander* 3.16.2 says two thousand.

14. Arrian *Anabasis of Alexander* 3.16.2 and Curtius *History of Alexander* 5.9.15.

15. Curtius *History of Alexander* 5.11.5–6.

16. Probably the Sarin Kuh Pass, the Tereh Mumag Pass, and the Basme Aftar Pass on the road leading out of modern-day Tehran, which passes Rey, ancient Rhagae. Each of these passes is a little more than twenty-two hundred meters high.

17. Siculus *Library of History* 11.69.2.

18. Arrian *Anabasis of Alexander* 3.19.

19. Curtius *History of Alexander* 5.13.

20. Inferred to mean the Greeks.

21. Arrian *Anabasis of Alexander* 3.21 and Curtius *History of Alexander* 5.13.

22. Justini *Epitoma Historiarum Philippicarum* 11.5.

23. Curtius *History of Alexander* 5.13.4.

24. Arrian *Anabasis of Alexander* 3.21.7.

25. Curtius *History of Alexander* 5.13.9.

26. Curtius *History of Alexander* 5.13.11.

27. Curtius *History of Alexander* 5.10.

28. Arrian *Anabasis of Alexander* 3.21 and 23 describes him as the virtual head of the Persian court and second only to the king.

29. Curtius *History of Alexander* 5.9.

30. Curtius *History of Alexander* 5.9.

31. Curtius *History of Alexander* 5.11. Darius was "not unacquainted with the Greek language," although he regularly used a Greek interpreter.

32. Curtius *History of Alexander* 5.11.

33. Curtius *History of Alexander* 5.13.8–10.

34. Curtius *History of Alexander* 5.12.17.

35. Arrian *Anabasis of Alexander* 3.21, gives no precise numbers for how many men were with Alexander when he came upon the Persian column, only that Alexander's men were greatly outnumbered. Curtius *History of Alexander* 5.13.21 says "barely 3,000 horsemen had been able to keep up with Alexander in his haste." Plutarch *Alexander* 43 says "only sixty," while Siculus *Library of History* 17.73 says that Alexander had cavalry with him but gives no numbers. The whole episode shows that perception is, under certain circumstances, far more powerful than reality.

36. Curtius *History of Alexander* 5.11.

37. Justini *Epitoma Historiarum Philippicarum* 11.15.1 names it Thara, an oasis.

38. Curtius *History of Alexander* 5.13.6 says it was a village.

39. Plutarch *Alexander* 40.3–4, Curtius *History of Alexander* 5.13.23, and Justini *Epitoma Historiarum Philippicarum* 11.15.

40. Siculus *Library of History* 17.73.4.

41. Siculus *Library of History* 17.73.3, Justini *Epitoma Historiarum Philippicarum* 11.15.16, Pliny *Natural History* 36.132.

Chapter Three

1. Archeological evidence from fairly recent excavations has generated a strong possibility that a number of low mounds located just outside the city of Damghan in northeastern Iran may be the remains of this ancient city.

2. Siculus *Library of History* 17.75 and Curtius *History of Alexander* 6.2.15.

3. Siculus *Library of History* 17.74 writes that eight thousand talents were found in the baggage of Darius plus a considerable amount of personal possessions. Curtius *History of Alexander* 6.2.10 writes that the amount looted was twenty-six thousand talents plus an equal amount that was pilfered by the men Alexander entrusted with recording and guarding the wealth.

4. Curtius *History of Alexander* 6.2.16.

5. Curtius *History of Alexander* 6.2.21.

6. Curtius *History of Alexander* 6.3.16.

7. Probably the modern-day Iranian city of Sari.

8. Curtius *History of Alexander* 6.2.9.

9. Curtius *History of Alexander* 6.5.23.

10. Barsine was Alexander's mistress. She was considerably older than Alexander and had been captured after the battle of Issus with the family of Darius. She bore Alexander a son named Hercules, and it is alleged that she was the first woman with whom Alexander ever had sex. Barsine remained with Alexander until he died.

11. Curtius *History of Alexander* 6.5.4.

12. Siculus *Library of History* 17.76.

13. Arrian *Anabasis of Alexander* 3.23.

14. Siculus *Library of History* 17.77, Curtius *History of Alexander* 6.5.24–32, Justini *Epitoma Historiarum Philippicarum* 12.3.5–7.

15. Today the area comprises a part of Turkey.

16. Curtius *History of Alexander* 6.6.30.

17. Curtius *History of Alexander* 3.12.17.

18. Plutarch *Alexander* 16.

19. Plutarch *Alexander* 4.5–6.

20. Arrian is curiously silent about the Amazon queen and her visit.

21. Plutarch *Alexander* 46.2.

22. Arrian *Anabasis of Alexander* 3.25 and Curtius *History of Alexander* 6.6.13.

23. Probably the modern-day city of Mashhad in eastern Iran near the border with Afghanistan.

24. Curtius *History of Alexander* 6.6.1–2, Siculus *Library of History* 17.77.2, Justini *Epitoma Historiarum Philippicarum* 12.3.8–10.

25. Plutarch *Alexander* 45.

26. A. B. Bosworth, *Commentary on Arrian's History*, Vol. 2 (Oxford, 1995), p. 47–48.

27. Siculus *Library of History* 17.77.

28. Plutarch *Alexander* 48.10.

29. Curtius *History of Alexander* 6.6.

30. Curtius *History of Alexander* 6.6.16.

31. Modern-day Herat in western Afghanistan.

32. The modern town is called Farah in Afghanistan.

33. Arrian *Anabasis of Alexander* 3.26.

34. Plutarch *Alexander* 48.5.

35. Plutarch *Alexander* 48.4.

36. Curtius *History of Alexander* 6.9.4.

37. Curtius *History of Alexander* 6.9.12.

38. Curtius *History of Alexander* 6.10.23.

39. Curtius *History of Alexander* 6.10.30.

40. Curtius *History of Alexander* 3.6.4.

41. Curtius *History of Alexander* 6.11.10.

42. Curtius *History of Alexander* 6.9.30.

43. Plutarch *Alexander* 49.12 says that Alexander actually hid behind a tapestry and listened to Philotas being tortured.

44. Curtius *History of Alexander* 6.11.23.

45. Curtius *History of Alexander* 6.11.38 says stoning, while Arrian *Anabasis of Alexander* 3.26.3 says execution in the traditional manner by javelins.

46. Siculus *Library of History* 17.80.3.

47. Curtius *History of Alexander* 7.2.17, Strabo *Geography* 15.2.10, Siculus *Library of History* 17.80.3. According to the sources, the journey under normal conditions and circumstances would have taken thirty days.

48. Curtius *History of Alexander* 7.2.32.

49. Curtius *History of Alexander* 7.2.35 and Siculus *Library of History* 17.80.

50. Plutarch *Alexander* 49.14.

Chapter Four

1. Siculus *Library of History* 17.81.

2. Curtius *History of Alexander* 7.4.34–38 tells us his hair was white by this time in his life.

3. Curtius *History of Alexander* 7.4.40, Siculus *Library of History* 17.83.6.

4. The modern cities of Kandahar and Ghazni.

5. Curtius *History of Alexander* 7.3.

6. Curtius *History of Alexander* 7.3.22.

7. Modern-day Kunduz.

8. The ruins of Balkh can be found today just a few kilometers away from the modern town of Mazar-e-Sharif in northern Afghanistan.

9. Syr Darya River, which flows from the mountains of Uzbekistan through the steppes of Kazakhstan to the Aral Sea.

10. Modern-day Uzbekistan, Kazakhstan, and Kyrgyzstan.

11. Curtius calls him Gobares.

12. The Amu Darya, which constitutes the modern-day northern boundaries between Afghanistan, Turkmenistan, Uzbekistan, and Tajikistan.

13. Probably the modern Uzbek city of Karsi.

14. Sir Aural Stein, *On Alexander's Track to the Indus* (London, 1929), 111.

15. Curtius *History of Alexander* 7.5.19–26, Siculus *Library of History* 17.83, Arrian *Anabasis of Alexander* 3.29.8–30.

16. Plutarch *Alexander* 43.6.

17. Siculus *Library of History* 17.83.

18. Curtius *History of Alexander* 7.10.10, Arrian *Anabasis of Alexander* 4.7.3, and Plutarch *Alexander* 43.3.

19. Arrian *Anabasis of Alexander* 4.7.3.

20. Tarn says that the site is near the town of Keleft, on the south bank of the river in Afghanistan. W. W. Tarn, *Alexander the Great*, Vol. 1 (Cambridge, U.K.), p. 67.

21. Now called Samarkand in Uzbekistan.

22. Near what is today the modern city of Chugend, in Tajikistan.

23. M. Cary, *Geographic Background of Greek and Roman History* (Oxford, 1949), p. 200.

24. Justini *Epitoma Historiarum Philippicarum* 12.5.8.

25. Siculus *Library of History* 17.99.18, Curtius *History of Alexander* 9.7.1.11, and Arrian *Indica* 5.27.5.

26. Modern Uzbekistan.

27. Curtius *History of Alexander* 7.9.22.

28. Zeravsan River.

29. Curtius *History of Alexander* 7.10.15 mentions six settlements north of the Oxus River in Sogdiana.

30. Because of the way Spitamenes had been able, even for a brief time, to unite the people of Sogdiana against the Macedonian invaders, he has become a national hero of modern-day Uzbekistan.

31. Arrian *Anabasis of Alexander* 4.8 and Curtius *History of Alexander* 8.1.20.

32. Plutarch *Alexander* 50.9.

33. Curtius *History of Alexander* 6.6.1.

34. Curtius *History of Alexander* 8.1.20.

35. Arrian *Anabasis of Alexander* 4.8.

36. Arrian *Anabasis of Alexander* 4.8.7.

37. Arrian *Anabasis of Alexander* 4.8.8.

38. Curtius *History of Alexander* 8.50 wrote that Alexander left the banquet hall and lay in wait for Cleitus to leave. Then he stabbed him to death in a darkened corridor (premeditated murder).

39. Arrian *Anabasis of Alexander* 4.9.1.

40. Arrian *Anabasis of Alexander* 4.8.9.

41. Curtius *History of Alexander* 8.1.21.

42. Arrian *Anabasis of Alexander* 4.9.7.

43. Curtius *History of Alexander* 8.2.12.

44. Curtius *History of Alexander* 8.4.30.

45. Plutarch *Alexander* 41.2.

46. Aristotle *Politics* 1253a.4–5, 25–29.

47. Plutarch *Alexander* 55.8.

48. Arrian *Anabasis of Alexander* 4.10.1–2.

49. Arrian *Anabasis of Alexander* 4.2.6.

50. Southwestern Turkey.

51. Curtius *History of Alexander* 8.5.5.

52. Arrian *Anabasis of Alexander* 4.11.

53. Curtius *History of Alexander* 8.5.21.

54. Arrian *Anabasis of Alexander* 4.11.

55. Arrian *Anabasis of Alexander* 4.12 and Curtius *History of Alexander* 8.5.

56. Curtius *History of Alexander* 8.5.

57. Plutarch *Alexander* 53.2.

58. Plutarch *Alexander* 54.3.

59. Arrian *Anabasis of Alexander* 4.12 and Plutarch *Alexander* 55.

60. Curtius *History of Alexander* 8.5. Arrian calls him Leonnatus in *Anabasis of Alexander* 4.12.

61. Curtius *History of Alexander* 8.5–6.

62. Arrian *Anabasis of Alexander* 4.10.

63. Curtius *History of Alexander* 8.6.3.

64. Siculus *Library of History* 17.65.1 and Curtius *History of Alexander* 5.1.42.

65. Arrian *Anabasis of Alexander* 4.14.2.

66. Xenophon *Cyropaedia* 1.4.14.

67. Curtius *History of Alexander* 8.6.10 and Arrian *Anabasis of Alexander* 4.13.4.

68. Arrian *Anabasis of Alexander* 4.13.5. and Curtius *History of Alexander* 8.6.16.

69. Curtius *History of Alexander* 8.6.21.

70. Curtius *History of Alexander* 8.6.22.

71. Plutarchus *Alexander* 55.23.8 and Curtius *History of Alexander* 8.6.27.

72. Plutarch *Alexander* 55.6–7 and Curtius *History of Alexander* 8.8.

73. Curtius *History of Alexander* 8.7.14: "miraris si liberi homines superbiam tuam ferre non possumus" (do you wonder that we, free men, are not able to bear your haughtiness).

74. Curtius *History of Alexander* 8.8.3.

75. Curtius, *History of Alexander* 8.8.17: "sed orbem terrarium subacturos venire."

76. Curtius *History of Alexander* 8.8.19.

77. Curtius *History of Alexander* 8.8.20. Arrian *Anabasis of Alexander* 4.14.3 says they were stoned to death, as does Plutarch *Alexander* 55.7.

78. A. B. Bosworth, *Commentary on Arrian's History*, Vol. 2 (Oxford, 1995), p. 98.

79. Plutarch *Alexander* 55.9.

80. Curtius *History of Alexander* 8.6.1.

81. Plutarch *Alexander* 55.

82. Plutarch *Alexander* 55.

83. Plutarch *Alexander* 55.9, Curtius *History of Alexander* 6.30.2.

84. Arrian *Anabasis of Alexander* 4.14.

85. Plutarch *Alexander* 55.

86. Curtius *History of Alexander* 8.8.22.

87. Ulrich Wilcken, *Alexander the Great* (New York, 1967), p. 172.

Chapter Five

1. Curtius *History of Alexander* 8.2.40.

2. Curtius *History of Alexander* 8.2.19.

3. Curtius *History of Alexander* 8.2.32.

4. Eight stades equal one mile according to the calculations of D. Cary, *Geographic Background of Greek and Roman History* (Oxford, 1949), p. 200. Thus, the rock was supposed to be nearly 3.5 miles high or 18,000 feet— hardly likely given that the mountains in that area rise to a maximum of about 12,000 feet.

5. Curtius *History of Alexander* 7.9.29.

6. There is a contradiction in two of the major sources on the chronology of events. Curtius *History of Alexander* 7.11 has the storming of the Sogdian Rock happening before the murder of Cleitus in 328 B.C., while Arrian *Anabasis of Alexander* 4.18.4 has the incident of the Sogdian Rock happening after in 327 B.C.

7. Arrian *Anabasis of Alexander* 4.19. 6.

8. Plutarch *Alexander* 47.7 and Curtius *History of Alexander* 8.4.23.

9. Plutarch *Alexander* 47.8 and Curtius *History of Alexander* 8.4.25.

10. W. W. Tarn, *Alexander the Great*, Vol. 1 (Cambridge, 1948), 18.

11. Ulrich Wilcken, *Alexander the Great* (New York, 1967), and Tarn, *Alexander the Great*, 1:18.

12. A son was born to Roxanne when Alexander reached India but died shortly thereafter.

13. The ruins at Ay Khanom were unearthed during the Soviet-Afghan War in the 1980s.

14. A "virguncula . . . ignobilis" as quoted in Curtius *History of Alexander* 8.4.25–30.

15. Plutarch *Alexander* 52.1.

16. Alexander's campaign took place in what is today Pakistan. His army reached only as far east as the Ravi River near Lahore and never entered modern-day India.

17. Arrian *Anabasis of Alexander* 4.26.

18. Arrian *Anabasis of Alexander* 4.27.4, Curtuis *History of Alexander* 8.10.33, and Siculus *Library of History* 17.84.1.

19. Plutarch *Alexander* 59.6.7.

20. Justini *Epitoma Historiarum Philippicarum* 12.7.9, Siculus *Library of History* 17.84.1, and Curtius *History of Alexander* 8.10.35.

21. The name could well derive from the Greek word *ouranos* (sky) or *vounos* (mountain).

22. Arrian *Anabasis of Alexander* 4.28.

23. Arrian *Anabasis of Alexander* 4.29–30 gives the most detailed account.

24. Plutarch *Alexander* 59.2–4.

25. A range of 55–95 as compared with 100–130 in the sweltering South.

26. Cary, *Geographic Background of Greek and Roman History,* 202–3.

27. Arrian *Indica* 5.3.5–19, Curtius *History of Alexander* 8.13, Justini *Epitoma Historiarum Philippicarum* 12.8.1, Plutarch *Alexander* 60.

28. Plutarch *Alexander* 60.15.

29. River Beas near the small town of Jalalpur in eastern Pakistan near the Indian border.

30. Siculus *Library of History* 17.94.2–3 describes the effects of seventy days of continuous rain on the men and their equipment.

31. Siculus *Library of History* 17.94.2.

32. Siculus *Library of History* 17.93.1 claims that the river was nearly a mile wide (seven stadia) and forty feet deep in places (six fathoms).

33. Arrian *Indica* 6.2.

34. Plutarch *Alexander* 62 writes that the figures for the Indian army were no exaggeration.

35. Arrian *Indica* 5.25.

36. Plutarch *Alexander* 62.9.

37. Siculus *Library of History* 17.94 only says that Alexander gave up the push east when the Macedonians refused to follow him. Curtius *History of Alexander* 9.2, Plutarch *Alexander* 7.62, and Justini *Epitoma Historiarum Philippicarum* 12.8 and 9–17 give the most detailed explanations of what happened at the Beas.

38. Siculus *Library of History* 94.5 writes about an assembly of the troops being convened to express their grievances, while Curtius *History of Alexander* 9.2.12 has the soldiers attend a gathering of the rank and file but exclusively for the Macedonian soldiers.

39. Arrian *Anabasis of Alexander* 2.7.6.

40. Curtius *History of Alexander* 9.2.30.

41. Xenophon *Anabasis* 6.6.36.

42. Strabo *Geography* 3.5.5.

43. Siculus *Library of History* 17.95.

44. Siculus *Library of History* 17.95.

45. Plutarch *Alexander* 7.66.1, Strabo *Geography* 15.1.

46. Tarn, *Alexander the Great,* 1:103.

47. Siculus *Library of History* 17.98.1 writes that the massacre of the

Malli happened before the combat, but Curtius *History of Alexander* 9.7.16 and Arrian *Indica* 6.14.1 are unclear since in their account ambassadors from the Malli are present for the contest.

48. Curtius *History of Alexander* 9.8.18 contends that Alexander tried to stop the combat, but the participants insisted on going through with it. Both men were "favorites of the king." Siculus *Library of History* 18.100.3 contends that Alexander backed Corratas because he was Macedonian.

49. Plutarch *Alexander* 63.

50. Plutarch *Alexander* 65.

51. Curtius *History of Alexander* 9.8.22.

Chapter Six

1. Main sources are Siculus *Library of History* 17.105, Curtius *History of Alexander* 9.10.8–17, Justini *Epitoma Historiarum Philippicarum* 12.10.7, Arrian *Indica* 6.23.4–26, and Strabo *Geography* 15.2.5–6.

2. Plutarch *Alexander* 66.4.

3. Siculus *Library of History* 17.105.

4. Plutarch *De Fortuna aut Virtute Alexandri* 1.5.328. Cicero also reported similar practices among the Bactrians and Hyrcanians in *Tusculan Disputations* 1.45.108.

5. Probably the modern town of Bela at the entrance to the desert.

6. In 1998, more than three thousand people died in a similar flash flood that struck the small city of Turbat.

7. March 2004 as reported in the *New York Times*.

8. Siculus *Library of History* 17.105.6.

9. Plutarch 66.4–5.

10. Most probably the ruins of Bampur just a few miles west of the modern Iranian city of Iran Shahr in the Sistan Province.

11. Plutarch *Alexander* 67.6.

12. Plutarch *Alexander* 67.8.

13. Curtius *History of Alexander* 9.10.20–21, 10.1.1–9, 30–42; Justini *Epitoma Historiarum Philippicarum* 12.10.8, Plutarch *Alexander* 68.2–3, Arrian *Indica* 6.27, 29, 30.

14. Plutarch *Alexander* 68.3.

15. Plutarch *Alexander* 68.3.

16. Siculus *Library of History* 17.108.4.

17. Curtius *History of Alexander* 9.10.21 and 29–30.

18. Plutarch *Alexander* 67.

19. Plutarch *Alexander* 67.6.

20. Arrian *Anabasis of Alexander* 6.28 says this drunken procession through Carmania never happened.

21. Curtius *History of Alexander* 9.10.27–28.

22. The modern-day city of Bandar-e-Abbas in southern Iran at the Straits of Hormoz.

23. Plutarch *Alexander* 68.1 and Arrian *Indica* 7.1.1.

24. Arrian *Indica* 6.30.

25. Arrian *Indica* 6.30.

26. Curtius *History of Alexander* 10.1.40.

27. Curtius *History of Alexander* 10.1.26.

28. Siculus *Library of History* 17.111.1–3.

29. Arrian *Indica* 7.3.

30. Plutarch *Alexander* 70.

31. Arrian *Indica* 7.4.5 and Appian *Roman History* 24.3.

32. Arrian *Indica* 7.4.7.

33. Curtius *History of Alexander* 10.3.13.

34. Curtius *History of Alexander* 10.3.14.

35. Arrian *Indica* 7.6.3.

36. Arrian *Indica* 7.6.1.

37. Plutarch *Alexander* 71 and Curtius *History of Alexander* 10.4 say this incident happened at Susa, while Arrian *Indica* 7.8 and Siculus *Library of History* 17.108 say it happened at Opis, a city on the upper Tigris River and much farther away.

38. Curtius *History of Alexander* 10.3.14.

39. Curtius *History of Alexander* 10.2.30, Justini *Epitoma Historiarum Philippicarum* 12.11.8, and Arrian *Indica* 7.8.3, who says Alexander merely pointed the ringleaders out to the guards.

40. Siculus *Library of History* 17.108.3.

41. Arrian *Indica* 7.6.3.

42. The quarrel between Alexander and his Macedonians differs materially between Plutarch *Alexander* 71 and Arrian *Indica* 7.8–11.

43. Plutarch *Alexander* 71 and Arrian *Indica* 7.12.

44. Curtius *History of Alexander* 10.4.

45. Plutarch *Alexander* 72 and Arrian *Indica* 7.14.

46. Plutarch *Alexander* 82.

47. Arrian *Indica* 7.16.5.

48. Arrian *Indica* 7.17.6.

49. Arrian *Indica* 7.18.2–4.

50. Siculus *Library of History* 17.115. Contains a detailed description of the pyre.

51. Arrian *Indica* 7.15.4 and Siculus *Library of History* 17.113.

52. Arrian *Indica* 7.25.

53. Siculus *Library of History* 17.117.1.

54. Curtius *History of Alexander* 10.4, Arrian *Indica* 7.24.4 and 25. Plutarch *Alexander* 74 says the pain was in his back.

55. Siculus *Library of History* 17.117.2.

56. W. W. Tarn, *Alexander the Great*, Vol. 1 (Cambridge, 1948), p. 49, goes on to write that "accusations of drunkenness have become a standing feature of all abusive propaganda against Alexander."

57. Ibid., 1:41.

58. Arrian *Indica* 7.25 and Plutarch *Alexander* 76.1–2.

59. David Oldach, *Emerging Infectious Diseases: A Peer-Reviewed Journal Tracking and Analyzing Disease Trends* (December 1998).

60. John Marr and Charles Calisher, *Emerging Infectious Diseases: A Peer-Reviewed Journal Tacking and Analyzing Disease Trends* (December 2003).

61. Siculus *Library of History* 17.118.

62. Siculus *Library of History* 17.118, Justini *Epitoma Historiarum Philippicarum* 12.14, Plutarch *Alexander* 77, Arrian *Indica* 7.27 and 28.

63. Plutarch *Alexander* 77.

64. Plutarch *Alexander* 77 and Arrian *Indica* 7.28.

65. Arrian *Indica* 7.27 says he "heard" the poison was made up by Aristotle.

66. Curtius *History of Alexander* 10.10.14, Justini *Epitoma Historiarum Philippicarum* 12.13.4, Plutarch *Alexander* 77, and Arrian *Indica* 7.27 all agree that he was poisoned.

67. Curtius *History of Alexander* 10.10.15 also identifies Craterus as a possible assassin.

68. Plutarch *Alexander* 77.2–3.

69. Arrian *Indica* 7.27 as reported in *Alexander Romance*.

70. Curtius *History of Alexander* 10.5.

71. Siculus *Library of History* XVII 117.4 says to the strongest, which in ancient Greek can also mean to the best.

BIBLIOGRAPHY

PRIMARY SOURCES

Manuscripts

Bibliotheca Scriptorum Graecorum et Romanorum Teubneriana. Teubner Library of Greek and Latin Texts.

Codex Vindobonensis. Twelfth century. Origin of all extant manuscripts of Arrian.

Scriptorum Classicorum Bibliotheca Oxoniensi. Oxford Classical Texts.

The following were men who were with Alexander when he campaigned and they wrote their memoirs shortly after his death. All their works are now lost and what we know of them comes down to us only through what Greek and Roman authors from the first century B.C. and later wrote. These authors reflect widely divergent views of Alexander from admiration of a great general and statesman to condemnation of a ruthless tyrant.

Aristobulus was a man of whom little is known. He was charged by Alexander with the restoration of the tomb of Cyrus the Great, and he wrote his history of the campaigns some twenty or thirty years after Alexander died.

Callisthenes was the official historian of Alexander's expedition and a nephew of Aristotle. Callisthenes was executed by Alexander in Afghanistan or Pakistan on a charge of treason.

Cleitarchus was considered by many scholars to have been an unreliable source because he recorded everything that was great and wonderful about the king. Aristobulus and Ptolemy are believed to have influenced the work of Cleitarchus, who wrote in approximately 310 B.C. He is considered the source of the Vulgate tradition on Alexander.

Nearchus was one of Alexander's boyhood friends and commanded the fleet that sailed down the Indus River.

Onesicritus was a cynic who studied philosophy with Diogenes and traveled with Alexander. Most noted for his interest in the Indian ascetics at Taxila. Served as an officer in the fleet.

Ptolemy was one of the most important commanders in Alexander's army and a boyhood friend of the king's. When Alexander died, Ptolemy became one of his successors and later pharaoh of Egypt. Ptolemy was alleged to be the son of Philip by a common woman and thus Alexander's half-brother.

Other Sources from the Time of Alexander

Alexander left no official writings of his own. Only fragments are left from the contemporary writers who described his career, his philosophy, and his political objectives.

Alexander Romance. A historical novel dating from a generation or two after Alexander's death. While interesting to read, it has been deemed worthless by some scholars as a reliable source for learning about Alexander.

Royal Diaries or Ephemeredes. Journals of Alexander's campaigns published after his death. One passage deals with Alexander's last days. The authenticity of the diaries has been disputed by scholars.

Vulgate Tradition or the Metz Epitome. Comprises several full-length histories of Alexander's reign written by Curtius, Siculus, and Justin several centuries after Alexander's death. The work of these three authors is based largely on what *Cleitarchus of Alexandria* wrote in the fourth century B.C.

Roman and Greek Writers (Second Century B.C.–Third Century A.D.)

Diodorus Siculus. A Greek historian (80–20 B.C.), Siculus wrote forty books on the history of the ancient world. He is considered a valuable source because of the details he provides scholars on the life of Alexander. Siculus drew from the works of Cleitarchus. Because Siculus wrote during the politically volatile period of the first and second Roman Triumvirates, there are aspects of Alexander's story that he treated with caution.

Flavius Arrianus. Greek historian and philosopher (A.D. 90–175). Arrian is considered by most scholars to be the most reliable source on Alexander. He lived during the reign of the Roman emperor Hadrian and wrote seven books based on what he had learned from the writings of men who were with Alexander such as Ptolemy, Aristobulus, and Nearchus. Arrian identified the driving force in Alexander as "pothos," or a desire to keep pushing farther and farther beyond the boundaries of where men had gone before. The problem with Arrian is that he wrote some four hundred years after Alexander died and thus at best can only be considered a secondary source.

Marcus Junianus Justinius. A Roman writer from the third century A.D., he has been referred to as the third-hand source by scholars who suspect that he relied too heavily on the works of Siculus and Curtius in producing his history of Alexander.

Plutarchus. A Greek philosopher and political biographer (A.D. 50–120) who wrote about the lives of famous Greeks and Romans. One of the lives he wrote about was Alexander's. In his *Life of Alexander,* he provides considerable information and insight into the character of the king. Plutarch's aim was to construct a moral portrait of Alexander rather than to write his history. In the preface to his *Lives,* Plutarch wrote "I am writing lives, not histories." Two other important works are *On the Fortune or Virtue of Alexander,* which is often used by scholars as the basic explanatory text for Alexander's treatment of his subjects, and *Eumenes.* Eumenes was one of Alexander's boyhood friends and the secretary to the king during the campaigns. Plutarch's work on Eumenes gives us many valuable perspectives into Alexander's personality.

Quintus Curtius Rufus. A Roman historian and biographer, most probably from the mid-first century A.D., he was the author of a history of Alexander in ten books based on Cleitarchus.

WORKS CITED AND SECONDARY SOURCES

Appian. *Roman History,* Vol. 2. London, 1948.

Aristotle. *Politics.* Trans. H. Rackham. Loeb Classical Library. Cambridge: Harvard University Press.

Arrian. *Anabasis of Alexander,* Vol. 1, Books 1–4, and Vol. 2, Books 5–7. Loeb Classical Library. Cambridge: Harvard University Press.

———. *Indica.* Loeb Classical Library. Cambridge: Harvard University Press.

Austin, M. "Alexander and the Macedonian Invasion of Asia." In *War and Society in the Greek World,* Rich and Shipley, eds., pp. 197–223. London, 1993.

Badian, E. "Alexander the Great and the Greeks of Asia." In *Ancient Society and Institutions.* Oxford, 1966.

———. "Alexander the Great and the Unity of Mankind." *Historia* 7 (1958): 425.

———. "Alexander and the Loneliness of Power." *Studies of Greek and Roman History,* pp. 192–205. Oxford, 1964.

Baynham, E. J. "Introduction to the Metz Epitome." *Antichthon* 29: 60–77.

Bosworth, A. B. *Alexander and the East*. Oxford, 1996.

------. *Commentary on Arrian's History of Alexander*, Vols. 1 and 2. Oxford, 1980 and 1995.

------. *Conquest and Empire: The Reign of Alexander the Great*. Cambridge, U.K., 1988.

Bosworth, A. B., and E. J. Baynham, eds. *Alexander the Great in Fact and Fiction*. Oxford, 2000.

------. *Cambridge Ancient History*, Vols. 5 and 6. 2d ed. Cambridge, U.K., 1994.

Briant, Pierre. *Alexander the Great: The Heroic Ideal*. Paris, 1996.

Cary, M. *Geographic Background of Greek and Roman History*. Oxford, 1949.

Cicero. *Tusculan Disputations*, Vol. 28 (London, 1929).

Cook, J. M. *Persian Empire*. London, 1983.

Curtis, J. *Ancient Persia*. London, 1989.

Curtius, Quintus. *History of Alexander*, Vol. 1, Books 1–5, and Vol. 2, Books 6–10. Loeb Classical Library. Cambridge: Harvard University Press.

Dascalakis, A. *Alexander the Great and Hellenism*. Thessalonica, 1966.

Delbruck, Hans. *Warfare in Antiquity*, Vol. 1. London, 1975.

Dover, K. J. *Greek Homosexuality*. Cambridge, Mass., 1978.

Droysen, J. G. *Alexander the Great*. Basel, 1877.

Ehrenberg, V. *Alexander and the Greeks*. Oxford, 1938.

Fox, Robin Lane. *Alexander the Great*. London, 1973.

Freud, Sigmund. *Civilization and Its Discontents*. New York, 1961.

Fuller, J. F. C. *The Generalship of Alexander the Great*. London, 1958.

Garnsey, P. *Ideas of Slavery from Aristotle to Augustine*. Cambridge, U.K., 1996.

Green, Peter. *Alexander of Macedon*. Berkeley, 1992.

Griffith, G. T., ed. *Alexander the Great: The Main Problems*. Cambridge, U.K., 1966.

Hammond, N. G. L. "Archaeological and Literary Evidence for the Burning of Persepolis." *Classical Quarterly* 42: 358–64.

------. *The Genius of Alexander the Great*. Chapel Hill, 1997.

------. *Three Historians of Alexander the Great*. Cambridge, U.K., 1983.

------. "The Royal Journals of Alexander the Great." *Historia* 37: 129–50.

------. *The Sources for Alexander the Great*. Cambridge, U.K., 1993.

Harbottle, Thomas. *Harbottle's Dictionary of Battles*. Revised by George Bruce. New York, 1981.

Heckel, W. *The Last Days and Testament of Alexander the Great*. Stuttgart, 1988.

Herodotus. *Histories*. Books 1–10. Trans. George Rawlinson. New York, 1943.

Hirsch, S. W. *Friendship of Barbarians: Xenophon and the Persian Empire*. Hanover, 1985.

Justini, Marcus Junianus. *Epitoma Historiarum Philippicarum*, ed. O. Seel. Stuttgart, 1972.

Koldewey, R. *Excavations at Babylon*. London, 1914.

Krefter, R. *Persepolis Rekonstrucktionen*. Berlin, 1971.

Lewis, D. M. *Sparta and Persia*. Leiden, 1977.

Livy. *Roman History*, Vol. 8. London, 1929.

Lock, R. A. "The Macedonian Army Assembly in the Time of Alexander the Great." *Classical Philosophy* 72: 92–107.

Merlan, P. "Isocrates, Aristotle, and Alexander the Great." *Historia* 3: 60–81.

Milns, R. D. *Alexander the Great*. New York, 1969.

Morkholm, O. *Early Hellenistic Coinage*. Ed. P. Grierson and U. Westermark. Cambridge, U.K., 1991.

Oates, J. *Babylon*. London, 1986.

O'Brien, J. M. *Alexander the Great: The Invisible Enemy*. London, 1992.

Olmstead, A. T. *History of the Persian Empire*. London, 1959.

Pearson, Lionel. *Lost Histories of Alexander the Great*. New York, 1960.

Pliny. *Natural History*, Vol. 10. London, 1933.

Plutarch. *De Fortuna aut Virtute Alexandri*. Loeb Classical Library. Cambridge: Harvard University Press.

———. *Lives of the Greeks and Romans*, Book 7, *Alexander*. Loeb Classical Library. Cambridge: Harvard University Press.

———. *Lives of the Greeks and Romans*, Book 8, *Eumenes*. Loeb Classical Library. Cambridge: Harvard University Press.

Pope, A. U. "Persepolis As a Ritual City." *Archaeology* 10 (1957): 123–30.

Price, M. J. *Coinage in the Names of Alexander the Great and Philip Arrhidaeus*. 2 vols. London, 1991.

Robinson, C. A. *History of Alexander the Great*. 2 vols. Providence, R.I., 1953.

Saggs, E. W. *The Greatness That Was Babylon*. New York, 1969.

Schackermeyr, F. *Alexander der Grosse*. Vienna, 1973.

———. *Indogermanen und Orient*. Vienna, 1940.

Seager, R. "The Freedom of the Greeks of Asia." *Classical Quarterly* 31 (1981): 106–12.

Siculus, Diodorus. *Library of History*, Books 16–17. Loeb Classical Library. Cambridge: Harvard University Press.

Stein, Sir Aurel. "On Alexander's Route into Gedrosia." *Geographical Journal* 102 (1943): 193–227.

———. *On Alexander's Track to the Indus*. London, 1929.

———. "An Archeological Journey in Western Iran." *Geographical Journal* 92 (1938): 313–42.

———. "An Archaeological Tour in Gedrosia." *Archeological Survey of India* 43 (1931): 52–144.

————. *Old Routes of Western Iran.* London, 1940.

Stoneman, Richard. *Alexander the Great.* London, 1997.

————. *The Greek Alexander Romance.* Harmondsworth-Middlesex, 1991.

————. *The Legends of Alexander the Great.* London, 1994.

Strabo. *Geography.* London, 1933.

Stronach, D. *Pasargadae: A Report on the Excavations Conducted by the British Institute of Persian Studies, 1961–1963.* Oxford, 1978.

Tarn, W. W. *Alexander the Great,* Vols. 1 and 2. Cambridge, U.K., 1948.

Walbank, F. W. *Historical Commentary on Polybius.* 3 vols. Oxford, 1957–1979.

Westerman, William L. *Slave Systems of Greek and Roman Antiquity.* Philadelphia, 1955.

Wilber, D. N. *Persepolis: The Archaeology of Persia.* Princeton, 1989.

Wilcken, Ulrich. *Alexander the Great.* New York, 1967.

Wood, Michael. *In the Footsteps of Alexander the Great.* Berkeley, 1997.

Xenophon. *Anabasis.* Trans. Rex Warner. London, 1949.

————. *Cryopaedia.* Trans. H. G. Dakyns. London, 1992.

INDEX